The Invention of the Crusades

CHRISTOPHER TYERMAN

University of Toronto Press
Toronto, Buffalo

First published 1998 by
MACMILLAN PRESS LTD
Houndmills, Basingstoke, Hampshire RG21 6XS
and London
Companies and representatives
throughout the world

First published in North America in 1998 by
UNIVERSITY OF TORONTO PRESS INC.
Toronto and Buffalo

ISBN 0–8020–4363–1 (clothbound)
ISBN 0–8020–8185–1 (paperback)

Canadian Cataloguing in Publication Data

Tyerman, Christopher
 The invention of the Crusades

Includes bibliographical references and index.
ISBN 0–8020–4363–1 (bound)   ISBN 0–8020–8185–1 (pbk.)

1. Crusades.   2. Crusades—Historiography.   I. Title

D160.T93 1998   909.07   C97–932119–0

This book is printed on paper suitable for recycling and
made from fully managed and sustained forest sources.

10   9   8   7   6   5   4   3   2   1
07   06   05   04   03   02   01   00   99   98

Printed in Hong Kong

In Memoriam
LIONEL BUTLER

CONTENTS

Preface   ix

Introduction   1

1   **Were There Any Crusades in the Twelfth Century?**   8

2   **Definition and Diffusion**   30
    Innocent III   35
    Innocent III's Legacy   36
    Papal Leadership   41
    Language   49
    Secular Law and the Crusader   55
    Preaching   62
    Crusade and Women   75
    The Cross   76
    Crusade and Reform   83
    Criticism and Decline   88

3   **Proteus Unbound: Crusading Historiography**   99
    The Sixteenth Century: Continuity and Change   100
    The Development of Modern Views   109
    The Modern Age   119

Notes   127
Select Bibliography   158
Index   162

PREFACE

One of the most striking developments in medieval studies in the last thirty years has been the growth of interest in the crusades. Anyone now attempting to produce a general synthesis therefore incurs manifold debts: mine are apparent in many footnotes and on most pages. Many individuals have immensely improved this book by their comments, discussion, criticism and by providing opportunities to air views. I am grateful to my pupils at Oxford for providing a stern testing-ground for my thoughts and to Hertford College for its intellectual fellowship. In particular, it is a pleasure to record my thanks to Peter Biller; Jessalyn Bird; Eric Christiansen; Helen Cooper; John Cowdrey; Barrie Dobson; Jean Dunbabin; Peter Edbury; Norman Housley; Jeremy Johns; Andrew Jotischky; Anthony Luttrell; Roger Pensom; Jonathan Phillips; Jonathan Riley-Smith and Jonathan Shepard. My errors, however, are my own. To the editors and publishers of *The English Historical Review* I am grateful for permission to use, substantially unchanged, my article 'Were there any crusades in the twelfth century?' (vol. cx, 1995). To Simon Winder I owe the invitation to write this book and to Peter Biller the idea of presenting my ideas in this form and the introduction to my publishers. What this book and its author owe to the encouragement, companionship and unsurpassed hospitality of the *familia* Biller cannot be measured in words. That there is a book at all is a tribute to the patience and understanding of my family. That this is yet another book on the crusades is, in no small degree, the result of the inspiration of my research supervisor whose genial but acute guidance first led me on my academic *passagium*. The loss of his wisdom, humour and humanity is still keenly felt: he would have made this a much better book. To his memory it is dedicated.

Oxford, 1 January 1997

INTRODUCTION

The crusades are one of the most familiar features of the Middle Ages. They appear to typify, even define, a whole period. Remote in aspiration yet retaining an attractive tang of relevance, crusading powerfully evokes a distant past while remaining topical. Although the word is not medieval, the image and resonance of 'crusade' provides the most prominent link between modern vocabulary, even thought, and the activities of twenty and thirty generations ago. The image of the crusader is unshakeable in western mentalities. However alien the motives or justifications, crusading still resounds in the imagination as much as the intellect, a persisting icon of western culture.

Some reasons for this are obvious. Crusading was a religious act closely bound up with perennial anxieties over the nature and purpose of existence in a world beyond human control or understanding. Crusading was political and social, a military activity in which internal spirituality matched external ambition. It expressed communal as well as individual attitudes to fundamental practical and ideological issues: faith; self-esteem; religious and social control; honour; pride; material and spiritual greed; the self-image of a civilization.

Thus, the crusades seem approachable to modern observers, whether delighted, intrigued or appalled. The purpose of this book is to examine how this occurred and to suggest that this convenient, glamorous and apparently coherent packaging of medieval society and religion into an institution distinct in essence, characteristics and operation, is not quite as it has been portrayed. The many layers of wrapping conceal nothing so much as more of the same.

Thirty years ago, H. E. Mayer ([1965] 1972) complained of the ambiguities and diffuseness of a phenomenon that, despite its popularity among scholars and public, lacked any agreed, precise definition.[1] Since then much discussion has concerned what could generically be called the 'what were the crusades?' question. However, Mayer's problem was in

1

no way new. It had been implicit or explicit in nearly all serious discussions of crusading from the thirteenth century onwards. That so many various conclusions have been presented may indicate something central to understanding. Although debate has narrowed to seeking a close definition, it could be argued that Mayer's problem was caused less by the slackness of scholars than by the nature of the subject they studied. It is not simply that intellectual slovenliness makes life easier for historians trying to find containable topics or saleable titles; nor that the crusades were so pervasive of culture and society that tight definition is unprofitable. Rather, the crusades lacked definition because, instead of illuminating all around them, they themselves reflected and refracted their surrounding context. Rather than a distinctive element in medieval culture, diverse and changing aspects of that society were gathered up, by observers, promoters and participants, into what we now know as the crusades.

The dynamism of the crusade was not originally self-generated. Only slowly did a tradition emerge which, even at its height of popular recognition in the two centuries after the Third Crusade (1188–92), possessed only sporadic life. Crusading may have been regarded by many as honourable and desirable, but never as a permanent or compulsory religious or secular obligation. In the four centuries after Urban II called for an expedition to relieve Jerusalem in 1095, the majority of western Christians did not become crusaders. Although the political, social and fiscal ramifications of active crusading inevitably had wide repercussions, if only on taxpayers and subjects, at no time in the Middle Ages was there a plain, categorical canonical definition or authoritative legal pronouncement of the associated forms of Holy War and spiritual exercises which now pass for crusading. Intriguingly, neither in Latin nor the vernacular was there a single, unique, still less universal word for the enterprise.

Therefore much of the controversy over 'what were the crusades?' may appear beside the point. Mayer has argued for the centrality of Jerusalem both as a military and spiritual goal of crusading and as the key feature of the crusade indulgence. This argument has been dubbed by its critics as 'traditionalist'. Against this J. S. C. Riley-Smith has insisted ([1977] 1992) that it was papal authorization that alone defined a crusade.[2] Thus where papal authority existed, there was a crusade. This has been called a 'pluralist' approach as it expands the scope of legitimate crusading to include all those many expeditions planned or launched with papally published indulgences, whether to Jerusalem or against heretics, Christians, pagans or non-Levantine Muslims. It also imposes a different time-scale. Traditionally, the loss of Acre in 1291 marked the end of the crusades, for Mayer as for Gibbon. The 'pluralists' include the later Middle Ages and beyond, when campaigns against the Holy Land remained stubbornly but conclusively on the drawing board.

Mayer has commented on the debate that 'the fronts have become hardened'.[3] In some respects this appears unnecessary. Not only may a number of the underpinning assumptions need revision, but both the novelty and extent of disagreement may have been exaggerated. Long before Riley-Smith, some accepted the widest chronological scope for the crusades. In 1960, even the *Grand Larousse encyclopédique* described the battles of Lepanto (1571) and St Gotthardt (1664) as 'véritables croisades'.[4] The 'pluralists' take their stand on what they regard as the hard canonist ground of papal authority, which, as N. Housley has noticed (1992), would logically exclude 'popular' crusades as well as some Baltic campaigning.[5] Yet Riley-Smith has admitted that equation with the Jerusalem expeditions was essential to proper indulgences. In this he follows, perhaps reluctantly, the thirteenth-century canonist Hostiensis who went as far as any in trying to codify the essentials of crusading. As Mayer has noted (1978), this puts 'Jerusalem squarely back at the heart of things'.[6] This is confirmed by Riley-Smith's recent assertion (1995), in a discussion of papal crusade policy, that 'everyone accepted that the crusades to the East were the most prestigious and provided the scale against which the others were measured', which is what I have argued elsewhere (in 1985).[7] This takes much of the wind from the opposing armadas.

Housley is less convinced, pouring scorn (1992) on any idea of a 'league table of crusades'.[8] He refuses to be swayed by evidence of popularity or reception, except where it supports papal policy. Yet although none could dispute that papal policy was 'pluralist', as Mayer (1988) has reaffirmed, 'what is at issue is not Church doctrine but the extent to which society found that doctrine acceptable'.[9] Evidence for a divergence between papal policy and wider acceptance of this can be found in the work of canonists and secular lawyers, as well as politicians, polemicists and propagandists.

In a sense the debate, while inevitably concerning technical intricacies such as the nature and form of indulgences or the criticism of intractable primary sources, is also about visions of the Middle Ages. 'Pluralists', while investigating the nature and potency of religious idealism, spirituality, faith and violence, often appear schematic in their view of the past. At times, this imposes an almost partisan adherence to medieval papal policy which can veer towards a neat Curial view of the world, with less attention being paid to the vacillation, confusion, delivery and acceptance of those policies across the different regions of Europe. Equally, 'traditionalists' truncate the evidence admitted for scrutiny. It is surely unnecessarily fussy to exclude from crusading history those who followed the precedent of 1095 and signed themselves with the Cross to fight a penitential, Holy War just because their stated goals did not coincide with those of the first crusaders. To ignore those writing, thinking and acting in ways they themselves deliberately associated with Holy Wars fought beneath the sign of the Cross, and enjoying privileges first granted warrior-pilgrims to the Holy Land, would seem unduly prim.

There is also the danger of mechanistic interpretations. Thus the crusade as an institution becomes a 'movement' which can, as in the hands of Housley (1995), take on life of its own. This Frankenstein's monster is anthropomorphic, its actions open to judgement. Its 'adaptability', 'resilience' and even 'panache' are praised, while its introversion was 'rather unhealthy', and its 'lack of focus' is 'sometimes irritating'.[10] This is bizarre when what are being described are events, actions, aspirations and motives of people living centuries ago. Who is irritated? Why? The best that can said for such an approach is that it chimes in with traditional (and pluralist) judgementalism, which has dogged the study of the crusades in all periods since 1095. It may be thought that much of these current debates are arcane, revealing more about modern historians carving out academic territories and empires than about the Middle Ages.

However, across all such discussion there is a shadow that is usually ignored, but cannot be dispelled. Most historians of the crusades have noticed that in every period there is uncertainty and confusion about what exactly is going forward. It was one thing for an anti-papalist in 1103 to ignore the implications for penitential warfare of the Jerusalem expeditions of 1095–1101; quite another for confusion over the operation of the indulgence to persist in the highest academic circles in the mid-thirteenth century.[11] The argument of this book is that such uncertainty was endemic because the crusade as an institution only existed as an expression of desires and policies to which Holy Wars were useful but tangential: the ecclesiastical and political ambitions of popes; the devotional practices of the laity, especially the nobility; the development of the cult of chivalry and a code of aristocratic self-esteem and honour; the economic expansion of parts of western Europe; the religious initiatives of Church reformers. The crusades were their creation, not vice versa. It was no coincidence that crusading was a product not of the frontier with Islam but of the heartlands of Christendom. When the enemy was actually at the gates of the West, from the fourteenth century, the institution appeared more not less fragmented. The crusade cannot adequately be defined in its own terms because it only existed in relation to the dictates of its shifting western context.

One consequence of this is the appreciation that neither 'pluralist' not 'traditionalist' interpretations are wholly acceptable. Instead of seeking precise legalistic formulae, it is perhaps more realistic to observe the fluidity and imprecision of the crusades, which were apparent to twelfth- and thirteenth-century canonists; were implicit in the ambiguities of the indulgence in the twelfth century as to what precisely was remitted, sin or its penalty; and evident in the growing transferability of crusader privileges from the 1190s. This legal, institutional confusion and flexibility were shared by the crusade campaigns themselves. Whatever the legal status of any war of the Cross, not all those who fought on them, even to the Holy Land, were *crucesignati*. Alternatively, to what extent did those signed with the Cross in, say, England in 1217 or 1265 or in some Italian wars of the thirteenth to early fifteenth centuries, see themselves in the same light as if they were on the road to Jerusalem? To exclude any or all of these would restrict the subject beyond what the evidence from the period dictates. As both 'pluralist' and 'traditionalist' must agree, it is impossible to open windows into men's souls. All degrees of crusade, crusader and crusading must be included. But that acceptance should not, in turn, impose blinkered partisanship.

What can be said is that contemporary mentalities felt easy with wide application of a form of Holy War that attracted spiritual and material privileges originally associated with armed pilgrimage to Jerusalem; understood that wars in defence of the Church, however defined, could be legitimate on similar terms; understood, nonetheless, that the emotions allied to fighting under the Cross were not the sole prerogative of those specifically papally authorized; recognized the primacy of respect engendered by war against the Infidel, as witnessed in rules for late medieval orders of chivalry; discriminated, as for any other political or military act, between the motives and honesty of separate actions, regardless of legal authority or rhetorical attempts at camouflage by equating all actions with honourable, selfless public good; and retained an impressively abiding obsession with the image, reality and uniqueness of the Holy City and the Holy Land sanctified by the founder of their religion. Crusading was, however, only one form of legitimate war, only one sort of spiritual exercise, only one strand in the rich polemic of Christian self-justification and self-awareness.

The invention of the crusades addressed and addresses two apparently distinct themes: the construction, nature and elevation of this particular form of Holy War by contemporaries and participants from a mass of religious and secular elements within society; and the subsequent confection of opinion and tradition by observers, medieval and modern. It is evident that there existed what we choose to call crusades. It is equally apparent that they did not possess the autonomous or uniform life that has usually been lent them. It has recently been insisted that the protean quality of crusading has been underestimated. However, the crusade was protean not because it had discrete existence of its own but because it answered the appeals and often assumed the guise of those who saw in its associated forms, rituals, rhetoric and traditions a means of fulfilling widely disparate and changing needs. In the association of war and penitential pilgrimage; wearing the sign of the Cross; and the overtones of sanctity connected with fighting, death as martyrs, even preaching, fund-raising and prayers, a Christian society found vehicles to express idealism and pursue spiritual and material ambitions that were extremely varied, often far from other-worldly, habitually many-layered and complex. Society drove the crusades and determined their form and fate. There were crusade institutions; but hardly a crusade 'movement'. Just as the former was an invention of contemporaries, the latter has been an invention of historians.

The argument of this book is conceived as a triptych, with a central chapter flanked by two necessary, balancing but smaller extensions. The first chapter considers the creation of crusade traditions and practices between 1095 and the Third Crusade, often seen as the heyday of crusading. In the long, focal second chapter the construction, nature and impact of what could be called developed crusading are examined by placing distinct, prominent aspects of the phenomenon, such as law, language, imagery, preaching, ritual and acceptance, in their ecclesiastical, political, cultural and social contexts to show how Holy War reflected rather than ignited its surroundings. Here the exchange between what was being promoted with its reception is parallelled by the

cumulative inadequacy of the reality and theory of crusading to provide a firm, lasting focus of identity for Christendom. The twin themes
of deliberate promotion and imprecise ambiguity run together. A final
chapter, by considering the historiography of the subject since the sixteenth century, completes the investigation of crusading as a series of
constructs as much as a sequence of events.

1

WERE THERE ANY CRUSADES IN THE TWELFTH CENTURY?

Guibert of Nogent, in a famous phrase, described the First Crusade as a new path of salvation which allowed laymen to earn redemption without changing their status and becoming monks.[1] This theme was taken up by later apologists and recruiters of further military expeditions to the Holy Land, notably St Bernard in his praise of the Templars in the late 1120s and his preaching of the Second Crusade in the 1140s, where the new opportunity was restyled as a unique bargain which God was offering his faithful. This identification of a fresh means of Grace, a new form of Holy War, has been generally accepted by modern historians. Carl Erdmann, after his painstaking excavation of the roots of crusading, insisted on the novelty of the First Crusade. The events of 1095–99 have been commonly regarded as marking an epoch in the Church's acceptance of secular militarism; in the development of theories of Holy War; and in opportunities for the legitimate expression of lay military and chivalric ambitions. Yet the evidence from the eighty years after the capture of Jerusalem hardly supports such categorical assumptions.

With hindsight, we may see the First Crusade as spawning a new movement which both characterized and shaped western Christendom for centuries. Contemporaries clearly did not. Their twelfth-century hindsight led them to different conclusions, namely that the First Crusade was unique and, especially after the fiascos of 1101 and 1146–49, unrepeatable.[2] The First Crusade was remembered as a symbol of loyalty and honour, a focus and inspiration for traditional secular qualities, not as a new way of salvation or a new form of Holy War. Thus in c.1143 the English baron, Brian FitzCount, saw the First Crusaders in terms of supremely loyal knights (*boni milites*).[3] Eugenius III said much the same in the Bull *Quantum praedecessores* of 1146 launching the Second Crusade. It was to the memory of the First Crusaders and to the honour of their descendants that Eugenius appealed.[4] His lead was followed by the popularizers and propagandists.[5]

Far from being a new way of salvation, the crusade was an old way of gaining reward, by loyal service to a master (the Pope or, more generally, Christ), only writ large. Besides the need to emulate the heroism of the first crusaders, Pope Eugenius identified two desired consequences of the proposed expedition: 'so that the dignity of the name of Christ may be enhanced . . . and your reputation for strength, which is praised throughout the world, may be kept unimpaired and unsullied'. It is the 'ancestral laws' which needed defending. Thus the religious rhetoric was underpinned by traditional themes of obligation, defence, honour and glory. Eugenius showed little interest in creating a new ecclesiastical institution or movement. He sought a specific response to a specific problem – the threat to Christian Outremer – and found it in calling for a repetition of the 1096 expedition. The lack of a clearly identifiable crusade institution by 1146 is further suggested by the ease with which Bernard of Clairvaux transmuted the enterprise into an occasion for mass repentance and spiritual reform. It is often argued that *Quantum praedecessores* marked a new stage in institutionalizing the crusade indicated by the statement of secular privileges, sumptuary regulations and the indulgence. However, the Second Crusade led nowhere. Although the papal bulls and the experience of the preaching and military campaigns provided a fresh set of precedents and memories, it is hard to see in, for instance, Eugenius's association of his indulgence with that offered by Urban II the presence of a definite current ideology, nor is it obvious that he wished to develop one.[6]

In this Eugenius was typical of the period before the Third Crusade when what we call the crusades in fact covered a fragmented series of military and religious activities that lacked coherence: general expeditions (only one between 1101 and 1188); private armed and unarmed pilgrimages, not all of which can be proved to have been undertaken in response to specific or general papal authorization; the interest of settlers in the East, such as Fulcher of Chartres or even William of Tyre, to create a process of constant reinforcement; and the birth and growth of the Military Orders. Each activity was distinct in motive, appeal and implementation, with nobody seriously trying to incorporate these diverse strands into one institution, theory, or even name.

The inability of an otherwise articulate and categorizing intellectual elite to propose or agree a term for the activity which later was named 'crusade' has tended to be noted without too much comment by modern observers. Yet the terminological vagueness of the twelfth century may be significant. To put it crudely, we know there were crusaders: they did not, or, if they did, their perception was far from the canonically or juridically precise definition beloved of some late twentieth-century scholars. The hesitancy of twelfth-century canonists has been tellingly exposed by Professor Gilchrist in two acutely revisionist articles in the 1980s.[7] His arguments can, however, be extended to wider aspects of twelfth-century crusading in order to suggest that the impact of this type of Holy War was less distinctive than many, myself included, have assumed. In a non-crusading context, crusading, popular or not, appears more as an extension of existing social or religious activities rather than a radical departure from them. Compare it to becoming a monk, as did some contemporary apologists.[8] Unlike monasticism, crusading was not a lifetime's vocation, guided by carefully elaborated rules inspiring a culture distinct from the rest of lay society. In law and action, its operation remained confused with other habits and forms. As an awareness of a continuing tradition – as opposed to a glittering memory of the First Crusade – it grew haphazardly. For official clarity, attempted definition and some uniformity, one must look at Innocent III and beyond. The twelfth century is crusading's Dark Ages.

An obvious question to ask concerns the effect of crusading on its participants. The charter evidence from the First and Second Crusades points to a strong pious impulse: the desire for active repentance and forgiveness of sins. The mechanism of the armed pilgrimage was different, but the inspiration – the desire for salvation – was traditional. It was closely allied to customary expressions of piety, especially donations to and associations with monasteries which, conveniently, acted as crusaders' material as well as spiritual bankers.[9] Crusading motives, where religious, were solidly embedded in contemporary spiritual anxieties and aspirations. However, the campaigns themselves did possess the special quality of a mission, with the element of pilgrimage central. During the Second Crusade, when Jerusalem was in Christian hands, the expedition to the East was, to Odo of Deuil, the 'via Sancti Sepulchri', and to Louis VII the 'sacrosanctae peregrinationis iter'.[10] The sanctity of the enterprise was reflected in attendant miracles and the belief that casualties were martyrs.[11] With martyrdom, however, the new cloaked the old. Radulfus Glaber, in the mid-eleventh century, had assumed that those who fell fighting the Infidel merited Paradise, even if it could be argued that technically they were not martyrs. In his *Decretum*, Gratian cited Carolingian authorities who recognized the same spiritual reward.[12] If perceptions of crusaders were formed by pre-existing attitudes, their experiences were often extraordinary. The physical circumstances of such long and hazardous campaigns made them so. Yet the expeditions were finite; experiences became memories, models of conduct and good stories. These hardly provided the basis for a new institution or formal ideology.

Veterans of the First Crusade were accounted heroes (or, if they had deserted, villains).[13] It could do them material favours, as with Robert of Normandy, who received especially pleasant conditions of custody between 1106 and 1134 because Henry I decided to treat him 'not as an enemy captive but as a noble pilgrim', a reference to Robert's inflated reputation as a leader of the First Crusade.[14] Responses to the survivors of the largely unsuccessful Second Crusade were, inevitably, more muted and confused. Their actions were not obviously taken as models or precedents even, it appears, at the time of the Third Crusade.[15] But crusading exerted no general influence on future behaviour, to the occasional disquiet of the church authorities. Unlike in the thirteenth century, there was no continuing institutional presence of crusading after the event, such as special prayers or parish collecting-boxes. Returning Jerusalemites in 1099, for all their expressions of contrition evident in their charters of three years earlier, appeared eager to pick up the familiar threads of their secular lives. Raimbold Croton was one of the heroes of the First Crusade, especially in the region of Chartres, where he enjoyed the reputation of being the first crusader to enter Jerusalem. Ralph of Caen, Albert of Aachen and Baldric of Dol all mention his heroism at Antioch and Jerusalem.[16] Yet, a few years after his return, Raimbold, incensed at a local monk who had beaten some of his servants for stealing hay, had the unfortunate cleric castrated. For this the church authorities forbade the former *miles christi* from bearing arms for fourteen years. Raimbold, apparently shocked into penitence, appealed to Bishop Ivo of Chartres who, knowing his canon law, declined to get involved directly but, in view of Raimbold's bravery at Jerusalem, sent him to Pope Paschal II for absolution. This Raimbold presumably received, for soon afterwards he met his death in one of the interminable and sordid petty wars in the Île de France.[17] The First Crusade may have widened the scope of knightly endeavour and provided

fresh heroes, but it did little to alter the realities of life, a point echoed by
Orderic Vitalis when lamenting the death of Robert of Flanders,
trampled in the royal retreat from Dammartin, a sad fate for a
'bellicosus Jerosolimitae'.[18]

The squalid career of Raimbold Croton, the political success and the
many personal failures of the ideal and practice of the First Crusade
may be seen to have consolidated a close relationship between the
Church and the *ordo pugnatorum*, at the very least an increased recognition of the mutual benefits. From all sides of religious debate, from Peter
the Venerable of Cluny, Suger of St Denis and Bernard of Clairvaux,
there was agreement of the potential virtue of the knightly order and its
violent activities, specifically when protecting ecclesiastical interests.[19]
Yet, consciously or not, these apologists were following a long tradition,
stretching back to papal approval of Carolingian militarism in the
eighth century and beyond, for example, the praise in Bede's *Ecclesiastical History* for Edwin, Oswald and Oswy.[20] In February 1145, Pope
Lucius II died from wounds received leading his troops in an attempt to
secure control of the city of Rome. But this was not a sign of any new
dispensation of acceptable holy violence. In the tenth century, both
John X (914–28) and John XII (955–63) personally took part in fighting.[21] Warrior bishops are not unusual in the twelfth century: Ralph of
Bethlehem; Rainald von Dassel of Cologne; Hubert Walter, then of
Salisbury. But they represented an old habit which, if anything, was
dying out, as the logic of Gregorian separation of functions and powers
seeped into law, custom and expectations, although there remained
some vigorous episcopal campaigners, such as Bishop Despenser of
Norwich in the fourteenth century, and episcopal war administrators
who occasionally donned armour, as, apparently, did Archbishop
Boniface of Canterbury, preparatory to mugging the prior of St
Bartholomew's, London, in 1250.[22]

The First Crusade was part of an old process of justifying wars against
pagans and enemies of the Pope in an atmosphere where war was a
familiar, necessary burden, not an inevitably abhorrent evil. Even
Burchard of Worms, in the early eleventh century, usually regarded as
extremely hostile to Christian approval of war, saw a role for legitimate
warfare fought with good intent.[23] The First Crusade only appeared as
the beginning of a coherent movement retrospectively when that
movement was constructed after 1187.

This impression is confirmed by a closer glance at papal responses.
Here we find a reluctance to define the crusade as an institution, maybe

because it was not regarded as such. Colin Morris has suggested one reason for this. Because Jerusalem was in Christian hands, 'there was no plan for an unrestricted offensive against the heathen and no need to discuss its justification'. He adds that pilgrimage and the Military Orders, not the crusade, provided the link between the Holy Sepulchre and the West.[24] But this is only part of the answer. Between the rare papally-launched general expeditions, men took the Cross to go east, and many were armed and fought; for example, in 1128 during Hugh de Payens's recruitment tour and on the departure of Fulk of Anjou in 1129, the military objectives were explicit.[25] Although it was only in 1146–48 that a general expedition was achieved, the papacy was involved in a number of plans which, if effected, could have led to more, for instance in 1106, 1150, 1157, 1165, 1169, 1181, and 1184/5.[26] Each occasion demonstrated the limitations of papal power and, after 1150, commitment.

In 1106, Paschal II gave Bohemond a papal banner and appointed as legate Bruno of Segni, a veteran of Urban II's preaching tour of 1095–96. A new *via sancti sepulchri* or *ire Hierusalem* was preached at a council held in Poitiers. The only practical result was Bohemund's unsuccessful attack on Epirus in 1107–08, a final outcome, for all Steven Runciman's chill condemnation, not necessarily envisaged by the Pope.[27] Papal loss of control of crusades was, after all, a constant feature of the Middle Ages.

In 1150, Eugenius III was involved in a scheme to redeem the disasters of the Second Crusade by a new expedition to the East. St Bernard himself tentatively accepted leadership of this enterprise, perhaps to vindicate his role in launching the Second Crusade. Any prospect of a new expedition was drowned in conflicting objectives: Outremer after the military disaster of Inab in 1149 or an assault on Byzantium, as preferred by the Sicilians and some French. But Eugenius III, in his bull *Immensum pietatis opus* of April 1150, was distinctly lukewarm.[28] However, what finally killed the idea was the explosion of criticism of the Second Crusade and even the ideal itself, hostility which was still vivid twenty years later. In a letter of 1169 from the entourage of Thomas Becket, the Second Crusade was condemned as 'grievous to the church', being an illustration that 'gifts offered from theft and wrongdoing are not pleasing to God'. The same letter mocked the reputation as a holy warrior of William IV of Nevers who had died in Palestine of a fever who, said the writer, 'was not even killed by Parthian darts or Syrian swords, so that not even a hero's glorious death could bring him consolation; but widow's tears, poor men's sorrow and complaints of churches are thought to have snuffed him out ingloriously'.[29] In such an atmosphere, papal approval of crusading was liable to be cautious.

Repeated calls for assistance from the East received muted replies. One reason for this was the widespread suspicion of the *pullani*, the inhabitants of Outremer (who were in no formal sense crusaders at all). Westerners, reared on the increasingly embroidered legends of heroism from the First Crusade, often failed to grasp the policies and habits of those who lived permanently in the Levant.[30] A further reason was that, as Colin Morris remarks, with Jerusalem in Christian hands the rhetoric of Clermont was inappropriate.[31] When it became suitable, after 1187, the response from a generation wedded to the Jerusalem pilgrimage was massive.

Domestic problems also distracted papal attention: enemies in Italy (from the 1130s to 1170s) and Germany (from the 1150s to 1170s); feuding of French provincial dynasties, characteristic of the period to the 1140s, was partly subsumed in the feuding between Capetians and Angevins from the 1150s; and on the frontiers of Christendom, in Spain and Germany, there were local holy causes to occupy putative crusaders to Palestine. Inevitably, with this absence of political concentration on the Holy Land (often forgotten by crusader historians), papal responses lacked originality. In 1165, Alexander III replied to appeals from the East merely by reissuing *Quantum praedecessores*, and two other of his encyclicals, *Inter Omnia* (1169) and *Cor Nostrum* (1181) were heavily dependent upon Eugenius III's model, a pattern of unadventurous plagiarism continued by Lucius III when he reissued *Cor Nostrum* in 1184/5. The contrast between these cautious and conservative encyclicals and Gregory VIII's explosive *Audita Tremendi* of 1187 is striking in urgency, originality, theological apparatus and tone. Yet even here the indulgences, legal immunities and sumptuary proposals followed very closely those of *Quantum praedecessores*.[32] In 1176, when Pope Alexander called upon the chivalry of France to go to assist Manual I Comnenus secure a road to the Holy Sepulchre across Asia Minor, he did not explicitly mention any spiritual rewards.[33] For much of the 1160s and 1170s, Alexander appeared more concerned to use the cause of the Holy Land as a diplomatic lever to move Henry II and Louis VII towards reconciliation.[34]

One novel approach was proposed in 1157 by the English Pope, Hadrian IV. Apart from appealing for warriors to hasten to free and defend the Holy Places, he offered indulgences to those who, unable to campaign in person, instead sent horses, military equipment and other aid. This extension of penitential advantages to those indirectly involved was to become a pivotal feature of crusading from the reign of Innocent III onwards. But there is little sign of Hadrian's offer being taken up, let alone built upon in practice or theory.[35]

Yet it was not as if twelfth-century popes held back from sanctioning war or in associating spiritual benefits with it any more than they had in the previous three centuries (cf. Leo IV, 847–55 and John VIII, 872–82).[36] Papal supporters in Flanders, Germany and Italy continued to receive remission of sins. At Pisa in 1135 those who fought against the anti-pope Anacletus were offered the same indulgence as Urban granted at Clermont.[37] Elsewhere, good causes were frequently described by clerical commentators as attracting spiritual rewards. In 1115, French royal troops attacking the bandit lord Thomas of Marle (himself a veteran of 1096–99) were described as 'the general assembly of the christian army' who attacked Thomas's castle as an act of penance meriting salvation.[38] According to Henry of Huntingdon, the English soldiers who defeated the Scots at the battle of the Standard in 1138 were assured by the bishop of the Orkneys of the justice of their cause and that those who perished would enjoy remission of the penalties of their sins.[39] Across Europe national or communal interests attracted spiritual rewards. Full indulgences for those who fell in battle were offered to those who fought against *routiers* in Languedoc in 1139 and against enemies of Norway in 1164.[40] In 1148, the German campaign against the Wends was explicitly linked to the Second Crusade by St Bernard.[41] Contemporaries depicted numerous campaigns in the Iberian peninsula and western Mediterranean in 1147–49 in ways equivalent to expeditions to the Holy Land, although they were essentially continuations of local enterprises aimed at territorial or commercial gain. The Genoese attack on Almería in 1146 was described in an entirely secular way, but the same writer, Caffaro, placed the successful capture of Almería the following year in the context of religious conflict and papal authorization.[42] In 1166, the Synod of Segovia promised anyone who fought for Castile remission of enjoined penance 'as he would gain by going to Jerusalem', although whether this can be taken as meaning the Jerusalem pilgrimage or crusade is typically unclear.[43] A diversity of ecclesiastical authority for such indulgences, by no means all papal, is evident, suggesting that, despite the activity and rhetoric, the papacy did not construct a new institution and that, in any case, it would have been difficult to achieve any uniformity of application.

This is not to say that the events of the First Crusade had no effect. The model of Urban II's Holy War was adapted and applied to campaigns against the Muslims in Spain and the western Mediterranean. Members of the Italian and Catalan expedition to the Balearic Islands (1114–16) were given crosses and indulgences, an offer applied by Calixtus II in 1123 more generally to all who fought the Infidel in Spain. At the Lateran Council of 1123, the Jerusalem privileges of 1095 were explicitly associated with campaigning in the Iberian peninsula. However, this application was not universal or consistent. In 1118, in the pre-1095 tradition, Gelasius II offered plenary remission of sins only to those who died in the siege of Saragossa. Similarly, the northern Italian involvement in the Balearic campaign should be compared with the Pisan and Genoese attack on Mahdia in 1087, which had equally been surrounded by the language of pilgrimage and Holy War. The account of the successful siege of Santarém in March 1147 talked of God choosing 'new wars in our days' and called the achievement miraculous. But there are no specifically crusading elements, such as indulgences or pilgrimage. The banner raised over Santarém was that of the king of Portugal. A few months later, at Lisbon, it was the banner of the Cross the same king displayed in triumph.[44] Here, as elsewhere, novelty and tradition are difficult to disentangle, probably because contemporaries were unaware of distinctions observed by modern historians.

The same can be said of the formulae of crusading which infected political responses to national wars, as in Spain in 1166 or the Baltic in 1148, and the literature of war. In Geoffrey of Monmouth's *History of the Kings of Britain* (1136), before Arthur's battle with the pagan Saxons, Archbishop Dubricius exhorts the Christian troops: 'You who have been marked with the sign of the Christian faith . . . if any of you is killed in this war that death shall be to him as a penance and an absolution for all his sins.'[45] These motifs would have been familiar alike to the educated cleric who had heard the epic accounts of the First Crusade and the layman who had listened to the early redactions of the crusade *chansons*. But it is almost impossible to identify what is old and what new: honour; justice; defence of home, country and comrades; God's favour; salvation for those who die; absolution; and remission of sins.

One source which, perhaps more than most, illustrates this confluence of tradition and innovation is the apparently eye-witness account of the siege of Lisbon in 1147, the *De Expugnatione Lyxbonensis*, long taken as an example of the establishment and extension of crusading.[46] What actually emerges from the *De Expugnatione* is an enterprise ideologically much less distinct or coherent than might be expected after the celebratory accounts of the First Crusade by contemporaries – or even modern crusader camp followers. In its lack of clarity and definition, the *De Expugnatione* shows how the activity of crusading could not, and cannot, be disassociated from pre-existing and concurrent attitudes to legitimate war, and how crusading, as a distinct attitude to war, at least by the time the text was written (probably in mid-century), had failed to alter patterns of military endeavour, even when that endeavour was part of a crusade.

A key passage in the *De Expugnatione* is the famous speech in which the bishop of Oporto tries to persuade the crusaders to turn aside from their voyage to Palestine and help the king of Portugal capture Lisbon from the Moors. Often quoted is the bishop's remark: 'the praiseworthy thing is not to have been to Jerusalem but to have lived a good life while on the way'.[47] Yet in some ways this sermon, whether delivered or not, was unnecessary. It had long been accepted that fighting the Infidel was meritorious, not least in the Iberian peninsula. Crusaders in 1096–99 had stopped *en route* to capture Muslim cities both on and off the route. The bishop of Oporto seems to be trying to persuade crusaders to do what they would have been happy to do anyway, their stated reservations being pragmatic and tactical, not ideological. Of course, although sometimes taken as such, the bishop's speech was not a crusade sermon. To divert the crusaders' *iter*, he falls back on the traditional themes of the *bellum justum*: self-defence; right intent; rightful possession; just cause; divine authority. Here at least, despite Gilchrist's argument that there was little Augustinian theory in twelfth-century martial rhetoric, is a strongly Augustinian justification. Although the weight of quotation is biblical, there are references to Ambrose, Jerome, Isidore of Seville and John Chrysostom as well as Augustine, all of which suggest that the author, or his source, was no run-of-the-mill hedge priest.[48]

The bishop of Oporto, in his initial appeal, stops short of offering explicit spiritual rewards, merely a share in the loot. Oblivious to the irony, he is following long custom when he declares 'quit you like good soldiers; for the sin is not waging war, but in waging war for the sake of plunder'.[49] With the right intent, then, the crusaders could – and did – receive generous material payment. When, during the assault itself, the bishop and an anonymous cleric, possibly the author, offer absolution and remission of sins – but only for those who die in battle and only after fresh absolution, beyond the contract of the crusaders' vows –

they are also following a tradition which had papal approval as far back as the early ninth century.[50] Like those who attacked Constantinople in 1204, the troops who assaulted Lisbon in 1147 (or those who sacked Messina in 1190 or Cyprus in 1191) were conducting battles familiar long before 1095: they were crusaders, in that they had taken the Cross, but these battles did not fulfil their vows.[51]

The reaction of the lay crusaders in *De Expugnatione* is equally devoid of any awareness of a new knighthood. The Flemish and Rhinelanders are portrayed as bloodthirsty and greedy despite 'the guise of pilgrimage and religion'. One group of Anglo-Normans preferred to push on into the Mediterranean unless payment and subsistence could be guaranteed. Most telling of all are the views attributed to the hero of the account, Hervey de Glanvill. In persuading the doubters to join the Lisbon siege he appealed, like Brian FitzCount and Eugenius III, to 'the virtues of our ancestors', the valour of the Norman race, glory and 'the counsels of honour', hardly specifically crusading qualities.[52] Unlike accounts of the First Crusade, there is little consciousness of uniqueness, of being the new Maccabees, the *militia* of Christ. (There is not much more in the account of Louis VII's crusade by Odo of Deuil, either.[53]) At Lisbon, even the final military confrontation is seen in terms which owe nothing to crusading as such. A parley was arranged with the Moors 'so that we might not appear to be attacking except unwillingly'. To establish a just cause, the Muslims are requested to surrender their rule of what had been Christian land. Then, in the manner of twelfth-century *chansons des geste*, Christian indignation is aroused by Muslim blasphemy and taunts at the possible misbehaviour of the crusaders' wives left at home. In general, a chivalric gloss is given to the conflict, which is called a 'trial of the sword', with God as the judge.[54] This chivalric strain is echoed in the precisely contemporary crusading song, *Chevalier, mult estes granz*, where the Second Crusade is described as a tournament between Hell and Paradise ('un turnei enpris entre Enfer e Pareis').[55]

The fusion of traditional behaviour and fresh attitudes is apparent throughout the Second Crusade. As has already been noted, the freedom with which St Bernard shaped and developed his preaching, even to the point of apparently embracing Sibylline prophecies of the Last Emperor, testifies to a lack of definition in the crusade.[56] Observers recognized that some of the expeditions of 1146–48 had particular features, especially those destined for the Holy Land. But in many theatres of war, in Spain, the western Mediterranean and the Baltic, religious elements were grafted on to existing political ambitions. Normal temporal aspirations were not suspended. Possibly because of its outcome, the language of participants tended to be less spiritually intense than that used of the First Crusade.[57] It is a measure of the combination of the secular and the spiritual that Conrad III and Louis VII, like Hervey de Glanvill, thought their crusades offered hope of temporal fame. In July 1147, in a letter to Wibald of Corvey, Conrad expressed the hope that his journey would lead to 'the prosperity of the whole church and the honour of our realm'. Louis echoed the sentiment writing from Antioch in the spring of 1148: 'either we shall never return or we shall come back with glory for God and the kingdom of the Franks'.[58]

The central point is that there was little that was new. However, this continuation of earlier church attitudes and papal policy has been misinterpreted as being a consequence of the First Crusade or, at least, the initiatives of the Gregorian papacy. The First Crusade may have confirmed or extended existing beliefs in the goodness of battle, and may eventually have aided the growth of intellectual structures within which the perception of the goodness could be translated into specific, popularly intelligible rewards, spiritual and material. But, as Gilchrist has suggested, it can hardly be said to have done so in Causa 23 of Gratian's *Decretum* (1140). Despite its extensive and detailed discussion of ecclesiastically sanctioned warfare, Causa 23 ignores anything that could be called specifically crusading.[59] Thus the debate about the centrality or not of so-called 'political' or non-Holy Land 'crusades' misses the point. There was Holy War in the twelfth as in earlier centuries which attracted spiritual benefits of various sorts. For some of these wars, fairly randomly except those directed towards the Holy Land, warriors adopted the Cross, perhaps to evoke the morale of the First Crusade. But to worry whether in such cases 'the full apparatus of the crusade was brought to bear' is to suppose that such apparatus existed.[60] If, as has been argued, there had emerged 'by 1198, a fairly stable group of crusading institutions centring on the legal ceremony for taking the Cross', it was a development which largely post-dated 1187.[61]

The main institutional novelty before 1187 connected with crusading was the development of the Military Orders. They were quickly accepted. By the early 1140s, the conservative Orderic Vitalis was describing them as 'admirable knights who devote their lives to the bodily and spiritual service of God and, rejecting all things of this world, face martyrdom daily'.[62] But to join the Templars, at home or, as many did, in the East, was not synonymous with becoming a crusader, it was an

alternative. The commitment and experience were of a different nature. The Military Orders were obviously one inheritance from the
First Crusade, but they were for a minority and did not necessarily ac-
celerate the elaboration of the theory or practice of crusading.[63] Rather
they were seen, as by St Bernard, as a new stage in the much older process of the Christianizing of knighthood.[64]

The legacy of the First Crusade certainly included ceremonial adoption of the Cross and the enjoyment of some sort of remission of the
penalties of sin (or, as Eugenius III called it, simply 'remission of sins')
and an array of temporal privileges associated with those of pilgrims: in
Quantum praedecessores these included protection by the Church; legal
immunity for the duration of the expedition; permission to raise mortgages and a moratorium on the repayment of debts.[65] However, formal
organization was rudimentary and papal and ecclesiastical control un-
systematic. The origins of crusade institutions at a local level are extremely obscure. Contemporaries, no less than modern historians,
could be perplexed.[66]

The First Crusade certainly lent pilgrimage to the Holy Land a new
dimension, but did not create a separate tradition. The twelfth century
was the golden age of pilgrimage to the Holy Land, not least for reasons
of practicality. However, the distinction between a pilgrim and a crusader is often hard to detect, an uncertainty which reflected reality. Not
all armed pilgrims fought, and not all westerners who did fight in Syria
had necessarily taken the Cross. In 1172, Henry the Lion, duke of
Saxony, led a substantial armed pilgrimage to Jerusalem, but neither
the images of crusading nor the intent to fight were involved. It is
wholly unclear whether the pilgrims described by Albert of Aachen as
eager for the fray in 1102 or 1107, or, in William of Tyre's misleading
ignorance, the Doge of Venice in 1124, had adopted the Cross or not.
The sources do not mention it, not do they distinguish between crusader and pilgrim, because all are called *peregrini*. Those settled in the
East in defence of the Holy Land rarely, if ever, took the Cross.[67]

Pilgrimage and crusade were fused together. *Crucesignati* bore the
staff and satchel of the pilgrim: pilgrims bore crosses and carried arms.
Both shared an indiscriminate vocabulary of the *peregrinatio*; some of
the privileges and the status of quasi-ecclesiastics. Louis VII of France
took the Cross at Vézelay at Easter 1146 and the pilgrim's wallet at St
Denis in June 1147, his response to the pull of crusade as distinct from
pilgrimage being decidedly ambivalent, if Professor Grabois is to be
believed.[68] In charters of the twelfth century, it is rarely possible to

distinguish the two exercises: Giles Constable's analysis of charter evidence which claims to show how crusades were funded applies equally, often identically, to pilgrims. As Constable admits: 'The charters gave no evidence . . . that (the crusader) differed in any essential respect from other pilgrims, or that he was required to go with any army or to fight the pagans, though many of them did.'[69]

It is often presumed that those who adopted the Cross, following the action of the First Crusaders, did so consciously to signal their martial intentions. Those who abandoned Robert of Normandy's army at Bari in 1096 marked their departure by 'taking up again their pilgrim staves'.[70] The Cross was closely identified with the special form of penitential warfare begun in 1096 and, as Michael Markowski has noticed, came to be associated particularly, although not exclusively, with expeditions to the Holy Land.[71] Although commonly referred to as *peregrini*, from 1097 at the latest crusaders were distinguished as being 'signed with the Cross'.[72] The *Gesta Francorum* describes how crusaders sewed crosses on to their garments.[73] By the first Lateran Council of 1123, beside the language of pilgrimage, popes referred to warriors assuming the Cross: for instance, Eugenius III in 1145 and 1148; Alexander III in 1169 and 1181 and Gregory VIII in 1187.[74] Yet chroniclers continued to use the word 'pilgrim' indiscriminately, even eye-witnesses such as William of Tyre. Perhaps he did not see much of a difference?

The notions of unarmed pilgrimage and armed crusade were less discrete than the apparent contradiction of purpose and function might imply. The Cross tended to suggest violence. But this was not universal. The English hermit, Godric of Finchale (d. 1170), according to his twelfth-century biographer, visited Palestine twice. On each occasion he contented himself with seeing the Holy Places, fasting and other self-imposed physical privations. Yet Godric had apparently taken the Cross both times and had borne the 'vexillum crucis' throughout his pilgrimages.[75] The biography was written in the late twelfth century and gives pause to those seeking easy categorization of crusade and pilgrimage. Orderic Vitalis, writing a few years after the event, describes the reaction of those supporters of William Clito not pardoned by Henry I after William's death in 1128: 'many others, distressed by their master's death, took the Lord's Cross and, becoming exiles for Christ's sake, set out for his sepulchre in Jerusalem'.[76] This may be regarded as euphemistic cover for a prudent act of self-preservation in the face of political disaster. Whether they intended to fight or not is impossible to judge.

This elision of themes, so characteristic of the period, is neatly summed up in a charter of 1120, written on behalf of one Guillaume le Veneur from Touraine who was declared to have 'accepted the Cross as a sign of his pilgrimage (*in signum peregrinationis*)'.[77]

The development of the liturgical rite for taking the Cross confirms this conjunction of practices. J. A. Brundage finds no explicit evidence of formal liturgical ceremonies from the first half of the twelfth century. However, they may be presumed. St Bernard dispensed crosses at Vézelay in 1146. Godric of Finchale had, his biographer claims, been given the Cross on one occasion by a priest and Guillaume le Veneur's charter indicates that taking the Cross was already, by 1120, a formal solemnization of a special pilgrimage vow. The ceremony began explicitly to be associated with a particular form of pilgrimage: Guillaume le Veneur's charter describes taking the Cross as 'the habit of these kinds of pilgrims' and a mid-twelfth-century Angevin observed that Fulk of Anjou's assumption of the Cross in 1128 was 'following the custom of such pilgrimages'.[78] Unfortunately, these sources fail to make clear exactly what was distinctive about these journeys. Was it that they had military intent (unlikely in view of Godric's experience), or, perhaps, that they were directed towards Jerusalem? Perhaps each region was different. If so, this may account for a flexibility of application in, say, Italy, while in northern France (where the two sources were written), the Cross implied a Jerusalem pilgrimage. This uncertainty in the evidence may itself support the idea that even the giving of the Cross implied no sharply defined or uniformly applied institution.

All surviving twelfth-century rites for taking the Cross so far discovered are closely associated with ceremonies for departing pilgrims.[79] Two particular features of such ceremonies are worth emphasizing. First, in papal references, taking the Cross marks the moment when the offered privileges came into force, the wearing of the Cross being a sign of the validity of the claim to protection. As Michael Clanchy has shown, such a ceremonial guarantee of a contract was commonplace in a society in which literacy was still patchy among the secular elites.[80] The symbol rather than the letter secured the contract. Some of the surviving rites from the twelfth century confirm the papal linkage between taking the Cross and protection, but on a much broader and more fundamental level. As the so-called Lambrecht Pontifical of the second half of the twelfth century has it, the Cross is a sign of God's protection and a surety of personal immunity from dangers both physical and spiritual: 'Accept the sign of the Cross of Christ in heart and body so that you may be protected from all your enemies and from all wiles of the Devil.'[81] This formula remained unchanged for centuries. The Cross was more than a focus of piety, a symbol of devotion, a public confirmation of a vow or, like a pilgrim's badge, a sign of the wearer's special status. It was a talisman, appealing to the deepest anxieties of the traveller and warrior, a guarantee of safety as well as salvation. As such, the pacific Godric of Finchale had as much need of it as Richard the Lionheart.

Another significant aspect of the surviving twelfth-century rites is that while they are all linked to pilgrim ceremonies, they are different from each other.[82] The impression is that there was no standard ceremony for taking the Cross. Indeed, despite the inclusion of a rite in the thirteenth-century Roman Pontifical, there remained no standard ceremony for the rest of the Middle Ages. In the face of increasing attempts to impose uniformity and in view of the importance attached by the papacy to crusading after 1187, this is remarkable. But it exposes one characteristic of twelfth-century crusading too easily belittled by those historians in search of precise canonistic definitions. In the twelfth century, diversity of local custom and individual response was the norm. The papacy was not in control of a homogeneous movement. Disparity of practice, uncertainty of focus and the absence of legal definition suggest an elusive and protean phenomenon. The crusade meant different things for different people at the same and at different times.

This is not to deny the seriousness of crusading, nor the new range of experiences associated with it. But these functioned as part of existing habits and traditions and, in the twelfth century, marked no sharply defined new era beyond the occupation and thus accessibility of the Holy Places. The development of crusading as an institution depended on its familiarity, not its novelty; on its acceptability as much as its challenge. If the activity was innovative in being especially physically demanding, the tensions which were assuaged – spiritual, social, political or economic – were not.

This new exercise was obviously not without effect. Crusaders' privileges, for example, had extensive implications, their legal and fiscal immunity being guaranteed by the Church and upheld, in theory, by the secular authorities.[83] The effectiveness or consistency of either is hard to assess, the evidence from the twelfth century being limited and contradictory. In 1106, Hugh du Puiset, who had taken the Cross to join Bohemund's crusade, appealed to Pope Paschal II to defend his and his vassals' property, threatened by Count Rotrou of Perche. Hugh claimed protection under papal decrees as a 'Hierosolymitanus'. Paschal passed the buck to the Archbishop of Sens and Ivo of Chartres. The latter, in turn, submitted the case to a committee of clerics who, in some confusion, were unable to decide between feudal rights and ecclesiastical immunity, not least because 'the institution of committing to the church's care the possessions of *milites* going to Jerusalem was new'. Ivo, in spite or perhaps because of his expertise as a canon lawyer, sent the case back to the Pope unresolved. Even if this instance is taken as a sign of the operation of crusading institutions, it is apparent that the local clergy had little idea of what to do. Furthermore, the immunity claimed by Hugh itself derived from Urban II's association of the privileges of crusaders with those which existed under the earlier eleventh-century provisions of the Truce of God, as well as those customarily enjoyed by pilgrims.[84]

In Hugh du Puiset's case, any superior lay power was absent, which, although unsurprising in the final year of King Philip the Fat, may explain the ineffectiveness of the immunity. Local ecclesiastical officials remained unsure of their ground. In November 1146, Eugenius III had to instruct the bishop of Salisbury that church jurisdiction did not extend to disseisin committed before the victim took the Cross. *Quantum praedecessores* had itemized the crusaders' immunities, but some still found their operation confusing. Being promulgated for specific journeys, such as the 1145–46 call to arms, the privileges had no permanent application, hence the repeated papal renewals up to *Audita tremendi* in 1187.[85] However, later in the century, at least in north-west Europe, the secular, not the ecclesiastical, arm seems to have taken the lead in defining protection and, perhaps, even extending the range of the temporal privileges. The *De legibus et consuetudinibus* attributed to Glanvill (*c.*1180) described special immunities for pilgrims to Jerusalem, including a unique variant of the writ *mort d'ancestor*, but failed to draw a distinction between crusade and pilgrimage. Significantly, perhaps, that had to await the lawyers of the thirteenth century.[86] In 1188, the Anglo-French crusade Ordinances, not papal bulls, extended the financial privileges with a precision and detail not seen before.[87] Although as early as 1166 Alexander III had offered plenary indulgences to those who fought in the Holy Land for at least two years, the first mention of the crusader's term of immunity and protection in action is on the Pipe Roll of 1191/2.[88] During the Third Crusade, as in the First, the practice of crusading fashioned the institution, not vice versa.

In a wider social dimension, it is equally hard to assert much independent or unique impact. The financial needs of departing crusaders certainly aided the concurrent opening of freer local land markets through mortgages and sale of property. Warfare in the East gave fresh scope for military enterprise, but, by its nature, was of limited significance. There was no channelling of violence away from domestic conflicts. There was only one general expedition between 1101 and 1188. Successful crusaders were those who had trained in the hard school of European war. If war in twelfth-century western Europe was more ordered, less anarchic or fragmented than in the tenth century, then crusading, with its large capital sums and structured recruitment, was a symptom of change, not a cause. The same can be said for the variety of motives contemporaries observed in crusaders, from those such as Etienne de Niblens (*c*.1100), who was said to lament the pollution of his life, and Ulric Bucel, who was described as being 'more concerned for the health of his soul than the honour of his earthly existence', to those who, in the words of the hostile Würzburg annalist, 'lusted after novelties and went in order to learn about new lands'.[89] The crusade was not the only outlet for such diverse emotions: not all adventurers bothered to seek Jerusalem; not all pious lay knights either. Warfare nearer home or the patronage of monasteries could, and did serve just as well.[90] Pursued by a minority of free society, crusading provided an extension of prevailing habits rather than an alternative to them.

Crusading was far from escapist; it was integrated into existing patterns of thought and behaviour, a reflection, not a rejection of social attitudes. To take one example, companionship and comradeship formed central features in contemporary accounts of crusading, as in society in general. In both, the cohesive power of friendship and association should not be ignored. Where institutional bonds lacked either strength or inspiration, the group, community or commune formed by mutual self-interest provided a necessary sense of belonging and a structure of material support. To such emotions did the Cistercians appeal with great initial success. It is no coincidence that Ailred of Rievaulx, one of the Cistercians' more effective recruiters, wrote a treatise *De Amicitia*: neither is it that the Cistercians played a central role in the inspiration of and recruitment for the Second Crusade. St Bernard himself saw crusade armies as sworn associations, modelled on monastic communities, bound together by love of God.[91] The important ties of the *familia* can be traced in the vernacular romances of Chrétien de Troyes no less than in the growth of corporate identity among the clerks and courtiers of Angevin kings, as chronicled by Walter Map.[92] Crusading fitted this pattern. It is not just in the stories of campaigning that we find evidence of cameraderie. After all, we should expect to find them there. But repeatedly in descriptions of crusade recruitment there are references to groups of relatives, friends and neighbours. Some entered into formal communes, as in 1147, 1189 and 1217.[93] The young crusaders described as *coniurati* who terrorized the Jewish communities of England in Lent 1190 were not untypical, bound together by shared location, kinship, class and friendship.[94] Crusading could create or more often reinforce such communion, inexplicable if divorced from its social and cultural context.

Did crusading create new patterns of virtue to admire? It may be that Urban II had some hopes of it. Those who interpreted Urban's thoughts in the subsequent generation depicted him as offering the crusade as an alternative, which brings us back to Guibert of Nogent. But the holy warrior was not new and the Jerusalem *iter* soon became the consummation, not the expiation, of a chivalric career.[95] Crusading heroes were regarded in terms of existing typology – honour, loyalty, etc. It is consistent with this response that Peter of Blois, in his panegyric on Raynald of Chatillon, the *Passio Reginaldi* written shortly after 1187, should be eager to claim his hero as an example of Apostolic Poverty, that is, not a specifically or exclusively crusading virtue.[96]

The *Passio Reginaldi* has been described as a piece of crusade hagiography. Although standing in the long, pre-crusading tradition of justification of violence and sanctification of holy warriors, the *Passio* marks a new beginning in its intensity, imagery and purpose. There is a distinctive quality which can only be called crusading. Peter of Blois chose to describe the celebrated killing of Raynald by Saladin in the Sultan's tent after the battle of Hattin (4 July 1187). Reynald's opportunistic career of excess and self-advancement is transmuted into one of moderation and self-denial. Claiming that his knowledge of Reynald's last moments came from an eye-witness, Aimery of Lusignan, Peter has Raynald display fortitude and constancy in the face of the infidel's blandishments and threats. Facing death, Raynald attempts to convert Saladin. At the end, Raynald's death is seen as a victory, a memory of Christ's passion, a doorway to everlasting life, a consummation of his pilgrimage. The image of the Cross is everywhere, just as it was to be in most surviving crusade sermons from the 1190s onwards. The concentration on the Cross in this and other Third Crusade *excitatoria* was fuelled by the loss of a relic of the Holy Cross at Hattin. For Peter of Blois the Cross is 'the Ark of the New Testament, the banner of salvation, the title of sanctity, the hope of

victory . . . the foundation of faith, the conqueror of Hell etc etc.'
Oddly echoing Saladin's own nickname for Raynald, Peter declared:
'as elephants are roused to battle by the sight of blood so, and more
fervently, does the sight of the Holy Cross and the remembrance of
the Lord's Passion rouse Christian knights'.[97]

At last, crusade propagandists had worked out a coherent imagery,
concentrating on the Cross as an all-purpose symbol of militant loyalty
to Christ and spiritual redemption, allied to a strong vein of secular romance both in depicting Christian warriors and their infidel foes. The
sacrifice demanded of the faithful soldier of Christ is distilled into a vision of glory which shines with remorseless consistency through the
exempla of later crusade sermons and propaganda, as well as forming a
growing theme of vernacular poets.[98]

The *Passio Reginaldi* is just one instance of the new impetus towards
defining the crusade provided by the battle of Hattin, the capture of a
relic of the Holy Cross and loss of Jerusalem in 1187. Almost immediately the customary vagueness in describing crusaders vanished. Perhaps in consequence of recruiting requirements and the implications
of crusader privileges for raising money as well as men, the status of a
crusader, contrasted with that of a pilgrim, was defined with precision.
The adoption of the Cross was now clearly established as separating the
two activities of crusading and pilgrimage. The terms of the Saladin Tithe
of 1188, both in Angevin and Capetian lands, granted exemption
from payment of the tax to those who had taken the Cross, a privilege
widely abused, according to a contemporary crusade song (*c.*1188).[99]
For the first time on a Pipe Roll the term *crucesignatus* was used in
1191/2, although *crusiatus* appears on the Pipe Roll of 1188/9.[100] By the
mid-1190s, the designation in Latin was standard: crusaders were
crucesignati (or equivalent words) and as such merited a different order
of privileges to pilgrims as they performed a markedly different function. In the vernacular, although the language of pilgrimage persisted
as long as crusading lasted, a distinctive crusading vocabulary was soon
developed. In French, the verb *croisier* or *croiser* can be found at the time
of the Third Crusade, as well as in the chroniclers of the Fourth Crusade, Robert of Clari and Geoffrey de Villehardouin. By extension,
croisié described those who had taken the Cross.[101] Words for the institution itself are contained in William of Tudela's poem (*c.*1213) on the
Albigensian Crusade: *crozada; crozea; crozeia.*[102]

It could be argued that the difference between pilgrimage and crusade had been inherent since 1095, but only after 1187/8 was it recog-

nized in law and government action, that is, secular law and secular government. The running was made not by canonists or Curial legists but by servants of temporal powers. It has even been suggested that Innocent III himself was introduced to the word *crucesignatus* by Gerald of Wales in 1199 (previously, popes had favoured more laborious phrases based on *crucem accipere*). Gerald had been a clerk of Henry II and a preacher of the Cross in Wales in 1188. Gerald had been using the word since before 1191.[103] The distinctive word for crusaders did not first appear after 1187. The phrase had occurred since the First Crusade. In letters, chronicles and in some of the rites for taking the Cross, 'crux' and 'signare' appear together. A solitary source from the Second Crusade uses the word 'cruziatur'.[104] However, it was only during and after the Third Crusade that the term *crucesignatus* (and *crucesignata*) gained wide currency: and the initiative seems to have come from temporal authorities, not the papacy. It would be entirely in keeping with a view of crusading as not being originally a clearly defined phenomenon if the pressure for legal and practical definition came from secular, not ecclesiastical, law and government, remembering always that both were administered by educated clerics.

Whatever else, the Third Crusade marked a watershed. I have argued for this in institutional terms. It also appears to have been true in more popular aspects. In the corpus of surviving crusade sermon *exempla* (mainly of the thirteenth-century and later) there are few stories which refer to crusades before 1187, and not even the First Crusade is exploited.[105] There are two good reasons for this. One is that Hattin and its aftermath redefined crusading in practice and then, with Innocent III, in theory. The other is that crusading before Hattin was hardly a discrete activity. Like King Lear's wit, it was pared on both sides, by pilgrimage and Holy War.

Ironically, the essence of pre-1187 crusading is to be found not in the content of Peter of Blois's *Passio Reginaldi*, but in its subject. Raynald first appears as a mercenary of Baldwin III at the siege of Ascalon in 1153. Two excellent marriages made him successively prince of Antioch and then lord of Kerak and Oultejordain. He believed in aggression as the best method of advancement. In his career he pillaged Cyprus and terrorized the Red Sea. He became identified with an actively hostile policy towards Saladin. His end, on 4 July 1187, hacked to death by Saladin himself, was entirely appropriate: extreme violence in the best of company. He was an adventurer who had tasted the pleasures of success as well as the miseries of a Muslim prison for sixteen years. His opportunism ended in death and his transfiguration into a martyr: an 'athlete of the Lord', indeed, as Peter of Blois put it in a cliché famous long before 1095. But there is no evidence that Raynald ever took the Cross.[106] In the twelfth century he did not have to because, in some senses, there were no crusades to fight.

2

DEFINITION AND DIFFUSION

The expeditions from western Europe to recover Jerusalem between 1188 and 1192 reforged the ideology and practice of crusading, casting the past in a new light and the future in new directions. Failure to achieve their ultimate goal ensured that *subsidium Terrae sanctae* – assistance for the Holy Land – remained prominent in contemporary religious and political rhetoric. Diverse mechanisms of thought, organization and action coalesced into recognizable patterns of belief, argument, aspiration and strategy sustained by distinctive legal, ritual and liturgical customs. Funding, recruitment and preaching developed in ways that flowed from the exigencies and experiences of the 1190s rather than the 1090s: clerical taxation; vow redemptions; armies paid by central funds; the use of sea transport; central control of regional preaching campaigns. Built on the disparate practices and habits of the previous century, crusading was fashioned to suit changing religious, ecclesiastical and political objectives.

However, despite an edifice of organization, it remains inappropriate to talk of crusading as a coherent or cohesive movement. The form of Holy War primarily associated with the struggle for control of the Holy Places became an institution of the western Church but, unlike Confession after 1215, it was neither compulsory nor universally applicable.[1] Available and advisable, it was also ephemeral and peripheral. Like the Inquisition, the crusade lacked a separate administration, head or permanent agents, its organization being conducted by papal Curia, local provinces and dioceses or secular rulers.[2] This variety of organization and participants lent crusading a possibly deceptive universality. So, too, did the popularity of the extraordinary spiritual privilege associated with taking the Cross. Each campaign offered indulgences which were specific and separate: the benefit may have been permanent but the exercise deserving merit was not. Yet increasingly the advantages of this form of penance became disassociated from active or strenuous participation in the Holy War which was its initial justification. General prayers for the Holy Land became customary, not least as a means of explaining the special power of the indulgence rather than the practical action which it originally rewarded.[3]

Thus, although provided with an administrative pattern by the end of Innocent III's pontificate (1216), crusading lacked consistent focus. For all its prominence in religious rhetoric, clerical commentary and secular interest, the ideas, descriptions and behaviour linked to this form of Holy War remained noticeably imprecise and malleable, lacking definition in law or language. Much of the interest of crusading lies not in arguments over its health or corruption, nor in some anthropomorphic transformation into a movement with a life of its own. More revealing is how it was interpreted and manipulated by apologists, critics and actors; in its reception at different levels, times and places in western European society; in variety of response as well as variety of application. Identifying the reality of these is complicated by the nature of the evidence, which is rarely objective. Literary, chronicle and much of the archival survivals are typically part of the exercise of crusading itself, biased, partial, apologetic. In western Europe, the long thirteenth century, from the fall of Jerusalem (1187) to the Trial of the Templars (1307–14), saw the elaboration of the *negotium crucis*, protean in diversity as much as universality, significant in what it reflected as much as in what it inspired.

Ambiguity and hesitation were not swept away by Gregory VIII's *Audita tremendi* in 1188. A Norwegian writer recorded that news of the fall of Jerusalem and the papal call to arms were received at the court of Canute VI of Denmark in stunned silence. A layman, Esbern, brother of the militant Slav-basher Archbishop Absolom of Lund, delivered a speech rousing the Danes to action. As reported, stirring emphasis was laid on the fame and heroic success of the Danes' Viking ancestors, whose glory nonetheless paled beside the 'greater and more profitable conquests' opened up by this Holy War. The Danish court was seemingly being introduced to crusading for the first time. There is no sense in the account, *De profectione Danorum in Hierosolymam*, of the Holy Land crusade being familiar, still less habitual, even though explicit church sanction for wars in the region had existed for at least a generation, with Archbishop Absolom heavily involved. According to the *De profectione*, the response to the papal bull and Esbern's address was limited. Only seven notables embarked. After batterings from storms and hostile locals, a remnant reached the Holy Land only after the truce between Richard I and Saladin in 1192. Although perceived as generally meritorious and personally rewarding, there is no standard rhetoric of the Cross in the description of the reception and execution of this crusade appeal. The Danes appear tentative and stumbling, especially when contrasted with other European rulers.[4]

Very different appears the world fifty years later. Adam von Beham, a papal legate, charged with disciplining German bishops sympathetic to the excommunicate Emperor Frederick II, recorded that on 3 August 1240 the dean of Passau 'publicly preached the Cross against me and gave many people the Cross for their salvation (*multos cruce signavit in salvationem animarum*)'. The dean of Passau and the Imperialists were making a neat propagandist point by appropriating the very weapons of Holy War employed so vigorously against them by successive popes. The proclamation of an anti-crusade, even as a gesture, suggests that at least the trappings of distinctive language and ceremonial had penetrated contemporary mentalities. The Passau anti-crusade was a backhanded compliment to the effectiveness of promoting the crusade as a panacea for the ills of the established Roman Church.[5]

The thirteenth century saw the wide application of crusading ideology and machinery to problems of the defence, expansion and policing of Christendom. *Crucesignati* were found in Syria, Egypt, Greece, Spain, France, the Baltic, England, Germany, Majorca and Italy, on battlefields as far apart as Mansourah and Lincoln, Lewes and Lake Chud. *Crucesignati* fought for and against Henry III of England as well as Frederick II of Germany. Enemies of the Cross included Muslims, Russians, Albigensians, Aragonese, Greeks, Italians, Bosnians, Slavs, Balts, Moors and Mamluks, infidels, heretics, rebels and political rivals of the papacy.[6] The institutions of the *negotium crucis* reached all parts of Christendom that acknowledged papal authority. By the 1220s, church and secular authorities voiced familiarity with the rituals and privileges of crusaders, *crucesignati riti*, as the General Statutes of the Scottish Church called them.[7] Even the exiguous settlements in Greenland apparently contributed walrus tusks for the cause in the early fourteenth century, while wills everywhere testified to the social embrace.[8]

The *negotium crucis* became emblematic of a variety of otherwise separate activities and aspirations. Associated preaching, ritual, vow, liturgy, recruitment, indulgence, penance, finance and military action were employed in refining ecclesiastical approaches to the laity and lay attitudes and procedures in spirituality, war and justice. The piety and politics of a Louis IX of France or a Simon de Montfort were closely bound up with a set of spiritual values and expressions of faith which included active crusading. Fashionable intellectual opinion received the support of warlords and politicians eager for recruits, cash and moral approval for their policies. The coincidence of self-interest and convenience for popes, lay rulers, clergy and laity was central to the prominence of crusading, which did not impose itself on the faithful as a discrete activity, but was rather adopted and adapted by them for reasons pious, sordid, noble, selfish, heroic or hypocritical.

Responses to crusading were neither crudely one-dimensional – for or against – nor uniform. Observers could be in favour of some or all crusades, or none. Many ignored them. In the early fourteenth century, the Venetian Marino Sanudo spent half a lifetime trying to encourage and advise a new *passagium* to the East. Close to the courts of Naples, Avignon and Paris, he nonetheless urged an end to the papal crusades in Italy, identifying them as the prime cause for the loss of the Latin East.[9] Frederick II took the Cross, went on crusade, although excommunicated, and had crusades launched against him. Simon de Montfort, son of the leader of the Albigensian crusade, fought on and was fought by crusades. Unlike, say, twentieth-century Communism, crusading was not a monolithic ideology or autonomous movement, a free-standing, coherent force determining equally clear positive or negative reactions. Rather it presented two distinct faces: a form of holy warfare available to political leaders across Christendom; and a collection of religious exercises which could operate far beyond the battlefield. As such it attracted enthusiasm or scepticism less according to any intrinsic moral value but rather depending on the interest of the commentator. General conclusions from individual witnesses tend, therefore, to be unprofitable.

There is a clear contrast, for example, between two thirteenth-century contemporaries, the English Benedictine monk from St Alban's, Matthew Paris (d. 1259), and the German mission priest Henry, still alive in 1259, whose *Chronicle of Livonia* was written in the late 1220s. Each was conditioned by circumstance and purpose: Paris writing a general chronicle of his times; Henry a triumphalist account of the establishment of the Christian colony in Livonia; Paris the prejudiced observer; Henry the committed participant. Their images of crusading are worlds apart.

Paris was fiercely protective of the rights and property of his Order and, by extension, the English Church. Thus he appears anti-papal and nationalistic, often quoted by modern historians who see a decline in the popularity of crusades caused by hostility to papal campaigns in Italy and Germany. But Paris was enthusiastic for a certain form of crusading. His lively criticisms concentrated on three features of the administration of the crusade: creeping papal control of the English Church, epitomized in newfangled clerical taxation; the collection and misuse of crusade funds which made this possible; and some of the destinations for crusading proposed by the papacy. His hostility to the friars and their methods of preaching to obtain vow redemptions for cash, was fuelled by inter-order rivalry and jealousy (which he later toned down) and their prominence in this new papal scheme to extract money from the laity, money that otherwise might go to the Benedictines. Paris drew attention to the confusion caused in the late 1240s by conflicting crusade objectives: now the Holy Land, now Romania (i.e. Greece), now Frederick II. He encapsulated his attitude in the remarks he attributed to King Haakon of Norway to the effect that the King was always willing to fight the enemies of the Church but not all the enemies of the Pope.[10] As witnessed by his obituary on the double *crucesignatus* Philip d'Aubigny (d. 1236), his praise of those who died on Richard of Cornwall's campaign (1240–41), and his eulogy on the fate of William Longsword at Mansourah in 1250, Paris approved of campaigns against Christendom's external enemies, especially in the East.[11]

Henry of Livonia's concerns were local, his enthusiasm unalloyed, his perspective partial. He constantly emphasized the nature as well as popularity of the privileges offered those who took the Cross against the 'perfidious Livs', equivalent, he stressed, to those granted for the Jerusalem expeditions. To underscore the spiritual dimension of what, even from his own account, could appear as secular and ecclesiastical imperialism, Henry habitually referred to the crusaders as 'peregrini' or 'milicia peregrinorum'. As elsewhere in Christendom, this traditional association of crusading and pilgrimage was fraying thin, but Henry saw it as justifying the enterprise and underpinning wavering enthusiasm. To portray conquest of the bleak pagan lands of the Livs and Letts as pilgrimage was made possible because the sees of Riga and Livonia had adopted the Virgin Mary as their patroness. Just as Jerusalem was the land of the Son of God, so Livonia was the land of His Mother, soon to experience a bizarre transformation by other Baltic writers into a demanding war-goddess. Henry of Livonia presented the crusade in which he was involved in self-justifying religious terms, the special pleading of genuine conviction.[12]

Such writers played a crucial role in creating the phenomenon they were describing, Henry's ingenuity, no less than Paris's scepticism, providing the context as well as witnessing the consequences of the sharper definition given to crusading at the beginning of the thirteenth century by the Pope.

Innocent III

It is possible to exaggerate the dynamic leadership supplied by Innocent III (1198–1216). He codified and articulated existing trends rather more than initiating new ones. Nonetheless, his contribution to crusading could be described as a sort of creation. The foundation charters of the crusade as a coherent institution are the bull *Quia Maior* (1213) and the decree *Ad Liberandam* (1215) of the Fourth Lateran Council. To them must be added the imposition of taxation of the clergy (1199); the provincial organization of preaching and fund-raising; and the confirmation, in the campaigns summoned against Markward of Anweiler in Sicily (1198), Livonia (1198 and 1204) and the Albigensian heretics (1208), of the regular extension of the Holy Land privileges to other theatres of warfare on behalf of the Church.[13]

Although in nearly every instance, Innocent consolidated and extended existing practice, thereafter the essentials of the institution were in place. Summoning a new expedition, *Quia Maior* reiterated the propaganda themes of earlier years: the offer of salvation, 'the ancient device of Jesus Christ'; charity to oppressed Christians; the Holy Land as the patrimony of Christ and His followers; a test of Christian devotion. The apparatus of inducement was rehearsed in fresh detail. Plenary indulgences, forgiveness of all confessed sins, granted through the power vested by Christ in the Pope, were granted to those who campaigned in person, at their own or another's expense; and to those who commuted their service by sending others as proxies. This put an end to more than a century of confusion, hesitation and obfuscation evident in papal reluctance to define the precise nature of the crusade indulgence, whether the sin or the penalty of sin was remitted.[14]

Innocent went further by encouraging 'anyone who wishes' to take the Cross, allowing for redemption of vows for money according to means, thus massively extending the embrace of the advantages of taking the Cross. Widespread vow redemption was to radically alter perceptions and perhaps the actual thrust of crusade preaching: the enterprise was financially and militarily advantaged; its reputation rendered vulnerable to charges of 'crosses for cash'.[15] Here Innocent was extending and clarifying the precedent of Clement III (1187–91). Within a generation, redemption of vows by non-combatants became habitual and, in certain cases, compulsory. To those non-*crucesignati* who donated funds according to their means, *Quia Maior* promised proportionate indulgences.[16] Ecclesiastical protection of crusaders' property, the moratorium on crusaders' repayment on usury and their exemption from usury to Jewish creditors were repeated.

Innocent's concept was deliberately inclusive of the whole Church, lay and clerical. While bishops were to enforce some of the provisions, the secular arm was involved in policing those against Jewish usury. Secular communities were encouraged to band together to supply adequate troops. To ensure the *negotium crucis* as a regular feature of lay life, monthly processions, fasting, almsgiving, preaching and prayers were instituted, including a special prayer inserted into the liturgy of the Mass. Repeating a directive of 1199, in each parish church a chest was to be placed to receive the indulgence-worthy donations of the faithful.[17] There were liturgical precedents under Gregory VIII and Clement III, and the 1213 injunctions were open to modification, such as the ringing of a bell during the Lord's Prayer in Masses for the Holy Land, which appears in the Worcester diocesan statutes of 1229.[18] Nevertheless, the bull of 1213, incorporated into the decree of 1215, provided the basis for the infusion, to quote the prayer ordained by *Quia Maior*, of the liberation of 'the land which thine only-begotten son consecrated with his own blood' into the daily life of Christendom.

Innocent III's Legacy

The terms of *Quia maior* were reiterated in the final decree (no. 71) of the Fourth Lateran Council, *Ad Liberandam*, but with a greater urgency and focus on details of enforcement of vows and financing, such as a three-year clerical tax of a twentieth. These ordinances exerted an extraordinary hold over succeeding papal legislation. The crusade decrees of the Lyons Councils of 1245 and 1274 were, in essence and words, copies of *Ad Liberandam* and continued to form the basis of crusade negotiations in the 1330s. Even the lack of comparable precision or verbatim borrowing in the equivalent decree *Redemptor noster* of the Council of Vienne (1312) may indicate that Innocent's decrees had established accepted crusading procedures.[19] By the 1340s, Clement VI, in authorizing preaching for a campaign against the Turks in the Aegean, referred to 'indulgentias consuetas' and, with reference to both the Turkish campaign and the defence of Caffa in the Crimea in 1345, indulgences 'usually granted to those who Cross the sea (*transfretantibus*) to help the Holy Land'. This unspecified formula was typical of later papal grants. However dynamic the impulses to campaign against the enemies of the Church, the legal conventions remained sclerotically static. Those who agreed to campaign against the infidel in the fourteenth century sometimes attracted additional privileges, such as the right to appoint their own confessors, but on the central apparatus of privileges, no pope after Innocent III and no medieval council after Lateran IV felt the need to go beyond the 1215 decree.[20] Even so, the reception and application of Innocent III's model was neither coherent, cohesive or straightforward.

The emphasis on the Holy Land in *Quia Maior* and *Ad Liberandam* was self-evident. In the twelfth century there appears to have existed a hierarchy of Holy War indulgences, combatants against Christians receiving them only if they died on campaign rather than, as with the full Holy Land privilege, if they survived as well.[21] In the 1213 encyclical, except for Provençals and Spaniards, the indulgences offered against the Albigensians and Moors were rescinded, an insight into the priorities of the Pope, who did more than anyone to extend the range of the *negotium crucis*. The centrality of the Holy Land in the system of remission of sins was acknowledged in the third decree of Lateran IV, *Excommunicamus*, in which those who took the Cross to exterminate heretics were offered the indulgences and privileges 'as is granted to those who go to the aid of the Holy Land'. Similarly, Constitution II: 2 of Lyons I equated the rewards of aiding the Latin Empire of Constantinople with those 'granted to those who come to the help of the Holy Land'.[22] What was true for heretics and schismatics was also true for pagans in the Baltic and papal enemies in Germany, Italy and elsewhere. Although there are examples, especially from the fourteenth century onwards, of plenary indulgences being granted without mention of the Holy Land, for instance with regard to conquests in the Atlantic and the Americas, the traditional link was never completely broken.[23] This did not prevent popes employing crusade privileges widely, but, with the prayers, processions and alms all explicitly and universally invited for the Holy Land, the *negotium crucis* did not exist entirely divorced from its original inspiration.

The theoretical basis of the exercise, so far from being clarified in Innocent's decrees, was glossed over. In his *Decretals*, Gregory IX (1227–41), who as Cardinal Ugolino had been intimately involved in crusading preparations in the 1220s, included *Ad Liberandam*, shorn of the passages relating to the juridical status of *crucesignati*.[24] In general, Innocent III did little to settle abiding academic anxieties over the relation of crusade to traditionally justified Holy War. Later canonists were free to render the crusade as they pleased, a striking licence in an age of increasing legalism and persecuting orthodoxy. No specific category of war was designated, the crusade merely feeding from a range of concepts and analogies: feudal, penitential, Roman. Theory tagged along behind or apart from practice. For example, the peculiarity of some Albigensian crusaders taking service for a customary vassalic term of forty days is ignored, despite its signal difference from other campaigns of the Cross. The canonist Hostiensis, who recognized the absence of precise legal vocabulary and any law explicitly authorizing crusades against Christians, nonetheless was able to argue for the greater importance of the *crux cismarina* over the *crux transmarina*, insisting that the internal threats to Christendom were greater than those outside, and even that the internal crusade was more just. But he had to admit that the Holy Land crusade was more popular.[25]

The impression left by the thirteenth-century theorists is that Innocent III's definition was superficial. The ambiguities and diversity of the twelfth century persisted beneath the carapace of papal certainty and uniformity. Beyond the assertion of papal plenitude of authority to order wars and indulgences, precise justifications and legal distinctions never coalesced into a clear, comprehensive, dictinctive body of accepted Canon Law. The best that Hostiensis, a pupil of Innocent IV, could manage was that a crusade was a papal just war. The authority rather than the purpose of the enterprise received a prominence that was reversed in practice.[26]

This concentration on authority ultimately prevented the development of a distinct theory of crusade. Instead there existed a series of concepts and justifications borrowed from elsewhere – just war, papal supremacy, relations with infidels – that were never incorporated together into laws or canons. This probably made no difference to those engaged in crusading, yet for such an apparently central feature of western Christendom to lack a settled legal explanation except as merely one aspect of papal power is notable, although not unique. Again, there is a parallel in the thirteenth-century Inquisition, which was *ad hoc*, local, diocesan-based, individual *inquisitiones* not amounting to a coherent legal or bureaucratic 'Holy Office' as later, with the fifteenth-century Spanish Inquisition. The lack of theoretical substance allowed for dilution and, in the long term, suggested ephemerality. While the general theory of indulgences lay at the heart of some fierce debates within and outside the Roman Catholic Church, the crusade, a prime means of earning an indulgence, was not. As a concept it remained elusive. At the end of the fourteenth century, after nearly two centuries of Innocentian ideals in operation, answering the question 'By what law or on what ground can war be made against the Saracens?', Honoré Bonet, in the *Tree of Battles* (1387), employed wholly traditional arguments. Although well versed in canon law and history, Bonet's justification of war against the infidels depended solely on a just cause – occupation of Christian land or rebellion against Christian rule – and papal authority. 'All the great expeditions . . . beyond the seas against the Saracens were made with the consent of the Holy Father of Rome.' Not only was there no recognition of an independent legal concept, there was no definitive word for what we call a crusade. In this Bonet imitated his predecessors as well as his contemporaries.[27]

Another central element in the crusade, the vow, was also left oddly ill-defined. More interested in legal theory, thirteenth-century canonists were concerned with crusade vows only in so far as they raised problems of authorization of violence. The peculiarites of the crusade vow went unresolved. Innocent III allowed the accumulated habits of more than a century to continue unregulated, except as regards authorization. Only papally appointed clerics could dispense the Cross. Otherwise, obfuscation prevailed. Following the precedent of the 1188 Saladin Tithe ordinances, *Quia Maior* assumed that taking the Cross symbolized the vow. This public rite was unlike the swearing of other lay vows, being more akin to entering religious orders. It matched the uniqueness of the supposed crusader's vow which attracted plenary indulgences, conferred special, quasi-ecclesiastical status and imposed upon the votary unusual public communal obligations to serve Christ and the Church. Such vows may be assumed to have been made privately, yet nowhere do they survive separately from taking the Cross, the act of which was regarded as triggering the benefits, spiritual, material or miraculous. Yet in such ceremonies, the nature of the crusader's privileged position and his obligations were not precisely stated, nor were oaths or liturgy uniform.[28]

The development of crusading was fuelled by practice, not theory: the demand for the powerful spiritual and material benefits; and the requirements of secular politics. The institution was created by those who participated and by those who described, not by academics or canon lawyers. This matched Innocent III's own apparent pragmatism in extending commutation, donation and redemption and, notoriously, making it easier for an individual to commit himself to the cause by allowing husbands to take the Cross without the consent of their wives.[29] Such rules were meant to work. Innocent's insistence on the authority of the Pope was designed for flexibility, not legal clarity.

In the absence of explicit direction from the Curia, it has been argued that canonists 'created a monster' of protean guises and infinitely malleable uses.[30] Imprecision could be said to be an intrinsic feature of the crusade as developed in the thirteenth century. Even Hostiensis, with his distinction between *crux transmarina* and *crux cismarina*, resorted to metaphor, if not euphemism. Others came less close even to his definitions, relying on the analogies of pilgrimage, journey, expeditions and even extermination (for heretics). There was a marked reluctance, shared by the Curia and canonists, to use the language of war, *guerra* or *bellum*. In official decretal collections, the crusade bulls of the past were generally omitted (Calixtus II's *Eis qui Hierosolymam* of 1123; Eugenius III's *Quantum praedecessores* of 1145) or emasculated (*Ad Liberandam*). Of more concern to theorists, including Thomas Aquinas, were wars within Christendom, between Christian rulers or against heretics, conflicts in which the association with pilgrimage, a central feature of crusading, sat uneasily as a legal fiction. No inclusive canonical theory matched the crusade's public ideology or rhetoric.[31] What legal theory there was lay rooted in the practical operation of politics, government, ecclesiastical organization, armies and the law courts.

Institutional flexibility, not, as some argue, definition, allowed the crusade to be employed widely as a military and spiritual exercise. Innocent's decrees left the papacy with free rein to use the mechanics of preaching, recruitment, Cross, vow, indulgences, privileges, alms, taxation, redemptions, and so on. The implications were considerable.

Once the link between vow and personal service had been relaxed, if not broken, in *Quia Maior*, those who fought on crusades did not have to be *crucesignati*. To be *crucesignatus* increasingly denoted status, not activity. On the other hand, targets for crusades ceased to require justification beyond constituting a threat to ecclesiastical interests. Innocent III bequeathed a paradox. By fashioning a more sensitive instrument of church policy, he ensured the crusade a more pervasive role in Christian society while at the same time diluting its distinctiveness as a Christian activity.

Papal Leadership

Of the enthusiasm to employ the apparatus of the *negotium crucis* amongst Innocent III's successors there is no doubt. The conflicts to which the papacy directed crusades fell into seven broadly distinct areas.[32]

The oldest enemy was the clearest cause: defence of Christendom and recovery of what rightfully belonged to it. Muslims in the eastern Mediterranean not only threatened and then extinguished Christian rule in the Holy Land (1291) but, increasingly, pressed against Christendom itself, in the Aegean and, with the Ottoman advance in the later fourteenth century, eastern Europe.

In Spain, the Muslims, after the Christian victory of Las Navas de Tolosa (1212), were in retreat, the operation of *reconquista* often being synonymous with secular dominion, a process largely complete, except for Granada, by the end of the thirteenth century.

Linked materially to this Spanish crusading, but expanding the underlying theory of defence and reconquest to one of extending (*dilatio*) Christendom, from the fourteenth century spiritual and temporal privileges were applied to the conquest and conversion of pagan lands in Africa, the Atlantic and the Americas.

The subjugation of the pagan Balts, Livs and Letts in the Baltic was increasingly devolved from secular powers and the local Church to the Teutonic Knights who, from the pontificate of Alexander IV (1254–61), ran a more or less privatized, eternal crusade.[33]

After the establishment of the Latin Empire of Constantinople in 1204 and the subsequent conquest by westerners of large parts of

Greece and the Aegean (known in the West as Romania), crusades were proclaimed to protect these acquisitions, particularly as the balance of advantage tilted decisively against the Latins from the 1230s. Continued efforts into the fourteenth century to prop up Latin Greece, often disguised, as in 1312, under 'help for the Holy Land against the schismatics in Romania', ultimately ran counter to parallel schemes, from the 1270s until the 1430s, for the reunion of eastern and western Churches.[34]

Within western Christendom there were two main targets for crusades. Those against the Albigensian Cathars had been successful, from a papal and northern French perspective. The theoretical justifications of Holy War against heretics caused little concern and some enthusiasm. Whatever the theory, however, practical differences from other campaigns were evident in, for example, the forty-day service limit, unique for a crusade, reflecting, even if accidentally, the essentially and increasingly political nature of the operation. The Albigensian example was attractive. Acquisitive secular rulers could easily obtain accusations of heresy against their enemies, whether German peasants in the Netherlands or Lower Weser in the 1220s or Bosnian opponents of Hungarian aggrandizement for a century after 1234. The Hussite crusades of the fifteenth century suggest that this cocktail of religious outrage on a base of political ambition remained potent, at least to organizers.[35]

Tangential to these wars against religious opponents of the Church were crusades against Christian enemies of the papacy, at once the most controversial and characteristic crusades in the two centuries after 1215. Although there were precedents from the twelfth century, and Innocent III had launched a crusade against Markward of Anweiler in 1199, the crusades against Frederick II, his Hohenstaufen heirs and their allies in Germany and Italy from the 1230s marked the start of a new focus and energy for papal crusading policy, one well established by the death of Innocent IV in 1254. Thereafter, crusades against papal enemies in Italy stretched from the wars of Charles of Anjou in the 1260s and the Sicilian Vespers in the 1280s to the struggle against Ladislaus of Naples in the early fifteenth century. These campaigns were not only conducted against local rivals, such as the Colonna, Visconti or Venetians, but could involve the great powers: Henry III in Sicily in the 1250s or Philip III of France against Aragon in 1285.[36]

As this range of activity suggests, crusading proved a tenacious feature of European politics because it served two of the powerful social and cultural forces of the High Middle Ages: the external expansion of western Christendom beyond its early medieval frontiers; and the internal development of structures of authority and order, what has been called the growth of a persecuting society.

To support campaigns the papacy developed a structure of recruitment and finance. In the regularization of preaching and the collection of funds, the thirteenth century differed sharply from the twelfth. A papally organized bureaucracy grew up to attract, administer and audit crusade money. The diocesan structure of preaching was replaced first by direct appointment of bands of preachers who operated alongside existing episcopal arrangements. In this the friars played an increasingly important role from the 1230s, useful in their centralized organisation and local presence. Taxation of the Church was systematized in the century after its inception until, in 1274, Gregory X divided Christendom into twenty-six collectorates. Extensive surviving records testify to the intricacy and painstaking, if not always efficient, administration of these measures.[37]

Despite bureaucratic developments which lend an air of uniformity to the various enterprises, where conflicting secular interests and crusading were involved, opposition was inevitable. So was uncertainty. Whereas crusaders intending to embark against Muslim enemies knew their objective and were confident in the rightness and respectability of their holy cause, the same could not be said, for instance, of the followers of Malatesta da Verruchio of Rimini, who set out along the Via Emilia in 1248 a Ghibelline but returned a Guelph.[38] The identification with local political advantage was too obvious to escape charges of self-serving abuse.

Indeed, self-interest was, reasonably enough, exactly what papal crusades in Italy were, their purpose to secure and further papal political independence and temporal authority in the peninsula. As a consequence their status has sparked controversy. Some modern historians regard these campaigns as 'pseudo-crusades', severely damaging to the reputation of the papacy.[39] For other historians who emphasize the legitimacy of these crusades, the blatant and unashamed partisan nature of such campaigns and the hostile reactions of those who, for whatever reason, opposed papal temporal interests, should make them appear even more harmful to the reputation of the papacy and the ideal of crusading. Whether legitimate or not, the crusades in Italy called papal authority into question. By insisting that papal political crusades were on a par with those against the Infidel, popes were seeking to promote a narrow Curial interpretation of Christian affairs upon contemporaries, a line followed by modern apologists. Unsurprisingly, not everybody was convinced.

The motives of critics were partial and selfish, neither more or less representative, right or wrong, wise or foolish, honest or devious, noble or corrupt than papal advocates and allies. Criticism of papal crusades in the thirteenth and fourteenth centuries came from some who were otherwise by no means anti-papal.[40] Equally, the same campaigns attracted vociferous support. Opinion is inevitably a matter of taking sides, as objective and as biased as each other. To argue, as have modern observers, over the relative popularity of crusading or certain crusades is diverting, in every sense. It is not very illuminating. It is incontestable that the wide use of crusading apparatus was divisive, that the view from the Roman Curia was not the only one. There is little to be gained now by adopting partisan positions. Yet the papacy cannot be said to have undermined the ideal, given that it had as many facets as destinations. Critics who lambasted the Italian wars were often sympathetic to the restoration of a Christian Holy Land, for which papal leadership was considered essential.

The range of thirteenth-century crusading can be illustrated by the Registers of Innocent IV, a distinguished canon lawyer who himself wrote on the theory of just war. Between 1243 and 1254, Innocent called for the Cross to be preached against Frederick II; Conrad IV; the duke of Bavaria; supporters of the Hohenstaufen generally; the Livs and Balts in Livonia and Prussia; the Mongols; the irreligious in Sardinia; Muslims in Spain, Africa and the Holy Land; Greeks; heretics in Italy, Lombardy and Bosnia; and Ezzelino of Romano.[41]

This apparent coherence of papal policy ignores the tensions and confusions caused by concurrent crusades, as in the 1230s, 1240s and 1250s. Even though most crusades, apart from those directed to the East, tended to be preached only in particular areas, administration could be a nightmare. In the mid-1250s rival sets of Dominican and Franciscan preachers competed for recruits and funds for different crusades in the same regions of Bohemia and Poland, hurling anathema at each other.[42] In 1248, two groups of papal agents in Normandy quarrelled over the right to collect crusade vow redemptions.[43] In 1263, Cardinal Gui Foulquois (later Pope Clement IV) was commissioned to preach a crusade against English rebels. These included, prominently, Bishop Walter Cantelupe of Worcester who, only a few months earlier, had been put in charge of organizing a crusade to the Holy Land.[44] Elsewhere, fraudulent, i.e. unauthorized, preachers and collectors appeared: in Germany in the 1220s; in Frisia in the 1240s.[45] The profits from redemptions and alms, made available by the provisions of Innocent III, were tempting.[46] So, too, was the ideology of Holy War which could be appropriated by opponents of the papacy and its allies. One direct consequence of the opening of Pandora's Box was the ersatz crusading of supporters of Frederick II and the followers of Simon de Montfort in England in 1263–65. The neatness of papal theory or propaganda scarcely reflected practice.

The plethora of alternative crusades on offer caused problems for *crucesignati* as well as ecclesiastical officials. Some evidently treated the whole exercise like shopping at a supermarket. The Frisians who joined the crusade in Germany against Frederick II in 1248 had actually signed up for the Holy Land.[47] Others could become enmeshed in a web of actual or potential commutations from one destination to another. Few managed quite so badly as Henry III of England, who took the Cross in 1250 for the Holy Land, yet, for diplomatic reasons, simultaneously held out the prospect of commutation to the African or anti-Hohenstaufen crusades. It is hard to demonstrate that this enhanced his reputation.[48]

The overlap of objectives had serious repercussions. It has been noticed that elements of the so-called Shepherds' Crusade of 1251, who reacted fiercely to the failure of Louis IX in Egypt and attacked friars who had preached the Cross, came from areas where the anti-Hohenstaufen crusade had recently been publicized.[49] More disruptive of papal peace of mind and *plenitudo potestatis* was refusal to follow Curial leads. In 1238, the counts of Brittany and Bar-le-Duc declined to commute their Holy Land vows to help Baldwin II of Contantinople. The following year, Richard, earl of Cornwall and other noble *crucesignati* in England swore an oath reaffirming their commitment to the Holy Land and rejecting redirection elsewhere. In 1240, the rectors of Berkshire denied the legitimacy of the crusade against Frederick II. Bishop Walter Cantelupe successfully petitioned Innocent IV not to allow able-bodied crusaders to be compelled to redeem their vows for cash or forced to fight against anyone except Saracens. In 1255, clergy of the archdeaconry of Lincoln rejected the proposed diversion of crusade taxation from the Holy Land to Sicily. At the same time, clergy in the diocese of Lichfield also opposed the redeployment of the tax 'since the reason for the levy which at first sight appeared pious now, it seems to us, is changed and is not pious'. This sentiment was echoed by the

English baronical proctors at the Mise of Amiens in 1264, who complained about the 'absurd' cancellation of Henry III's Holy Land crusade and the conversion of a crusade 'against the Saracens who are foes of Christ's Cross into an attack on fellow subjects of the same Christian religion'. The preaching of the crusade against Aragon met vociferous local opposition at Lille in 1284.[50]

Of course, there was another side. Italians, Germans, Spaniards and French on occasion flocked to support their local crusades, against Hohenstaufen, Ghibellines, Baltic pagans, Moors and Albigensians, for the chance of material profit and temporal glory as well as spiritual gain. However, popular or not, crusades other than to the Holy Land (and some of them met with disapproval) were different, in intention and action; and contemporaries noticed. When in the mid-fourteenth century the Florentine Giovanni Villani compared the constant support given by Christians to the Holy Land in the previous century with the regular aid received by Granada from Morocco, he was implicitly drawing a sharp contrast with the nature of Christendom's relationship with internal crusading, support for which was neither continuous, institutional, habitual or universal.[51]

Despite the best endeavours of popes and their agents, crusading other than against the infidel could not expect automatic, general approval. Contemporaries do not appear to have seen crusading as a united movement entire unto itself. Responses were fragmented. There was awareness of the differences of destination, motive and circumstance. Even devotees of popes and crusades could voice opposition. The abbot of Vaux resisted the diversion of the Fourth Crusade. Humbert of Romans condemned the Baltic crusades as unnecessary in the 1270s. Joinville and others disapproved of the Tunis crusade of 1270. Philip V and Charles IV of France refused to support crusades against the Visconti in the 1320s.[52]

Popes were not without discrimination. Most intimately concerned with the whole paraphernalia of crusading, they adopted a realistic attitude to the difficulties of running crusades on many fronts. Most took care to target preaching to regions deemed sympathetic. Northern France was the recruiting ground for the Albigensian campaigns. After the 1250s preaching of the Italian crusade avoided England and, in general, 'political' crusades tended to have restricted constituencies.[53] Between 1319 and 1322, John XXII argued against a general *passagium*, citing the hornets' nest he himself kept stirring in Italy. In 1336 Benedict XII cancelled Philip VI of France's Holy Land crusade because of discord in western Christendom, which was, in its Italian and German dimensions, partly the Pope's own responsibility, Benedict authorizing a new crusade against Ludwig IV of Germany in 1337.[54]

There was a realization that words and theories could not be used entirely indiscriminately. In 1318 a French attempt to identify the Flemish as suitable targets for a crusade as excommunicates impeding the *passagium* to the East, and thus on a level with Saracens, proved too much even for John XXII.[55] His rejection of harnessing the crusade to French foreign policy was followed by his successors at Avignon. Until the Great Schism of 1378, the Hundred Years War did not involve crusading. Even when, in 1383, the Roman Pope Urban VI issued crusade bulls on behalf of Bishop Despenser of Norwich's attack on Flanders, the campaign was recognized – and criticized by some – for what it was: a continuation of the war with France.[56]

Despenser's crusade exposed the obverse to papal extension and manipulation of crusading, its exploitation by others. Ostensibly a campaign to fight the schismatic supporters of the Avignon Pope Clement VII, in fact most of those described by one English contemporary as 'enemies of the Cross' were Urbanists.[57] One central tenet of some recent studies of crusading is that Curial control matched papal theoretical authority. This underestimates the uncertainties surrounding the despatch and reception of papal commands. Sometimes bulls only reached their targets after their message had become redundant. John XXII's crusade bulls of July 1333 were published by the archbishop of Canterbury in May 1335 and recorded as being received by his suffragans between June and September. In the province of York collecting chests were commissioned only in May 1336 and the Minster chapter got round to acknowledging receipt of the 1333 bulls in December 1336, after Benedict XII had cancelled the whole operation. The slowness and complexity of the timetables proposed for Holy Land crusades in 1290, 1312 and 1333 themselves invited abortion.[58]

All crusade plans required negotiation between ecclesiastical authorities and secular commanders, for privileges, legacies, and, increasingly, funds. Direct ecclesiastical control was rarely envisaged nor effective, Cardinal Pelagius's role during the Fifth Crusade being largely fortuitous in the absence of the promised arrival of Frederick II.[59] Outside Italy, papal direction rarely tended to be much more than administrative, concerned with finance, recruiting and preaching. Calls for crusades were frequently stimulated by events and the appeals of the beleaguered faithful, from Alexius I Commenus in 1095 to John Hunyadi of Transylvania,

Ladislaus V of Hungary and Frederick III of Germany in the 1450s, with pleading from Outremer and Romania almost constant.[60]

Many crusades found the Pope not the leader but the led. Louis VII had initiated his own crusade plans without reference to the Pope in 1145. In some campaigns, as in the Baltic and Spain, the papacy was complicit in local control. Elsewhere, events moved out of Curial control. Although crusade preaching had been authorized, Frederick II took the Cross without warning or prior papal blessing in 1215, as did King John of England in the same year. The first crusade of Louis IX of France (1248–50), one of the most famous of all, stories of which resonated through the rest of the Middle Ages, owed its inspiration and most of its organization to the King, not the Pope, a pattern repeated in the choice of Tunis as a destination in 1270.[61] The most notorious example of the flouting of papal wishes was the crusade of Frederick II (1228–29).

There was an irony to these developments. While even the crusade to the Holy Land could slip from papal control, as spectacularly occurred in 1202–04, those campaigns especially close to papal concerns, the wars in Italy, were more directly supervised. From the 1250s, more effective effort was expended by popes on Italian crusades than on any other. The reasons were many. No major *passagium* was possible to raise for the relief, later recovery of the Holy Land. There was little left to be reconquered in Spain and few heretics with a clear geographical or political base to attract crusades until the Hussites of the fifteenth century. Against this, papal interests in Italy appeared urgent and receptive of military solution. Despite support for those willing to combat Muslim threats in the eastern Mediterranean, it seemed to some in the fourteenth century that crusading had become the weapon popes used primarily against their political foes, to the detriment of Christendom's resistance to Islam. In England, for example, the tradition of Matthew Paris was maintained by William Langland, John Gower and John Wyclif and, it has recently been argued, Geoffrey Chaucer.[62] The requirement to equate the Italian campaigns with traditional crusading had encouraged popes to adopt a wide, not to say strained, interpretation. At a time when Christendom seemed in danger, not everybody was impressed. This may have made an impact even on the Curia. In the fifteenth century, after the Great Schism and with the Ottoman advance renewed and unmistakable, the Curia abandoned its policy of two centuries by not calling for crusades against its enemies in Italy.[63]

The nature of the *negotium crucis* in the thirteenth century and beyond appears less coherent when observed away from Curial propaganda. The lack of innovation by lay and ecclesiastical authorities to the pattern of crusader privileges after the first quarter of the thirteenth century was at odds with significant shifts in attitudes and practice. This legal and ideological caution in the face of apparent continuing enthusiasm for spiritually beneficial warfare, and the undimmed rhetoric of activists and apologists, hints at a discrepancy between the image and reality. Responses to crusade calls were difficult to control then and assess now, many of the more eulogistic accounts being themselves part of the process of promotion and image-building. Innocent III had presented with new clarity weapons of war, penance, finance, social control, persecution, political aggrandizement and faith, weapons which his successors exploited with determination and skill. To that extent, the crusade was not an organic growth but a manufactured creation. Although using the language of precedent and tradition in *Quia Maior*, Innocent's carefully turned innovations admit as much. Thereafter, papal leadership was patchy, its efficiency and authority honoured as often in the breach as on the battlefield.

Language

Despite Innocent III's codification of crusade organization, one supreme peculiarity survived the twelfth century to persist until modern times: the lack of a precise, specific and universally accepted name to describe the activity. Even after the term *crucesignatus* became fashionable in Latin texts after the Third Crusade, the expeditions themselves were still represented either by non-specific words of journeying – *iter; expeditio; profectio; passagium; passage; via; voiage* – added to an epithet of holiness or geographical destination (Holy Land, Jerusalem, etc.); or by the traditional *peregrinatio/pèlerinage*. There were some attempts to apply distinctions. The English chronicler Roger of Howden characterized Hugh of Bar's choice in 1181 as between a 'profectio' to Spain and a 'peregrinatio' to Jerusalem. Another Englishman, Ralph of Coggeshall, saw that, in 1203–04, Constantinople was not a crusading goal as such when he wrote, only a few years after the event, that the city had been captured 'by the army of Latins going to Jerusalem'.[64] However, no clear system of categories was established.

Descriptions of participants were more precise but no more uniform. Their identification as pilgrims was widespread into the fourteenth century and beyond in literary and official sources, applied with varying degrees of credibility to crusaders in Languedoc, Greece, the Baltic, and even, in the 1260s, Italy.[65] The other technical term, *crucesignatus*, was by no means exclusively employed. In the context of crusading, Erard de Valéry, in a letter from Acre to Louis IX in 1267, referred to 'chevaliers pèlerins'.[66] Elsewhere, the word *crucesignatus* was used with no association with the crusade, for instance by the Inquisition when it imposed cross-wearing as a penance on reformed heretics.[67]

To say, with one modern expert, that in the fourteenth century 'contemporaries usually called [the crusade] either a *sanctum passagium* or a *cruciata*' ignores evidence of variety.[68] Distinctive vocabulary did emerge, mainly in the vernacular and then only patchily, especially, it seems, in southern France, possibly a result of the immediacy of the Albigensian crusade. As has already been observed, the verbs *croisier*, *croiser/ croisé* are apparent in the early thirteenth century in *langue d'oil*, and the nouns *crozeia*, *crozea* and *crozada* in *langue d'oc*.[69] Regional variants are apparent. By the end of the thirteenth century, *croiserie* as well as *croisé* (as a noun) were current in northern France and in England, but alongside *passage* and, popular into the fifteenth century, *voiage*.[70] While *crozada/ cruzada* became standard in southern France and Spain, *crociata/ cruciata* are found in northern Italy.[71] However, even in these regions there was no uniformity.

The language of official documents was no more specific. Papal sources tended to concentrate on issuing privileges and preaching, describing the actual expeditions in the composite language mentioned above. The Curia came to the Italian-Latin word *cruciata* around 1300 and its use, as we shall see, was not without ambiguity. Some close to official thinking were happy to use simply the word *crux*. The canonist Hostiensis wrote of the *crux transmarina* and the *crux cismarina*.[72] The Dominican Inquisitor Bernard Gui described how the 'crux cum plena peccatorum indulgentia' was preached against the early fourteenth-century heretic Dolcino.[73] A study of just over three hundred Latin documents dating from between 1096 and 1270 which mention specific crusading activity, chiefly charters but including a few records of lawsuits, mainly from France, the Low Countries and England, is suggestive.[74] Just over half refer to the crusade using verbs of motion (e.g. *eo*, *proficiscor*) coupled with a destination. There is one use of 'cruisiavit'. Of the nouns used, *iter* appears fifty-six times; *peregrinatio* sixty-six times, *via*, twenty-two; *expeditio*, thirteen (none in the English sample); *profectio*, one. *Peregrinatio* is combined with *iter* (eight times); *via* (six times); and *expeditio* (twice); *iter* with *expeditio* twice. Here, as elsewhere, the difference between an armed crusade and a pacific pilgrimage was not always clear, even after the late twelfth century, when increasingly such distinctions were being made elsewhere with some clarity.

No less apparent is the flexibility of language of individual writers. In his great work *Secreta Fidelium Crucis* (1309×1321), Marino Sanudo Torsello of Venice was heavily dependent for his early historical material on Jacques de Vitry and, through him, William of Tyre. This conditioned his crusade vocabulary, which is derivative, while his sources lasted. No distinctive fourteenth-century language imposed itself on his sources, perhaps because none existed, the fluidity of his texts remaining perfectly acceptable. For crusaders Sanudo usually used *peregrini*, but occasionally *crucesignati*; for the expeditions *peregrinatio, passagium; iter, exercitus* and, for the Shepherds' Crusade of 1251, *crucesignatio*. It appears unlikely he used these words to depict shades of meaning.[75] A contemporary text, the *Directorium ad passagium faciendum* (c. 1332), is equally free: *bellum Dei; sanctum negocium; iter; exercitus Domini; passagium.*[76] This last was most common in fourteenth- and fifteenth-century works of crusade advice from across Europe. While its connotations were, in context, clear, when compared to the modern 'crusade' or, indeed, to some other contemporary words (e.g. *cruciata*), it lacked definition.

Diversity of language continued. Henry Knighton, an Augustinian canon from Leicester (d. c.1396) described Despensers' crusade of 1383 as a 'cruciata', 'croyserie' or 'voyage', its soldiers being described in the official document he quoted as 'peregrynes'. In the fifteenth century, Thomas Basin seemed unaware of any precise technical term when describing the Burgundian crusade plans of the 1450s: *expeditio; sanctum opus; peregrinatio.*[77] Jean Germain, bishop of Châlon and intimate of the duke of Burgundy, used *voyage* and *passage* interchangeably, with *passage* describing pilgrimage as well as crusade. In his *Discours du voyage d'Oultremer* (1452), he had to explain more specific vocabulary when talking of 'the old *voyages* and *passages* of Outremer which are called *croisiez*'.

The Burgundians themselves, according to the contemporary provost of Péronne, Mathieu d'Escouchy, referred to the proposed expedition as the 'saint voiage': observers from the Imperial court wrote of the 'sainte besoigne' and 'sainte oeuvre'.[78] By this time, however, not only had the rhetoric become indistinct, but so had the activity. Although both had indulgences granted them, accounts of the Tunis expedition of crusade of 1390 and the campaign that ended in disaster at Nicopolis in 1396 do not mention a single person actually taking the Cross.[79] Similarly, the Vow of the Pheasant in 1454, perhaps the most notorious and colourful expression of crusading enthusiasm in the fifteenth century, was not attached to a cross-taking ceremony, only one of those who swore oaths actually mentioning his ultimate desire, once the Turks had been defeated, to pursue the 'saint voyage de Jherusalem'.[80]

The divorce of crusading from *crucesignati*, which, although by no means universal, was a feature of the later Middle Ages, was signalled in the ambiguities of language which had evolved in the thirteenth century. These are evident in Joinville's account of the crusades of Louis IX. Writing in the early fourteenth century, at much the same time as Sanudo, Joinville's customary formulation for the crusade was the 'pèlerinage de la croix', a phrase also used by another of Joinville's contemporaries, Philippe de Rémi de Beaumanoir, in his description of the *Coutumes de Beauvaisis* (1280×1283).[81] Heaven, Joinville insisted, rejoiced at those 'qui en ces dous pèlerinages moururent vrai croisé'.[82] This exactly reflected the common Latin juxtaposition of *crucesignatus* with *peregrinatio*, which persisted into the fifteenth century. As I shall discuss below, the liturgical cross-taking, the cult of the Cross, also wielded influence. The 1270 campaign is called 'la croiserie' as well as a 'pèlerinage de la crois'. Louis's expeditions were described in one place as his 'dous croisemens', which allowed Joinville to equate the King's death, 'croisiez' at Tunis, with Christ's death 'en la croix'.[83]

There is an impression of writers and observers playing with language and ideas, particularly involving the Cross. It could be argued that there was a deliberate attempt by the Curia to use the image of the Cross and the euphemism *negotium crucis* to de-territorialize and unfocus the ideal, and, where appropriate, to disassociate it from the Holy Land and concentrate on a less earth-bound image of Christ Crucified. General service to Christ and the mystical symbolism of the Cross is everywhere in surviving crusade sermons, as well as ecclesiastical exhortation. However, the repeated emphasis by lay and clerical observers on the element of pilgrimage showed how difficult it was to hide the Holy Sepulchre in the shadow of the Cross. In 1226, in a letter to Frederick II, a number of French bishops and nobles described Louis VIII and his fellow-invaders of Languedoc as 'sicut peregrini'.[84] Technically, as Louis and his troops were *crucesignati*, the association was apt. But such easy equations in Languedoc or Italy fooled no one.

Even careful extensions and reformulations of crusading could not be disguised by language. There is an unmistakable edge of bitterness in the early thirteenth-century French vernacular continuation of William of Tyre, a view from Outremer, when describing preaching authorized by Innocent III. The author readily adopted new vocabulary. Although sometimes crusaders were *pèlerins*, more commonly they were *croisiés*; the Fifth Crusade was a 'croiserie'; the commitment *se croiser*. Preachers such as Robert Curzon preached 'pour croiser [les gens] de la crois d'Outremer'; Jacques de Vitry 'en croisa moult'. But, despite the need for *croisiés* at Damietta, the Pope ordered bishops to 'descroiser' the ordinary people ('les menus gens'), legates being despatched 'por descroiser', to raise money or to ensure that those 'qui ne descroisoient' should set out.[85] 'Decroisier' perhaps sums up the contradictions inherent in the expansion of crusading in the thirteenth century and beyond. By the 1260s the poet Rutebeuf could present a recognizable, if deliberately unsympathetic type, the *Descroisié*, eager to enjoy the spiritual privileges through vow redemption, fearful of the sea and reluctant to relinquish his material position at home, speciously justifying his position by arguing that God could be sought and found as well in France as in Outremer.[86] Whether admirable or not, papal policy had got through.

This success helped determine the language employed and thus the way ideas were expressed and events described in the later Middle Ages. The thirteenth-century failure to construct an officially uniform, consistent or specific Latin vocabulary of crusading was a significant omission by the Curia and canon lawyers. However, it facilitated the obfuscatory, even misleading manner in which crusading was sometimes presented. The imagery of the Holy Land and the Cross was exported across all fronts, not always convincingly:

> Our men ... having the banner of the Holy Cross before them ... thought that victory in this cause was glory but death reward ... those who suffered death would be martyrs ... Our men were eager to avenge the insults to the Cross ... and thus the blessing of the Cross was achieved, and the crucesignati gloriously captured the town and there destroyed the enemies of the Cross so that not one of them survived.[87]

This over-written account, saturated in traditional crusade epithets and justifications dating back, in places verbatim, to the twelfth century, in fact described Bishop Despenser's attack on Gravelines in 1383: Urbanists slaughtering Urbanists. Even on the terms of the papal bulls themselves, and accepting the validity of Despenser's original project as a crusade, the chronicler's language concealed what, in the attack on Urbanists by Urbanist crusaders, was a misuse and distortion of the ideal. In 1512, did Henry VIII believe that his army, 'roused' by papal indulgences, actually, as he claimed, considered their French opponents as 'Turks, heretics and infidels'?[88] These are extreme examples. However, similar instances of literary fancy could be excavated from all other European theatres of crusading from the late twelfth century onwards. Here language exposes a complicated relationship between observation and event. If, in these examples, the only consistency crusading managed was linguistic, the diversity of crusading vocabulary may cast the coherence of the activity into further doubt.

The word that some have seen as identifying just such a coherent activity, *cruciata*, is no less revealing in its application. Whatever its first coinage, and an original Scandinavian use has been posited by some, it is a Latin equivalent to the many related words in Romance languages already noted meaning the activity of those who had taken the Cross. It may have been a Latin transcription of the vernacular, not vice versa.[89] Current by the fourteenth century (especially perhaps in Italy), even common, but by no means in universal circulation, by the fifteenth century the term was being used by academics, chroniclers and agents of John XXIII and Martin V to mean a crusade, in Italy and Bohemia respectively.[90] However, the word seems to have implied a particular, specific and significant subsidiary meaning: money. In the accounts of the papal treasurer of the March of Ancona for 1322, the heading *crutiata* referred to the cash collected to promote preaching.[91] In 1397, *cruciata* still implied the proceeds of crusade fundraising.[92] The connotations of the attendant mechanisms of this, particularly the sale of indulgences, are reflected in Wyclif's condemnation of Despenser's crusade in 1383, *De Cruciata*.[93] By the early sixteenth century, it was explicitly synonymous with money levied for a crusade from the sale of indulgences, as Leo X put it, the 'indulgentiae sanctissimae cruciatae'; the 'sancta cruciata', in the phrase of Emperor Maximilian in 1518; or, as Francis I wrote in 1517, 'la croisade'. In 1587, in his plan for a new general campaign against the Turks, the Huguenot François de la Noue suggested raising money in the traditional fashion favoured by popes, 'which he called *croisade* or *contribution*'.[94] The road from *Quia Maior* was long but direct.

With Francis I's use of 'croisade' we are on the rim of modern language, if not concepts. Francis and Pope Leo were using *cruciata* and 'croisade' in the same sense as the sixteenth-century Spanish *cruzada*, a grant of the sale of indulgences for the benefit of the ruler.[95] It may, therefore, be no coincidence that the French only coined the word 'croisade' in the mid-fifteenth century, Georges Chastellain using the word in a chapter heading of his *Chronique*.[96] Yet the word is an unexpected hybrid, replacing the French *croisé* or *croiserie* with a word constructed from the northern French *crois* with the Provençal/Spanish suffix -*ada*. The Spanish link, by the early sixteenth century, may not have been fortuitous, but specific and fiscal. When talking of what we call crusades, most sixteenth-century writers referred to the *guerre sainte* or *bellum sanctum* (the Holy War), not 'croisades'.

In English, French precedent held sway. In the fifteenth century 'croyserie' described the crusade against the Hussites, as it had Despenser's crusade in 1383.[97] Borrowing continued. From the sixteenth to the eighteenth centuries, apart from Holy War or passage, the French word, occasionally with variant endings -a or -o, held sway, although a few writers, such as Francis Bacon, employed the Spanish 'cruzada'.[98] The now universal use of the word 'crusade', derived from the Spanish, probably owes its rise to dominance to David Hume and Edward Gibbon in the eighteenth century, which is perhaps appropriate, as they penned some of the most memorably trenchant descriptions of the exercise yet seen in this or any language.[99]

If language mirrors culture, attitudes and behaviour, the history of crusade vocabulary raises a series of questions about the nature and perceptions of the activity. The linguistic profligacy, euphemism, imprecision, malleability, archaism and spurious uniformity should give pause before the crusade is defined as a concrete institution with an existence outside the interpretation of observers and promoters. Whatever else, their failure to construct or agree on a consistent, clarifying vocabularly was not the least distinctive part of the phenomenon.

Secular Law and the Crusader

Something of the nature of crusading as well as its penetration into the workings of lay society can be traced in the procedures used in secular law courts to sustain and enforce the temporal privileges granted to *crucesignati*. A general pattern is evident. Crusader privileges derived from and remained closely linked to those as enjoyed by pilgrims to the Holy Land. As a consequence, Jerusalem and Outremer were central in the assumptions of those describing how these rights were administered. The act of taking the Cross and the status thereby conferred stood at the heart of the application of the legal and fiscal immunities. Inevitably there was variety of custom over time and place. The records of law courts and custumals provide an alternative barometer of responses to crusading which indicates that, north of the Alps at least, from the later thirteenth century fewer and fewer people took the Cross, until by 1400 rules for crusaders appear to have become obsolete.

The crusader's temporal privileges had grown up over the twelfth century, reaching full elaboration in the decrees of the kings of England and France at the time of the Third Crusade and the subsequent legislation of Innocent III.[100] They addressed the intimate material concerns of the *crucesignatus*: protection for him, his family and property; accelerated litigation before departure; essoin of court (i.e. permission to delay answering summonses); immunity from prosecution while *crucesignatus*; freedom to sell, lease or mortgage property with the consent of interested parties (usually relatives); moratorium on debts; exemption from interest; and immunity from taxation. The privileges were effective the moment the Cross was adopted (no separate vow being recognized).

The basic principle was the withdrawal of the crusader, like the pilgrim, from a purely lay condition, placing him under the protection and authority of the Church, as if he had taken temporary Holy Orders, which, in a sense, he had. The purpose of the temporal privileges was to recognize the importance of this commitment and to encourage and support its fulfilment. As a Somerset *crucesignatus* put it during a lawsuit in 1220: 'the crusade (*crussignatio*) ought to improve my condition, not damage it'.[101]

Acceptance in secular courts of these legal immunities was rapid. The oldest surviving Norman custumal (*c.*1199/1200) referred, as had the English law book attributed to Ranulf Glanvill (*c.*1180), only to Jerusalem pilgrims as recipients of essoins of a year and a day.[102] By 1205, however, an inquest held at Rouen acknowledged the equivalent legal status to a cleric of a *croisié*.[103] By mid-century, law books from England, the French royal demesne, Normandy and Touraine admitted the special status of crusaders without question.[104] Lay authorities and courts faced problems of enforcement and clarification. Successive papal bulls ignored repercussions of taking the Cross. This left the secular arm not only to protect crusaders' rights but also to define them in practice, as they touched important issues in the relationship of individuals to the community: crime; tax; land; inheritance; debt. It was left, for example, to the Norman judges at Falaise to determine whether or not a champion *croissié* could engage in trial by combat, hardly a burning issue at the Curia or in the lecture-rooms of Paris and Bologna, yet of some interest in provincial France.[105] It was the responsibility of secular authorities to establish, case by case, the claims of individual crusaders within their jurisdiction and, in many instances, to restrict their immunities in accordance with local custom and effective justice. The rights of church courts were recognized, but the point at which Canon Law and ecclesiastical protection operated was often a matter for lay courts and often modified by them.

The practical ramifications of papal privileges were not taken for granted because they were often ineptly or incompletely drafted, the bulls being as much literary exercises in exhortation as bases for legal obligations and rights. In 1188 the Capetian and Angevin ordinances for the recruitment and financing of the Third Crusade went beyond Gregory VIII's *Audita Tremendi*.[106] The bull, for example, made no specific mention of crusaders' immunity from tax, although it was implied by the blanket ecclesiastical protection. The levy of the Saladin Tithe made clarification essential. Gregory VIII had explicitly exempted crusaders from paying interest on loans and from any diminution of their goods. This cut two ways: in protecting the crusader's resources (and state of Grace) from usury, it threatened to destroy his creditworthiness, and hence his ability to fulfil his vow (thereby jeopardizing his means of Grace). In the thirteenth century, such pressures forced *crucesignati* voluntarily to waive such exemptions.[107]

In 1188, in Capetian lands, the papal exemption was modified to the point of contradiction by a royal edict issued with the approval of French prelates as well as barons.[108] This show of unity suggests that fears over debt repayment by and to the Church were keen, another sign that papal pronouncements formed only one part of crusade preparations, and not one everywhere decisive. In addition to clauses on mortgages, the French debt ordinance allowed creditors, Jews as well as Christians, to reclaim outstanding loans, including interest, up to the day the debtor took the Cross, the repayments being scheduled over two years, in three stages, to be collected from lands and revenues assigned to the creditors by the departing crusader debtor. *Crucesignati* were not permitted to avoid debts by alienating money and moveables.

The ordinance ends, however, by reasserting *crucesignatus* immunity from land suits, in accordance with the papal bull. It is, perhaps, no coincidence that the decree *Ad Liberandam*, agreed at a General Council attended by representatives of lay rulers and local churches, went into greater detail than had *Audita Tremendi* about crusaders' debt repayment.[109]

The gap between papal theory and secular practice persisted. An ordinance was issued by Philip II of France in March 1215 on crusaders' privileges (*libertates*) and church protection which went into much greater detail than the papal bull of 1213. Once more the King was eager, in consultation with his bishops, to protect lay interests, in particular concerning exemption from fiscal and public obligations, debt and legal immunities. While acknowledging the rights of *crucesignati*, the ordinance asserts the competing claims of customary law. Crusaders were not exempted from secular justice in criminal cases, their clerical status confined to lesser non-capital offences, not incurring death or mutilation. In civil suits, *crucesignati* had to answer pleas concerning feudal obligations and rents initially in the court of the relevant lord. In minor civil disputes, the *crucesignatus* could choose lay or ecclesiastical justice, there being no compulsion in such instances to appear in a secular court.[110]

The stated purpose of the 1215 enquiry and ordinance was to safeguard the 'law and customs of Holy Church and similarly . . . the law and customs of the kingdom of France, and the authority of the Holy Roman Church'. Such accommodation was apparently echoed by Innocent IV in 1245 when he denied that crusaders should automatically be exempt from the customs of the realm of England.[111] Given the vagueness of papal legislation, responsibility for deciding the detailed limits of crusader privileges were left to local bishops and, possibly chiefly, lay authorities. The terms of essoins in lay courts were variously specified for departed crusaders: in 1188, three years; in the thirteenth-century English law book known as 'Bracton', an indefinite period; elsewhere in thirteenth-century England five years; in a mid-thirteenth-century Norman custumal, seven years.[112] This lack of uniformity points to a lack of fixed, universal rules and to the strength of local ordering of the institution.

The limits to legal immunity in the 1215 French ordinance were not unique. In civil law, Philippe de Rémi de Beaumanoir's *Coutumes de Beauvaisis* (1280×1283) recorded that the crusader's immunity extended to contracts, personal property and chattels, not to crime or patrimonial land, and that once a crusader had begun a suit of his own in a secular court, the Church should not intervene.[113] Such distinctions were familiar to some courts. In 1219, an Englishman was denied crusader's immunity over a writ of *novel disseisin*.[114] At Rouen, in 1236 and 1246, it was pronounced that crusaders could not avoid charges involved in fiefs and pledges.[115] The rights, laws and customs of Communes were safeguarded against crusaders who had not yet departed for the Holy Sepulchre, in royal charters such as those granted by Philip II to Tournai and Péronne.[116]

Exploitation of the temporal privileges was recognized as a problem in the attention lavished on backsliders in the decree *Ad Liberandam*. In 1246, Louis IX of France complained to Innocent IV that many *crucesignati*, instead of abstaining from excess because of their privileges, were committing theft, murder and rape. The Pope ordered the French bishops not to protect these miscreants. The abuse appeared stubbornly endemic: in 1273 Gregory X had to reissue the 1246 order.[117] A wide variety of suspected criminals and those facing awkward lawsuits took advantage of the immunities offered. Such problems were compounded by the increasing habit of vow redemption. Early in the thirteenth century, a Lincolnshire man took the Cross to avoid accusations of illegal possession of land, only to redeem his vow by paying money to the dean of Lincoln.[118]

Whatever the strains and confusions, crusaders' privileges did not lead to any institutional rivalry between church and secular courts. Within the limitations set by lay rulers, with the acquiescence of ecclesiastical authorities, each jurisdiction respected the other. In 1238, the Bishop of Séez was instructed by the Norman exchequer to hold in prison the crusaders who had wounded a local knight until the resolution of the case.[119] Provided no fraud was attempted, crusaders' rights were upheld. In 1204, the English Justiciar, Geoffrey FitzPeter, intervened to halt a case of *mort d'ancestor* because the defendant was a crusader. Respect for the status is evident: at Worcester in 1221, two illegal wine-sellers had their fines remitted because they were *crucesignati*. In Normandy, if a convicted fugitive took the Cross he could opt for a choice of punishment: the King's or Bishop's prison or exile.[120]

Inevitably, there was vigilance to ensure abuse was held in check, even at high political cost. In 1270, in the royal court, the viscount of Melun lost a suit brought by the dean and chapter of St Martin, Tours when his proctor failed to sustain his claim to crusader essoin in the face of the plaintiff's demonstration that the viscount was staying in Apulia 'stipendiarius'.[121] According to a collection of Norman laws, in church courts anyone pleading crusader privileges had to show proof of his 'votum peregrinationis' on pain of a fine of 40 *livres tournois.* Once satisfied, the ecclesiastical judge had to ensure the accused actually departed 'ad general (*sic*) passagium', leaving 40 *livres tournois* as surety. Only measures such as these could convince the secular authorities to honour the arrangements for crusaders.

Genuine commitment by action was seen as crucial. Crusaders who stayed at home were guaranteed protection only for a year and a day in parts of France. In England, the three-year or longer term seems to have prevailed, but even then some were shown to have expired. In 1221 it took an elaborate official inquiry to show that Geoffrey de Lucy had received an additional eighteen-month extension.[123] Pierre de Fontaines, writing his *Conseil* in the 1250s, employed a more literary flourish in arguing that the privileges of crusaders who deserted ('qui s'enfui de la commune bataille des crystiens et des sarrasins') were placed in jeopardy.[124] However, privileges were not immutable. Followers of the Lord Edward in 1270 limited their own legal protection in certain property suits. A similar procedure was current in the Beauvaisis where vendors could waive all customary rights including, then and for the future, 'toz privileges de crois'.[125]

From the perspective of the implementation of crusaders' privileges in secular courts there emerges a picture of general principles cautiously applied in *ad hoc* circumstances. There was no corpus of crusade canon law, still less a secular law code. However, law books included discussions *De Cruce* and identified the position of crusaders in descriptions of other procedures. There was general acceptance that, as the so-called *Establissements de St. Louis* (*c.*1273) put it, a *croisié* received equivalent general legal protection to clerks 'ou aucun home de religion'.[126] There was a difference: both the individual status of each crusader and, as it turned out, the popular adoption of the privileges were impermanent. Clerics were so for life; the Church eternal. Crusaders enjoyed their status for the term of their vow; the apparatus allowing them to do this did not become a permanent feature of western society.

Behind the evidence for meticulous adaptability, legal records suggest an inherent conservatism in secular courts' approach to crusaders, reflected in the language used to describe them and their activities. The crusaders' essoin in 'Bracton' was associated with the 'general passage' beyond the sea of Greeks to the Holy Land. Pierre de Fontaines assumed that ecclesiastical protection was for 'li croisiez qui ala outre mer'.[127] Just as their destination was Outremer, so the conflict was with the Saracens. Beaumanoir identifies three reasons for legitimate non-appearance at court: royal or public service abroad; imprisonment by Saracens and the 'pèlerinage d'outremer en Jherusalem' (which his recent translator, interestingly enough, renders simply as 'crusade'). In presenting the extent of ecclesiastical jurisdiction over 'croisiés', Beaumanoir makes no other distinction than those 'croisié de la crois d'outremer'.[128]

This traditionalism, in the face of the extension of crusading across Europe, and especially in France, is notable. It has been argued that an Anglo-French version of a Norman custumal, written shortly after Louis IX's Egyptian campaign, recognized current fashion in translating 'peregrinatione in Jerusalem' as 'pèlerinage d'outremer'.[129] In general, however, the same sclerosis affected legal as well as ecclesiastical texts. From the point of view of jurists, the crusade remained firmly fused with Jerusalem because of the legal protection earned by Holy Land pilgrims which formed the basis of the crusader privileges, the pilgrimage that attracted most extensive legal privilege being that to Jerusalem. The expeditions of crusaders were called pilgrimages both by judges of the Norman exchequer in the 1220s and 1230s and by Beaumanoir in the 1280s, who used the phrase favoured by his contemporary Jean de Joinville: 'pèlerinage de la crois'.[130] In a compendium of Norman legal procedures, the *Summa de legibus Normannie in Curia laicali* from the 1250s, the expedition was consistently described as a 'peregrinatio', the vow a 'votum peregrinationis'. The fusion of crusade and pilgrimage was explicit. When discussing contracts, the author defined 'solemn pilgrimages':

> when pilgrims have received licences in their parish church [*parrochia* is ambiguous], with Cross and holy water and have been conducted out of the church [/parish] and set on their way to Jerusalem, Rome or St James [i.e. Compostella] or in another pilgrimage for a general crusade ['per generalem crucis signationem']. Similarly, *crucesignati* retain the privilege of the Cross for a year and a day.

The association of crusade and pilgrimage is inextricable, at least in one corner of western Christendom.[131] It is a link symbolized in action by men like Joinville in 1248 or the priest of Varangeville in 1265, who adopted the scrip and staff of pilgrims as well as the Cross of crusaders.[132]

There can be no doubting the impact of the crusade on secular society in the thirteenth century. It did not last. The decline in numbers taking the Cross without immediate redemption undermined the secular edifice. One characteristic right of lordship before 1300 was the fourth 'necessitas', a crusade aid, which operated on a national or, for example in the towns of Lautrec or Limoges, provincial scale. This depended, as in the Limoges charter of 1277, on the lord taking the Cross or contributing to the 'crucis expensas'.[133] Despite numerable small crusades, locally preached, such aids were soon a thing of the past. The last royal attempt in France to levy a crusade aid, by Philip VI in 1335–36, proved a very damp squib.[134] It was not that crusading as an ideal or objective had soured: but too few people, at least away from the papal front-lines, took the Cross to maintain its prominence as a social activity. When Andrew Horn (d. 1328), fishmonger and Chamberlain of the City of London, compiled his *Mirror of Justices* and included the essoin 'on account of a general passage of all crusaders to the land of Jerusalem', such an expedition was still a lively possibility and interest.[135] By the 1380s, the *Grand Coutumier de France* could include a detailed list of essoins with no specific mention of the crusade or crusaders. Provision for them had become redundant.[136]

Preaching

If the crusade was a movement, its voice was preaching. Crusading began with Urban II's sermon at Clermont in 1095. Some of the most famous images and defining moments were associated with preaching: St Bernard on the hillside at Vézelay in 1146; the bishop of Oporto urging the crusade fleet to turn aside to attack Lisbon in 1147; the archbishop of Tyre at Gisors, Archbishop Henry at Strasburg in 1188; Fulk of Neuilly before the Fourth Crusade; Jacques de Vitry in the Holy Land and Oliver of Paderborn in Frisia before the Fifth. The power of the image of the preacher and the need to identify charismatic leaders inspiring the faithful were rooted in the Bible. In descriptions of his Clermont address Urban II was self-evidently Christlike in quoting: 'take up your Cross and follow me'.[137] No less potent was the parallel literary tradition that attributed the origins of the First Crusade to Peter the Hermit.[138] There were two models, both apocalyptic and eschatalogical; both appear as certainly literary devices; either were possibly genuine: one authoritative, academic, political; the other populist, direct, rabble-rousing: Jesus and John the Baptist. By 1200, the two had merged, as preaching, even that described as being most magnetic and popular, was conducted by university-trained intellectuals. Jacques de Vitry, in his famous account of the preaching of the charismatic Fulk of Neuilly around 1200, emphasized that the preacher's success began after he had sat at the feet of the Paris masters, Jacques's own mentors.[139] Innocent III exploited this fusion in his provisions of 1213. Crusade preaching thereafter combined academic precision and spiritual rigour, later institutionalized in the employment after 1230 of the Friars to promote the *negotium crucis* throughout western Christendom.[140]

Sermons lent coherence and focus to subsequent events. As recorded they explained the need, identified the obligation and proclaimed the incentives. Through the techniques of *narratio* and *excitatoria*, story-telling and exhortation, the immediate *causus belli* was presented in a moral and providential context. However, the importance of crusade sermons in reality rather than as a literary convenience, especially in the twelfth century, is not as obvious as has often been assumed. For writers constructing a clear, didactic account, the significance of sermons is unquestionable. The classic example is the Clermont sermon of 1095, reconstructed, even by eye-witnesses, to suit the authors' purpose and circumstance.[141] Such manipulation of the record makes it hard to accept at face, or perhaps any value chronicle descriptions of the content of preaching, especially as no independent texts of twelfth-century crusade sermons survive until 1189.

Literary accounts of sermons may be as unconvincing as the speeches chroniclers placed in the mouths of commanders before battles. Nonetheless, they played a role in the development of crusading. Until the Third Crusade, there were few models of crusading to follow: by the end of Innocent III's reign there were many. In this creation of a new tradition, accounts of preaching provided models of how to deliver and respond to crusade appeals; of how to think of crusading, its history, importance and benefits. In some descriptions it is possible to detect this internal process of construction. Thus Günther of Pairis's account of Abbot Martin of Pairis's sermon at Basel in 1201 may have been coloured by Günther's own versification of Robert of Rheims's story of the First Crusade some years earlier.[142] More concretely, preaching and the concurrent extension of privileges formed part of a greater emphasis placed on popular evangelization in the life of the Church in the generation after the late twelfth-century preachers and pedagogues, Alan of Lille and Peter the Chanter.[143] Crusading, not least through its preaching, assisted in concerted moves to involve the laity more closely in spiritual exercises, often delivered in sermons which conformed to new methods established again by Parisian masters.

Around 1200, among influential sections of the *intelligentsia*, a new historical orthodoxy emerged on the origins of crusading, and, with it, a fresh model for preaching. If the survival of manuscripts is a guide, the heavily Francocentric account by Robert of Rheims was the most widely read version of the First Crusade.[144] The French tradition had little or no time for Peter the Hermit. However, by the time of the Fifth Crusade, two influential crusade preachers, Jacques de Vitry and Oliver of Paderborn, were familiar with the *Historia* of William of Tyre, who, following his source Albert of Aachen, gives Peter the Hermit the credit for initiating the 1096 expedition. During the thirteenth century the Peter the Hermit story usurped other accounts to become the standard view of the origins of the First Crusade for the next six centuries. Jacques de Vitry incorporated large sections of William of Tyre into his influential *Historia Orientalis* (*c.*1220). In his letters from Damietta during the Fifth Crusade, Jacques even used William's phrases for the First Crusade to describe events in the crusader camp.[145] The pattern of the charismatic inspirational preacher in the image of Peter the Hermit is strong elsewhere in Jacques's writings and in accounts of Oliver's preaching in Frisia, complete with attendant miraculous signs. The model influenced attitudes. Jacques de Vitry described contemporary preachers, such as Fulk of Neuilly, in terms reminiscent of Peter.[146] It may have been more than a literary fashion. Given the concern to spread the message of moral reform and apostolic poverty to the laity, a process in which the crusade was a significant element, Peter the Hermit could have been taken as a pattern for actual behaviour. As often in past and present, it is difficult to disentangle ideal and reality, precept and action, form and substance.

From the early thirteenth century preaching was integral to the idea and practice of crusading. It provided an apt setting for the revivalist urging of repentance and the public ceremony of taking the Cross, a form of active congregational participation distinct from other responses in the Mass or in Confession. It was embedded into the administrative and liturgical provisions of *Quia Maior* and thereafter in the organization of every crusade, the fulcrum balancing recruitment, indulgences, finance, propaganda and spiritual renewal.

This was something new. In the twelfth century there was little organized preaching. Apart from Urban's tour through France and the possible activities of Peter the Hermit, the evidence for preaching the First Crusade is thin. Few bishops bothered to record the Clermont crusade decree. The role of legates such as Abbot Jarento of St Bénigne, Dijon, was primarily diplomatic. Networks of communication were monastic and social, through ties of tenure, clientage and community, groups to which Urban himself addressed a number of letters advocating the crusade. It was probably through the Benedictines, via Abbot Jarento, that Urban's message reached the enthusiastic monks of Cerne in Dorset. There is no direct evidence that the popular evangelist of the poverty movement, Robert d'Arbrissel, specifically preached the crusade.[147] In many areas, such as Germany and Italy, passing crusaders were themselves the sole publicists.[148]

General preaching of the Cross remained unusual, heavily dependent on local secular approval and management, both on show during the tour by Hugh de Payens in 1128.[149] At the time of the Second Crusade, apart from St Bernard, the bishop of Langres and the unauthorized renegade, Rudolph, there was a marked absence of preaching. No general preaching campaign was authorized by Eugenius III. According to the contemporary account, the bishop of Oporto explicitly stated that there had been no preaching to inspire the crusaders he was trying to persuade to attack Lisbon ('nullo predicante, nullo admonente').[150] His audience came from Flanders, the Rhineland, Normandy and England. Commanders depended on assemblies of their vassals, St Bernard on circulars to whip up support. As he admitted in his letter to the English, he would have preferred to preach the Cross 'by word of mouth had I but the strength to come to you as I desire'. Instead, the channels of information were those of lordship, tax collection, the market-place, the parish church, the monastery door, travellers' lodgings, meetings of communities and families, not the set-piece sermon.

The Third Crusade followed this pattern. Although Gregory VIII's bull *Audita Tremendi* (1187) made no mention of organized preaching, it may have provided the basis for sermons of exhortation. In 1181, Alexander III had unsuccessfully instructed the clergy to publicize papal letters when promoting the crusade.[151] The Danish experience after 1187 suggests that interpretation was left to recipients. In any case, the initiative for organizing fleets and armies came from secular rulers, not the Church: the kings of Sicily, England, France and Germany; the counts of Flanders and Poitou. Any sermons were part of a political process to secure the material base for the expedition. The failure of Patriarch Heraclius in 1185 to do anything except encourage tears and a handful of Angevin courtiers to take the Cross attested to the fate of preaching not supported by prior political orchestration and support.[152]

By contrast, the satisfactory outcome of Archbishop Josias of Tyre's sermon at Gisors in January 1188 was, by all accounts, political, Philip II and Henry II becoming allies through the mediation of taking the Cross. Recruitment, aristocratic support and royal power provided the context for Archbishop Henry of Strasburg's address to Frederick I's court. Archbishop Baldwin of Canterbury and the bishop of Rochester preached at Geddington in 1188 in a similar exercise designed to publicize the Saladin Tithe and to secure the commitment of the English establishment. The collection of the Tithe required publicity through preaching, by such as Renier, bishop of St Asaph's. Archbishop Baldwin's preaching tour of Wales in Lent 1188 was in large measure an exercise in ecclesiastical and political overlordship.[153] Away from secular direction, there was little preaching. The main thrust of preparations, at least north of the Alps, was material, recruitment a matter of personal, geographic, familial or financial allegiances as much as popular devotion. The contrasting fates of the Saladin Tithe in Capetian and Angevin lands suggests an organization centred upon secular, not ecclesiastical, authority.

After the 1190s, there was ostensibly a greater ecclesiastical commitment to preaching. However, some of those authorized to preach the Cross, such as Fulk of Neuilly and Eustace de Flay, incorporated the crusade into their main interests in moral evangelizing, sabbatarianism, usury and the corruption of riches. Indeed, Fulk of Neuilly's reputation was shot to pieces by his involvement in the crusade. He was suspected of embezzling alms raised for the cause, one of many examples of the corrosive association of preaching and fund-raising.[154] Around 1200, the preaching authorized by Innocent III was finer in conception than on the ground, with a dearth of preachers and large areas for each to cover. Apparently, until Abbot Martin in 1201, nobody had preached the Cross in the Basel region since the papal bulls of 1198.[155]

A change came with the urgent preaching of the Albigensian crusade in parts of France and preparations for the Fifth Crusade, both of which produced deliberate and effective campaigns of mass evangelism. However, crusade preaching retained its intimate relationship with secular authority. In 1245, the wretched bishop of Beirut was refused a hearing in England by Henry III.[156] Nothing was more acidly political, i.e. based on interests essentially civil and secular, not spiritual, than preaching crusades against the Hohenstaufen, the Stedinger peasants or papal enemies in Italy. Such vituperatively controversial campaigns, although the testing-ground for papal policy, were not, however, the laboratories for the new idealists who tended to concentrate on heretics, Tartars (i.e. Mongols), Muslims and the Holy Land.[157]

Preachers under Innocent III such as Robert Curzon, Jacques de Vitry and Oliver of Paderborn employed the crusade in their efforts to put pastoral theology into practice. This was no less true of their successors Eudes de Châteauroux, Gilbert of Tournai or Humbert of Romans. It may be no coincidence that, as has been recently observed, all the authors of surviving thirteenth-century crusade sermons had, like Innocent himself, studied at Paris, the centre of ideas of practical moral reform and the more esoteric Christology of the poverty movement which so infected the rhetoric of some of these evangelists.[158] Encouraging personal confession and individual penance chimed in neatly with the extension of vow redemption, the goal of such evangelism increasingly appearing to be the indulgence, as much as the liberation of the Holy Land or defence of the Church.

This fed a central paradox. Preaching became widespread and familiar at a time when recruitment became divorced from such evangelism, a separation concealed by the integration of preaching into the formal apparatus of crusade preparation. The numerous thirteenth-century sermon *exempla* depicting audiences unexpectedly and spontaneously taking the Cross are in stark – perhaps deliberate – contrast to the reality of assembling armies.[159] The establishment of regular, ordered, large-scale preaching coincided – as a stated objective – with the widening of the scope of indulgences to the *décroisiés*. At the same time, while preaching was placed at the formal centre of recruitment drives, the methods of raising men were becoming more structured and less dependent – if they ever had been – on the chance of mass enthusiasm. The bonds of lordship, clientage, locality and family had always lain at the heart of crusading, and were now increasingly expressed in the form of written contracts and cash. Collecting troops supplied the efficient element in the constitution of the crusade, preaching the dignified. The marriage of religious and social loyalties was well caught by an entry in the Register of Cardinal Ugolino of Ostia, later Gregory IX, describing recuits from Savoy 'who have received the Cross for God and love of the marquis (of Montferrat)'.[160]

This Register, which records the fruits of the Cardinal's fund-raising tour of northern Italy in 1221, makes clear that not all those who joined the crusade were *crucesignati*. The latter, in accord with Innocent's decrees, were to pay for themselves or be subsidized by their lords or communities, and had been enlisted contractually after careful negotiations with the legate and representatives of the Emperor. The list of those to whom money raised by the Church was to be paid implied that some soldiers had not taken the Cross. Thus, from Viane, in Savoy, 1000 marks were to be paid to a hundred knights, 'except those who have taken the Cross'.[161]

The machinery revealed by Ugolino's register is paralleled by Master Hubert's preaching efforts in England for the 1227 crusade, when he was said to have kept a roll of the names of the *crucesignati* he had signed up.[162] Ugolino, however, raised his troops by bargaining, not preaching, a method recommended later in the century by Humbert of Romans.[163] All this is far removed from the impression given by Ugolino's contemporary and future colleague Jacques de Vitry, whose letters were studded with tales of the effect of his exhortations to take the Cross, although admittedly on occasion external factors, such as the fear of drowning and seasickness, contributed to the audience's susceptibility.[164] Such discrepancy was unavoidable because reports of sermons and their effectiveness were elements of the promotional exercise itself.

The converse was the case with critics, such as Matthew Paris, who delighted in exposing ineffectual or badly received preaching. However, in trying to establish the effectiveness of preaching, of more interest is the testimony of Hostiensis, the leading theorist of crusades against Christians, who admitted he encountered fierce opposition to the anti-Hohenstaufen crusades on the grounds, so he claimed, that the arguments for such crusade were not clear in law.[165] This could have been a reaction against novelty. However, given there were few sharper ideologues than Hostiensis, it was probably less the working-out of his argument that aroused hostility than its basic premise. Either way, the burden of recruitment fell mainly on rulers, not preachers, whose role effectively was to provide an attractive context of propaganda and spiritual benefits. The effectiveness of crusade sermons, therefore, did not depend on whether or not they secured fighting *crucesignati*. Increasingly that was a secondary function. These sermons should be viewed in their own context, stylized literary confections and tools of missions pastoral and political.

Crusade sermons were almost never spontaneous for preacher or audience; they were probably always ritualized: and they operated as part of wider religious, ecclesiastical or secular initiatives. One of the most detailed accounts of any crusade preaching is Gerald of Wales's *Journey through Wales*, which chronicles the tour of Archbishop Baldwin in Lent 1188 with Gerald as a close associate. Written shortly after the event, Gerald's book, though possibly sanitized and propagandist, and certainly self-satisfied and self-serving, is instructive.[166]

Crusade preaching differed from other forms by demanding a physical response from the audience. As Patriarch Heraclius discovered at Reading in 1185, tears and promises of repentance were insufficient. Such occasions could not be left to chance: they required the stage-management of a Billy Graham. The 1188 itinerary was worked out in advance. In tune with Gregory VIII's instructions for special Masses during Advent and fasts during Lent, the sermons were ostentatiously placed in a frame of confession and penance. The season, fortuitously, was Lent. The Cross was usually preached immediately after the celebration of Mass or after general confession. Gerald once actually described adoption of the Cross as conversion. There were, in Gerald's account, the usual minor miracles to demonstrate the sanctity of the cause.

Formal staging is explicit in Gerald's description of the opening sermon of the tour, at Radnor:

> I . . . was the first to stand up. I threw myself at the holy man's [i.e. Baldwin's] feet and devoutly took the sign of the Cross. It was the urgent admonition given some time before by the King which inspired me to give this example to the others, and the persuasion and oft-repeated promises of the Archbishop and the Chief Justiciar, [Ranulf Glanvill, Henry II's leading minister, was in the audience at Radnor] who never tired of repeating the King's words. . . . In doing so I gave strong encouragement to the others and an added incentive to what they had just been told.

Gerald later, in mitigation, admitted that it had been the 'exhortation of such great men' and the King's promise to fund his crusade that had persuaded him to play his part.[167] In the event he did not set out.

Such tricks were as old as the crusade. Bishop Adhemar of Le Puy's dramatic adoption of the Cross at Clermont in 1095 had been premeditated. Crowd psychology was important and, as Jacques de Vitry observed in a sermon, to gain *crucesignati* it helped to have somebody come forward promptly. Humbert of Romans suggested that preachers themselves could supply the required example.[168] Despite what preachers and chroniclers wanted their audiences to believe, throughout its history crusade preaching was marked by a lack of spontaneity. St Bernard's address at Vézelay did not come out of the blue: Louis VII had been preparing to take the Cross for months. The same can be said for subsequent set-piece addresses, down to the fourteenth-century instances of Cardinal Fréauville's in Paris in 1313 or Pierre Roger's in the same city twenty years later.[169] Innocent III's reforms imposed careful preparation. Taking the Cross in public was rarely done on impulse. According to Joinville's memory, everybody at court knew beforehand when Louis IX was going to take the Cross in 1267.[170] Attendant sermons, and their content, hardly came as a surprise. Occasionally there are reports of sermons, or speeches of exhortation, that broke from the mould, such as that by Pierre de la Palud in Paris in 1331 reporting on the threat from Egypt and calling for a new general *passagium*. Even here, his intervention, if coincidental, was convenient for a government whose interests were once again turning towards Outremer.[171] Sometimes the stage-management failed, as in 1252, when curmudgeonly Londoners failed to follow the lead helpfully provided by royal officials.[172]

It is in the context of prearranged formality that references to preachers being understood despite not using the audience's vernacular should be assessed. Elements of a literary topos are apparent. Gerald of Wales smugly compared the effect of one of his crusade sermons, delivered in Latin and French to an uncomprehending Welsh audience, with St Bernard's preaching in French to Germans. Both apparently elicited excited responses, despite the language barrier. However, there were interpreters: the bishop of Oporto employed them in 1147; Archdeacon Alexander of Bangor translated on the 1188 Welsh tour; Cardinal Ottobuono relied on the dean and some friars at Lincoln in 1267.[173] Surviving manuscript crusade sermons from the thirteenth and fourteenth centuries are in Latin, although some widely circulated *exempla* (uplifting anecdotes) are in the vernacular. In some parts of Europe, Italy for instance, simple Latin may have been widely understood. However, the gap between the preacher and his audience, of status, class, experience and region as well as language, was recognized, possibly at times even deliberately emphasized. Separation was not necessarily a hindrance. As with the Mass and the figure of the priest, the crusade preacher and sermon were witnesses to divine mystery, even though the object was increasingly and transparently mercenary.

Elsewhere, recognition of the need to employ the vernacular and simplify rhetoric for more bucolic or practical audiences suggests that some popular preaching did attempt direct appeals to audiences.[174] This came, however, at the end of a chain of evangelization that began in formal ceremonial. When Gregory VIII, Clement III or Innocent III ordered prayers and liturgical devices associated with the Mass, they were adding to existing religious rituals independent of direct, spontaneous, immediate communication. Like the surviving crusade sermons and preaching manuals, the Mass and the special prayers were in Latin. The power of all such rituals depended on familiarity and satisfying fulfilment of prior expectation. The predictable can be moving, often particularly so, understanding of its significance operating behind and beyond verbal reasoning.

Some of this is suggested in Günther of Pairis's account (c.1207/8) of Abbot Martin's 1201 Basel sermon. The account is highly contrived, composed by a 'recognized literary master', possibly as part of a defence of the Abbot after an inquiry into his administration and conduct in 1206.[175] Günther is anxious to stress the accessibility as well as force of Martin's oratory by describing acute expectant tension before the sermon. The large crowd in the church in Basel had been stirred up by rumours from other provinces of men taking the Cross after hearing sermons. Günther depicts the congregation in a heightened emotional state, well prepared for what Abbot Martin was going to say and do. Like the sermon itself, the whole response was ritualized. That Abbot Martin's sermon was the first in Basel says little for the idea that crusading or its preaching had become habitual. The congregation knew how to behave because they understood ceremonial and had been recently forewarned of what was about to happen.

The sermon itself reads like a spiced-up version of a papal appeal: the loss of the Holy Land, a relic and the heritage of Christ; the grand crusading past; the present crisis since Hattin; the spiritual and temporal benefits. Günther has it greeted by the customary display of released tension and religious hysteria, familiar, expected accompaniments to any account of a successful religious event. More practically, Martin had crosses ready to hand out and was soon organizing the troops for embarkation. The congregation's reaction was what both speaker and audience hoped and expected. In case anybody missed the significance, Günther decorated the conclusion with a poem on the symbolism of the Cross. His attitude, in an echo both of Gerald of Wales and Jacques de Vitry, was captured in his describing Martin subsequently 'converting many to the same militia of Christ'.[176]

The Basel ritual depended, if only in Günther's imagination, on shared expectations, not shared experience. The congregation at Basel, in Günther's eyes, were innocent of crusading: but they were experienced at what was expected of them in church, at religious festivals, Mass, etc., where generally passive audiences or congregations could be tutored to kneel, join in prayers or gaze and bow at the elevated host and chalice. It was the habitual religious conduct of the faithful that crusading began to exploit consistently and coherently in the thirteenth century. That, as much as, perhaps more than recruitment, was the role and context of crusade preaching.

This familiarity, this sense of ease with what was offered by preachers, is confirmed by an increasing lack of originality in the message, its delivery, language and recorded effect. Everywhere, as with Günther's modelling of Abbot Martin's speech on papal bulls, there was a growing similarity of rhetoric, of salient themes, stories, phrases and words, often derived from Scripture, frequently associated with the Cross. Repetition within sermons was a technique commended by Humbert of Romans.[177] The use of the Cross as a sort of mantra can be observed across generations and hierarchical position: in Archdeacon Gerald's account of his own preaching in Wales; in the post-1216 English preaching manual *Ordinatio de predicatione Sancti Crucis in Angliae*; in the sermon of the future Clement VI, Pierre Roger, before John XXII in 1333; or in a sermon by an early fourteenth-century Languedoc monk privately circulated by a canon of Rodez.[178]

Standardization characterized crusade propaganda in the later Middle Ages. Preachers and chroniclers of the thirteenth century spawned a religious literary genre with a life of its own, devoted to but often with only tangential links with the realities of the religious wars fought under the banner of the Cross. In fact, after its golden age in the thirteenth century, the heavily allusive and metaphorical language of the crusade sermon was sustained less by working preachers so much as by more desk- or court-bound propagandists. It has been estimated that, in a sample of 1147 mentions of sermons in northern France between 1350 and 1520, of the 262 that specify the occasion, excluding Lenten and Advent addresses, only twenty-two concerned the crusade, indulgences, Saracens and heretics.[179] The true heirs of Jacques de Vitry and Humbert of Romans were writers like the late fourteenth-century

Philippe de Mézières whose crusade works – extravagant, allegorical, mystical – had, at their heart, a call to arms not just against the infidel but against corruption within, the Holy War to be a vehicle and agent of spiritual and moral reform in a virtuous circle of righteousness and victory.[180]

The evidence of sermons indicates that, as a formulated, coherent institution, crusading was an invention of thirteenth-century intellectuals. By the end of the century, collections of crusade *exempla* were in circulation; there were preaching manuals, such as Humbert of Romans's *De predicatione S. crucis*; famous preachers included crusade sermons in their collections. Eagerness to embrace a wider audience is witnessed in the often rather strained anecdotes designed to reinforce the populist appeal.[181] Ever greater indulgences were offered to those who attended crusade sermons, which may say more of the promoters' hopes than of public enthusiasm.[182] In 1291, the archbishop of York instructed friars, rather unsurprisingly, to preach where large congregations could be assembled.[183] However, of what popular preachers said, there is silence, possibly because they lacked record-keepers of their own; possibly because their preaching was fairly perfunctory. After all, Humbert of Romans urged preachers to keep things simple, in marked contrast to those elaborately literary and learned sermons that have actually survived. Humbert probably had a point. The medium was the message.

For a form of evangelism so prominent in chronicle accounts of the period, evidence for the frequency of crusade sermons is ambiguous. Despite the taint of academic, literary and propagandist stereotypes, one dimension of crusade sermons was highly distinctive: the arousal of an audience to anger, a tradition that stretched back to Urban II and which depend on a fresh supply of atrocities to unveil. This made them unusual, to say the least. The other great penitential and eschatalogical themes were familiar from other aspects of ceremony and liturgy. Only twenty-one surviving thirteenth-century sermons with explicitly crusading titles have been identified.[184] This may suggest a rather rarified phenomenon, although survivals from the earlier fourteenth century appear to be relatively plentiful. It is, however, often hard to disentangle crusade from other sermons, notably sermons on the Cross. Pierre Roger, in his crusade sermon to John XXII in 1333, used as his peroration a passage on the Cross lifted wholesale from a sermon he had preached on doctrine.[185] Sermons *de cruce* lent themselves to a dual purpose.

For many of its promoters, the crusade provided a means for lay conversion, symbolized and recognized by the indulgences given not just to those who took the Cross, whether to redeem it or not, but also to those who simply listened to the preacher. The sermon was a holy event, suitably attractive in itself, knitted closely and deliberately into the general round of the church calendar and the general expectations of the faithful. Thus certain days in the year became suitable for crusade ceremonies, regardless or coincidental of any external crusading need. This can be traced in sermons from the late twelfth century designed for the Invention (3 May) and Exaltation (14 September) of the Cross, the latter being especially favoured, becoming a sort of crusade festival day. The penitential seasons were also popular: Lent, leading up to Easter, and Advent, leading up to Christmas. In 1215, Frederick II took the Cross at Easter; King John, Ash Wednesday; *Ad Liberandam* was promulgated just after Advent. The 1188 preaching tour was in Lent. The Yorkshire friars in 1291 were instructed to preach on 14 September. The apparent popularity of the crusade in Tournai in the 1330s may have been linked to its traditional week-long festival of the Holy Cross which ended on 14 September.[186] It was on 14 September that Philip IV ordered the arrest of the Templars in 1307; Clement V banned tournaments because of the forthcoming crusade in 1313; John XXII issued his first crusade bulls in 1316; and in 1317, in the Church of the Holy Cross in the rue St Merri in Paris, Louis, count of Clermont held the first assembly of his crusading *confrarie* of the Holy Sepulchre.[187]

Crusade preaching exposes something of the nature of crusading as devised in the late twelfth and thirteenth centuries, especially in its development beyond the specific task of recruiting to raise money and form a tool of general pastoral efforts by the church hierarchy. Because of this integration its apparatus could survive when private commitment to fighting for the Cross was overtaken by other concerns. The call to take the Cross had a redemptive purpose that did not depend on subsequent temporal battle. Conversion, indulgence, salvation, religious duty and Christian destiny drowned out the needs of the warrior. Merely to hear the words gained spiritual reward; to respond by taking the Cross earned social, political and fiscal, as well as divine, merit. Concentration of the 'signum victoriale',[188] the Cross, which formed so central a feature of this preaching, by embracing so much more than the crusade, ensured that in the long run it meant less to those wanting to fight in a Holy War against the infidel, or, indeed, against anyone else.

Crusade and Women

For one group in society, the military aspects of crusading had always been muted. The relationship of women to crusading mirrors the transformation of the crusade from a Holy War of particular hardship and merit to a widely available spiritual exercise involving no necessary extraordinary physical activity. From the beginning, women had gone on crusade. Amongst royalty and the nobility it was frequent: Godehilde of Tosni (1096); Ida of Austria (1101); Eleanor of Aquitaine (1147); the countess of Flanders (1157); Margaret of Provence (1248); Eleanor of Castile (1270). Most accompanied their husbands. Some, like Eleanor, countess of Montfort in 1240 or Beatrice, countess of Flanders in 1267, clearly took the Cross, once more suggesting that there were peaceful as well as violent connotations to the ritual.[189] In 1225, it appears that one adventurous Englishwoman departed for the Holy Land leaving her husband behind, his vow unfulfilled.[190] The habit of women taking the Cross was well established by 1200. Four or five Cornish *crucesignatae* failed to redeem their vows in the late 1190s.[191] Some years later, the Parisians Renard Crest and his wife were described as *crucesignati.*[192] Jacques de Vitry boasted of the crowds of wealthy Genoese women he persuaded to take the Cross in 1216.[193] In crusade armies were prostitutes and laundresses, who doubled as de-lousers. Women, it is not always clear whether westerners or locals, ferried water to the troops at Dorylaeum in 1097; helped fill the moat at Acre in 1190; sold provisions to Louis IX's army in Egypt; and raised the alarm at Mansurah when the count of Poitiers became surrounded.[194] The authorities generally disapproved. Restrictions on women's freedom, legal and domestic, were considerable. Unattached women were strongly frowned upon, unless they were sexually harmless old washerwomen. The church sought combatants or non-combatants who would provide for the troops, and was reluctant to afford women rights to take the Cross in any case, still less without the consent of their guardians or husbands. Women's control over their spouses' actions was further reduced by Innocent III in 1200 and 1201 when he decreed that men could take the Cross without their wives' prior agreement, although women accompanying their husbands were permitted.[195]

In the thirteenth century, with Innocent III's severance of activity and reward, women were drawn into crusading through their own donations, legacies, redemptions and indulgences transferred from their husbands. Sermon *exempla* customarily portrayed women as obstacles to their menfolk taking the Cross, a tension perhaps exacerbated rather than eased by Innocent III's rulings against conjugal rights. There were also severe practical diffuculties. A wife abandoned by a crusader, however legitimately in the eyes of the Church, was exposed to dangers not, as romancers would have it, sexual, but legal, material and, in some cases, homicidal. It was not a chastity-belt that such a wife required (in any case an invention of the seventeenth century), but a good lawyer or a strong guardian.[196] To mitigate wives' resistance to their husbands' crusading, it was soon suggested, by Jacques de Vitry among others, that wives and children of departed crusaders should enjoy a full share in the indulgence, a view ultimately accepted by Innocent IV.[197] Thereafter, wives and Church were in greater formal harmony as crusading became just one more avenue for feminine philanthropy, as revealed in wills throughout the later Middle Ages. Some may have resented such relative exclusion: in her will of 1269, Jeanne, countess of La Marche and Angoulême, left 200 *livres* to the Holy Land on behalf of herself and her daughter.[198] There may have been a certain personal feeling behind the bequest of Lady Clare in 1360 to the next *passagium* to the Holy Land.[199] Her mother, Joan, daughter of Edward I, had been born at Acre in 1271.

The Cross

If preaching were the voice of crusading, the Cross was its clothing, its symbol, its inspiration. The potency of the image was obvious and deliberate. The Cross mystically represented Christ, His Passion, the Resurrection and the Church, inspiring a literary devotional genre of its own. The most familiar religious artefact, it stood for Christianity itself. In the language of the Gospels, living a Christian life could be pictured as bearing one's own Cross in imitation of Christ. The True Cross, one relic of which sustained Christian armies in Outremer until its loss at Hattin, had specific association with Jerusalem. As military ensign, mystic symbol, badge of penance, talisman or charm, no icon was more potent.

As a universal religious symbol, wearing the Cross as a token was widespread, by no means the exclusive prerogative of the crusader. The Crutched Friars were known as *crucesignati*. Crosses were worn by military and monastic orders and religious confraternities, such as Bishop Fulk of Toulouse's White Company of 1209, who wore crosses and enjoyed indulgences in their factional urban war against heresy and usury. In northern England, the insignium of St Cuthbert, worn by his devotees and servants and soldiers of the bishop of Durham, was a black Cross.[200] As well as devotion, loyalty and zeal, the Cross could display penance and penitents. The imposition of crosses on reformed heretics as a humiliating sign of their past shame and present repentance had been begun by St Dominic in 1208, becoming a widely used penalty of southern French bishops and the Inquisition by the 1240s. A generation later, such recanted heretics were described as 'crucesignatus propter/pro haeresim'. By the early fourteenth century the noun *crucesignatus* was commonly applied to these ex-heretics in Bernard Gui's *Practica inquisitionis*.[201] The coincidence of language with crusading cannot have been unnoticed: the same inquisitors were also imposing penitential crusades. This was not, as today, when the word 'crusade' is applied to many good causes, a matter of analogy or metaphor but of alternative usage. Crusaders were not the only *crucesignati* whose compounded enthusiasm and penance was thus symbolized. Such fluidity of symbols makes crusading – and made crusaders – seem less distinctive than they have often been portrayed. Sometimes the vocabulary was wholly divorced from any specific spiritual or religious, let alone crusading, context. In mid-fourteenth-century Norwich, among those amerced (i.e. fined) by the Leet Court were 'diversis crucesignatis', men who had failed to appear in court when summoned and who had been, in consequence, forced to wear crosses.[202]

In crusading itself, although, by the 1190s, the imagery of the Cross permeated almost every aspect of the enterprise, differences in application remained strong and striking. The first variable was where the Cross was worn. *Crucesignati* to the Holy Land had them on their shoulders, in imitation of Christ in the *via dolorosa*. Crusaders against the Albigensians and the Moors in 1212 wore them on their chests; so did the royalists at the battle of Lincoln in 1217 and the Montfortians in 1263–65. Those who fought the Hohenstaufen and Ghibellines varied their practice. One English chronicle refers to the crosses of the followers of Simon de Montfort on shoulders and chests, an arrangement depicted clearly in a famous contemporary English drawing of a kneeling crusader.[203] The shape of crosses was, with the exception of the mid-twelfth-century Baltic campaigns, consistent.[204] The material tended to be cloth, occasionally silk, although there is mention of brass in the fourteenth century and iron in the fifteenth century.[205] Colour varied considerably. Red seemed the preferred colour before 1188. On the Third Crusade, to mark differing allegiances, Capetian followers wore red; Angevin, white; Flemish, green. The English remained attached to white: John in 1215; supporters of Henry III in 1217 and Simon de Montfort in 1263–65 all used white. But the adoption of the white Cross by the rebel Montfortians forced the royalist crusaders in 1265 to change to red, the colour of their French allies. This was retained for the rest of the Middle Ages: the crosses for the Despenser and Hussite crusades were red.[206] Two-toned, red and white crosses were worn against Manfred in 1265–66 and appeared on the banners of Italian crusaders of John XXII.[207] Parallel to this, the Military Orders had their own distinctive crosses which so characterized the wearers that, by the fifteenth century, the Teutonic Knights were described simply as *cruciferi*.[208] Whatever the iconographic symbolism, increasingly crusaders' crosses became, as at the battles of Lewes (1264) and Evesham (1265), badges of identification: uniforms.[209]

Lack of standardization is mirrored in the rite of taking the Cross. One of the most surprising features of the crusades is that the central defining act, the taking of the Cross, lacked consistency or coherence. A ceremony that concealed the vow in a physical gesture, a ritual that stubbornly resisted any attempts – if any were made – to regularize it was nonetheless of central importance. Taking the Cross was the visible witness of the interior, binding vow: as one mid-thirteenth-century canonist put it: 'no cross, no obligation'.[210] Instituted by Urban II at Clermont, the ceremony established the special religious status of both enterprise and individual. Fiscal and legal immunities were dependent on the ceremony. For at least two and a half centuries thereafter, no Cross, no crusade. However, even this plain definition became attenuated. After 1250, fewer in the armies of the Church were *crucesignati*. Even garrison troops sent to Outremer may not all have taken the Cross.[211] As already mentioned, Louis II of Bourbon's expedition to North Africa in 1390 and the Franco-Burgundian campaign to Nicopolis in 1396 both attracted indulgences and were described by contemporaries in terms of crusading, yet there is no explicit evidence that any of the participants took the Cross.[212] The famous Vows of the Pheasant taken by the Burgundian nobility at Lille in 1454 were to attack the Turk but, although it was discussed at the time, the votives did not take the Cross.[213] Where the Cross was adopted, it was recognized and recorded, as for the defence of Belgrade in 1458, although even here traditional literary formality may have helped clarify the language as much as events.[214] Early in the fourteenth century, the Venetian crusade promoter Marino Sanudo had envisaged the initial conquest of Egypt being accomplished by soldiers who had *not* taken the Cross, preaching being expressly to collect money through redemptions and alms.[215]

In general, taking the Cross was the *sine qua non*. In so far as it possessed one, the Cross gave its name to the whole enterprise, the canonist Hostiensis, who came nearer than most to providing an ordered definition of the institution, calling it the *crux peregrinatio*. He was also acknowledging the centrality of pilgrimage to the crusade in both its religious and legal dimensions. Taking the Cross in recognition of the vow was, in Villey's words, the 'point de jonction' between pilgrimage and Holy War.[216] As already discussed, the language contemporaries used, in chronicles or law manuals, was shot through with the image of the pilgrimage. Crusades in almost all theatres of war were, at one time or another, called pilgrimages – in the Baltic, against the Albigensians, even, in 1265–66, against Sicily, as well as in the East. Outremer crusaders were called pilgrims not only in literary accounts: the contract between Louis IX and Genoa in 1246 for shipping the French Army to Acre or Tripoli called the clients *peregrini*.[217]

From kings such as Louis VII, Philip II and Louis IX, nobles such as Joinville, to the priest from Varangeville in Normandy in 1265, crusaders took the scrip and staff of a pilgrim as well as the Cross, sometimes in separate ceremonies, as in 1146, or at the same time.[218] In the English Midlands at the beginning of the thirteenth century, there was a rite for taking the Cross that was appended to that of blessing the pilgrim's insignia. The Norman law-book's account of what constituted a 'solemn pilgrimage', already noticed, may be describing a similar ceremony: pilgrims, crosses, holy water, prayers, are common features between the two.[219] The confusion of crusader and pilgrim is not confined to language, ceremony or law. As with Godric of Finchale in the twelfth century, so with Robert Almer of Kent in 1462, pilgrims with seemingly peaceable intentions appear to have taken the Cross.[220] Of course, priests and, as already noted, women habitually took the Cross without martial intent.

Most chronicle references to taking the Cross are perfunctory over the details of the ceremonies. Extant notarized or registered accounts of ceremonies, such as the record of a Marseilles *crucesignatus* Hugh de

Fonte in 1290, Duke Hugh of Burgundy in 1314, or that of a Bavarian in the late fourteenth century, are more concerned with the conditions attached to the act.[221] This was natural, as the fulfilment of the conditions earned the rewards and was of vital concern to all crusade organizers from the first months of the First Crusade onwards. The mechanics of taking the Cross were of less importance.

The surviving examples of the rite for taking the Cross reflect the fragmented nature of the exercise which, away from the prestigious set-pieces, depended on local clergy as much as on papal agents. Common elements were the giving of the Cross in response to or recognition of a vow, although details, content and contexts of such rites lacked any uniformity. From the first century and a half of crusading, different rites have survived in pontificals from Bari, Lambrecht, Coventry, Ely and Canterbury. Different Roman pontificals included a variety of rites, the standard wording, finally adopted by Innocent VIII (1484–92), being the work of Guillaume Durand the Elder, known as the Speculator (1231–96). In the later Middle Ages, diversity persisted. Different rites have traced in fourteenth- and fifteenth-century England alone at York, Lincoln and Salisbury.[222] Such variety is a reminder of the essentially local experience of crusading and, indeed, of most medieval public worship. From the twelfth to the fifteenth centuries, local clergy, parish priests, cathedral officials and monks can be observed giving individuals the Cross. This itself may have been a cause of tension when papal agents from outside the area usurped indigenous custom, or even tried to use other rites. However, popes got round this potential awkwardness by using local bishops and, increasingly, neighbourhood friars, presumably in tune with the habits and liturgy of their regions. The contrast with – even absence of – the centralization of crusade policy, theory and administration at the Curia could hardly be greater.

It may be chance, but the surviving cross-taking rites confirm the significance of Jerusalem and the Holy Land. Not all mention the terrestrial goal of the journey; those that do all refer to the Holy Land, or the Holy Sepulchre or Jerusalem. The Coventry Pontifical supplements the Holy Land as an objective with 'another land to fight the enemies of the Cross', possibly a reference to Egypt.[223] In Durand's Pontifical the ceremony is of 'the blessing and giving of the Cross of those going to assist the Holy Land'. In some fifteenth-century copies 'overseas' (*ultra mare*) replaced the Holy Land, and later Innocent VIII altered the preamble by inserting the phrase 'to assist and defend the christian faith or the recovery of the Holy Land'.[224] Elsewhere, whether from Bari in the twelfth century or Lincoln in the fifteenth, the association with the Holy Land dominates. Men took the Cross for a variety of wars. In fifteenth-century Germany, vows were sworn explicitly to fight the Turk.[225] Reality obviously intruded. But the assumptions are self-evident. In Italy, where crusading meant local warfare, the Pontifical made for Bishop Ugolino Rossi of Parma in 1325 included a sole chapter concerning the Cross headed: 'Concerning the Cross of him who is going to Jerusalem'.[226]

The cross-taking ceremonies show how the Cross and, hence, crusade, were regarded simultaneously in temporal and spiritual terms. In the twelfth-century Bari version, as we have seen, the *crucesignatus* received the Cross 'in heart as well as body' to defend against terrestrial and diabolic foes, an idea that reappeared in a fourteenth-century blessing. The early thirteenth-century Coventry Pontifical called the Cross 'an especial means of assistance, a support of faith, the consummation of his works, the redemption of his soul and a protection and safeguard against the fierce darts of all his enemies'. In the late fifteenth-century Roman Pontifical the Cross figuratively represented Christ's passion and death and thus signified a defence for the body and soul of the *crucesignatus*.[227] Some rites made the military objective explicit, although if descriptions of crusading in charters were analogous, it is likely that many services were less specific.

The association of the cross-taking rites and the Mass was intimate. Throughout the history of the crusades observers, preachers and participants proclaimed the sacramental context. Given the nature of the spiritual benefits, dependent on confessed sins, there must be a presumption that the would-be *crucesignatus* had recently undergone at least general confession, probably in the Mass. On campaign crusaders regularly received communion in celebrating Mass before battle, in reaffirmation of the mystical communion which they had joined by taking the Cross. This formed a clear contrast with civilian life, where the Sacrament was taken infrequently. Some preachers urged that the Sacraments be displayed on altars throughout the crusade to emphasize the holiness of the enterprise.[228]

Not just a protective talisman and a symbol of status, the Cross was a sign of the penance that earned the *crucesignatus* the remission of sins made possible by Christ's Crucifixion and Resurrection. The penitential aspect, strong from the beginning, did not fade with time. In 1316, a group of French nobles led by Louis of Clermont took the Cross 'as a sign of penitence'.[229] This was easily exploited. In the diocese of York in

the mid-1270s, out of a list of three hundred *crucesignati* who had redeemed their vows, all but eleven had been forced to take the Cross as
penance for crimes ranging from irregular ordinations and assaults on
clergy to adultery.[230]

The wider moral and spiritual dimension of assuming the Cross received, if anything, a greater prominence in the promotion of Holy War
as it became an integral element in the reform of the church in the thirteenth century. Extended exegesis on the symbolism of the Cross was a
commonplace of preaching, extending from the Gospel associations to
the story of the conversion of Constantine. The rhetoric was often comprehensive. For Pierre Roger in 1333, the Cross was the sign of victory,
the hope of Christians, resurrection of the dead, guide of the blind, the
path for the wandering, consolation of the poor, protector of the naked,
etc.[231] As a banner for crusaders, the Cross was a natural choice, certainly since the early twelfth century. From the fourteenth century,
even armies in which there may have been few if any *crucesignati*
paraded the Cross. Philippe de Mézières in 1397 and the Emperor
Frederick III in 1454 looked to campaigns against the Turks fought by
troops under the banner (*bannière; vexillum*) of the Cross, with no mention of *crucesignati* as such.[232] Alternatively, in Italy during the pontificate of John XXII and in Flanders under Bishop Despenser, crusaders
continued to fight beneath banners of the Cross.[233]

The convenience of the symbol for church reformers was well caught
by Etienne de Bourbon's *Tractatus du diversis materiis praedicabilibus*, a
mid-thirteenth-century preaching manual and collection of *exempla*.
Etienne, a Dominican who became Inquisitor for large parts of southern
France in the 1230s, had preached the Cross against the Albigensians in
1226. Despite this he had no doubts as to the superior efficacy of the *crux
transmarina*. He insisted on the general efficacy of taking the Cross to attract absolution and mitigate suffering, 'especially that assumed for
across the sea'. He supported this with a number of stories of how taking
the Cross for the Holy Land brought benefits that varied from putting
demons to flight and saving souls to curing physical deformities. Taking
the Cross is depicted as part of a cycle of confession, penance, forgiveness
and redemption. It encompassed a social, philanthropic function. Men
possessed could be exorcised by the adoption of the Cross – the *crux
transmarina* is specified – by them or their friends, one such story being
placed in the diocese of Chartres in 1245. Etienne testified to a story of a
crusader against the Albigensians who secured an indulgence for his
dead father by promising to serve an extra forty days.[234]

Such transferability of the benefits of taking the Cross became widely accepted in the thirteenth century. Eudes de Châteauroux, crusade legate to France in the 1240s, argued that the Cross and consequent pilgrimage offered the chance of escape from purgatory for the *crucesignatus's* loved ones (*caros suos*).[235] Controversial – Jacques de Vitry supporting the idea of transferable indulgences, Hostiensis opposing – this was an issue over which the papacy appears not to have exerted much effective control. Similarly, although preachers such as Jacques de Vitry thought it standard for crusaders to bequeath or transfer their indulgences to wives or children, only with Innocent IV did the practice receive formal papal approval.[236] The Cross was even portrayed as having mystical powers of physical healing. There is an echo of this in the story of Louis IX's miraculous recovery from illness in 1244 leading to his assuming the Cross.[237] Ultimately, in some quarters, the dying and the ill were thought to be able to benefit by taking the Cross and even redeeming their vow. In the widest sense, again in the words of Eudes de Châteauroux, 'by assumption of the Cross men are marked and distinguished as servants of God against the servants of the devil, and as they accept the payment of the Lord so they shall not be killed by the sword of eternal punishment'.[238]

This use of the apparatus of crusading to effect or illustrate moral reform and spiritual regeneration could be seen as deflecting the thrust of the exercise, making the crusade in the thirteenth century both more elaborate and more attenuated than previously. Coupled with vow redemptions and the extension of the crusade as a weapon of papal policy, the harnessing of the crusade to reform secured its placed in Christian life. It also produced a consequential diffusion of the ideal which became, at its crudest, a way of buying remission of sins in all circumstances, a short cut to salvation. The traditional martial rhetoric could not conceal that, by 1250, taking the Cross was a form of spiritual self-help, with little necessary practical connection with the defence of Christendom.

Crusade and Reform

The association of crusading and Christian reform provided the perfect reconciliation of martial ambition and religious obligation. The crusade justified its soldiers and so became an important part of the self-image of the dominating military aristocrats of western Europe. Joinville recorded a story of how, after an affray with marauding Germans some time probably in the early 1240s, Josserand, lord of Brançion in southern Burgundy, prayed (rather pointedly in view of the early fourteenth-century date of writing) for God to take him 'out of these wars among Christians in which I have spent a great part of my life; and grant that I die in Thy service, and so come to enjoy Thy kingdom in paradise'.[239] It is clear from crusade songs that the justification for the laity was not solely religious.[240] As the early fifteenth-century biographer of a veteran of Nicopolis Marshal Boucicaut insisted, compared to war against the infidel, nobles and barons 'could not go on a more honourable expedition or one more pleasing to God'.[241] Emmanuele Piloti, a Cretan ex-patriot who spent many years in Egypt in the early fifteenth century, summed up the appeal of the crusade in traditionally inclusive terms: 'to the honour of Jesus Christ, and the salvation of the souls of relatives and infinite fame and glory in this life'.[242]

In this scheme of obligation, salvation and honour, the Holy Land, although often no more redemptive in terms of papal indulgences, was most ennobling. Moreover it was, in the words of an early fourteenth-century Hospitaller tract, 'the nearest way' to Heaven.[243] Since its inception, crusading had been portrayed as a process of spiritual regeneration for the individual and for Christendom, an integral element in the moral programme of the Church and the secular value system of chivalry. Experiences of 1200 to 1350 might have cast some doubt on the wider regenerative properties of crusading within Christendom. Whatever theorists and popes argued, the grimy reality of warfare in Europe was condemned regularly and, by the end of the fourteenth century, more or less universally, precisely because of its effect in hampering resistance to the Turk of aggression against the Mamluk.

Most of the uplifting stories that underpinned crusade publicity came from campaigns against the infidel. The Holy Land crusade was militarily and morally positive. In 1332, Venetian ambassadors to the French court prefaced their sober practical advice on crusade shipping with a prayer. Such expeditions could not only solve practical internecine problems such as that of the fourteenth-century Free Companies, but also, in Sanudo's phrase, the crusade to the Holy Land would destroy Islam and conserve the Faithful.[244] Writers like Sanudo, Mézières or the Frenchman Pierre Dubois saw in the Holy Land crusade the chance for the regeneration of Christendom through expansion, the winning of new empires and new markets and through what could be best described as a restoration of optimism. In a phrase current in the fifteenth century, the crusade was 'the public business of Christendom': it was also a public method of Christian renewal. Even a shrewd observer of politics, Sanudo, insisted, in an emotional epilogue to his great work *Secreta Fidelium Crucis*, that colonists must be good Catholics, if necessary recruited as young as six years old by offers of indulgences and freehold, and that the ruler of a restored kingdom of Jerusalem had to possess in high measure all the virtues: piety, mercy, fairness, righteousness, learning and a devotion to divine law and the avoidance of sin. The crusade could purge sin, but only those without sin could win the crusade. Sanudo promised one patron lordship of the world *and* paradise. When rejecting the sanctified land route of Godfrey de Bouillon, he argued, like the preacher he was not, that triumph would come only through divine aid. Despite his extravagant and meticulous, if not entirely convincing, detailing of necessary ships and arms, for Sanudo the whole exercise was ultimately profoundly moral and spiritual.[245] To quote Sanudo's contemporary, Pierre Roger, the crusade offered *remuneratio* to the crusader and translation 'from earth to Heaven, from exile to home, from poverty to dominion, from death to life, from work to rest, from sorrow to joy, from misery to paradise'.[246]

As the use of the Cross in ceremonial, in language and in preaching has shown, the crusade was identified closely with personal and collective renewal. In a deliberate creation of the late twelfth and early thirteenth centuries, ideas that spiritual reform and voluntary poverty were essential for the successful prosecution of a crusade were taken up almost as an official programme. The association is clear in Gregory VIII's *Audita Tremendi*, the subsequent sumptuary regulations promulgated by Cardinal Henry of Albano in Germany and Henry II at Geddington in 1188; and in Peter of Blois's *Conquestio* of 1188–89.[247] The theme is of penance, internal and in outward visible display, not vainglory. The emphasis is on poverty, not indigence, but a state of mind rejecting wealth; a humility of spirit rather than material want. As Gregory VIII put it: 'We are not saying "give up the things you have", but "send them off to the heavenly barn and entrust them to God".'[248]

Stress on the personal spiritual life and moral behaviour of Christians added definition to more traditional general exhortations against sin which went back to Urban II. Moral rearmers such as Fulk of Neuilly or Eustace de Flay incorporated the crusade into their prescriptions for reform. Even more than for St Bernard, the concentration is on the individual. As already seen, Gerald of Wales, Günther of Pairis and Jacques de Vitry described *crucesignati* as converts.[249] This analogy was drawn in greater detail by the Cistercian Caesarius of Heisterbach in his *Dialogus Miraculorum* (*c*.1223). Here the *crux peregrinatio* or *crux transmarina* are discussed under the general heading *de conversione* and compared with entering the Cistercian Order which, being more permanent, was, he argued, preferable. However, he noted that the vow for the crusade was comparable with that to join an order: 'these two crosses, namely of the order and of the pilgrimage, are equally health-giving'.[250] A similar comparison of the Orders of crusaders and monks was made by Jacques de Vitry at about the same time, each being described as a *religio*.[251] As such, the crusade involved the community of the faithful far beyond the warriors themselves.

Thus crusading was given new definition, and moulded to suit current cultural and intellectual fashions of reformers, in whose ultimate purposes the crusade played only a secondary role. In the preaching of many of the Paris-trained moralists who promoted the Cross for Innocent III, the emphasis was more on the redemption of souls and reformation of life than on the war against the enemies of the Church. Robert Curzon was accused of signing the old, the young, the infirm and women, non-combatants all.[252] Eustace de Flay's missions to England in 1200 and 1201 were remembered more for their vitriolic attacks on illicit trading and breaches of the Sabbath than for promotion of the Holy War.[253] Concentration by crusade preachers on usury was notorious. The Toulousain White Company waged war against usurers as effectively, if not more vigorously, as against Cathars. The priorities of some preachers were clear. The insistence by Curzon and Fulk of Neuilly on the rejection of usury and the abandonment of wealth in favour of a rigorous *via apostolica* placed many aspirant crusade contributors and participants in material and moral difficulties. Regardless of the practical problems caused to the crusade by the campaign against usury, Innocent III appears to have approved.[254] If politics are about priorities, the politics of Innocent's crusade were, in places, confused.

Unlike the Muslim *haj*, the crusade was never obligatory, merely, in Innocent III's legislation and all that flowed from it, available and convenient. These developments had a profound effect on the practical implications of crusading. The broadening of the religious appeals to embrace more or less all free society altered perceptions and habits. Louis VII had been a pious monarch and crusader, but the role crusad-

ing played in his spritual life pales beside its importance to his great-
grandson, Louis IX. For the younger Louis, the crusade was a central
theme of his life, at once setting him free, as a sort of personal and spiritual emancipation, and then continuing to define his behaviour even
when not actually on crusade. It became the most important element in
his life because of its incorporation into a system of practical spirituality
over the previous generation.[255] A similar integration of the crusade
into a wider puritanical seriousness of faith can be seen in the career of
Simon de Montfort, another leading *dévot* of the mid-thirteenth century. A crusader himself, whose father had fought in the Holy Land as
well as against the Albigensians, it was entirely in character that Simon
called on the images of crusading to sustain his cause in the years of rebellion and civil war from 1263 to 1265.[257] As F. M. Powicke remarked,
the crusade was part of the air such men breathed. This had not been
true in anything like the same fashion for rulers and nobles before 1187.
Even for a lukewarm crusader such as Henry III, the Cross had become
an accepted way of demonstrating his personal religious credentials,
almost regardless of whether he embarked.[258] For his uncle Richard I,
on the other hand, crusading had been a much more specific ambition,
no less intense, perhaps, but less integrated into his regular spiritual life.

These changes indicate a central feature of crusading. Throughout the
half-millennium when in some form or other it was recognized and
understood by contemporaries as a living phenomenon, however attenuated, the crusade reflected and refracted its religious, social and
cultural setting: the militant Christianity of the eleventh century; the
poverty and reform movements of the twelfth and thirteenth centuries; the elaboration of Canon and Civil Law; the growth of the
economy and secular government; the elevation of papal monarchy;
the colonization of frontiers. Not all areas responded equally: there
were crusades in Bosnia, but not in Ireland. But crusading did not exist
by itself; as a habit of mind or action it was at the mercy of other events
and attitudes. In the increase in organized, large-scale warfare across
western Europe after 1250, crusading occupied a not always discredit-
able but a diminishing place. Except in eastern Europe – Hungary or
Prussia – crusading played little part in the many wars between
acquisitive rulers and lesser neighbours in north-west Europe: England
against Wales and Scotland; France against Flanders. The crusades
were part of the internecine battles in Italy and the Schism, but at a high
cost in public attitudes. Again and again fourteenth- and early fifteenth-

century writers insisted that wars in Europe, crusades or not, were hindering the fight against Islam. Popes probably agreed but were trapped by their own political requirements, for increasingly crusading had become financially vital in the prosecution of certain wars.

Elsewhere, crusading was squeezed out of the expectations of the West by the Hundred Years War, despite the increasing threat to Christendom itself by the advancing Turks. This contradiction did not pass unnoticed. As a result, traditional crusading became increasingly irrelevant: contemporaries and chroniclers slowly lost active interest. Just as the crusade vanished from the law-books of the West, so the identification of the crusade with spiritual reform faded, itself a sure sign that its importance as a religious exercise was essentially, perhaps unexpectedly, ephemeral, far from the central Christian habit some have imagined. As it waned in significance, so its associated religious and social functions – almsgiving, prayers, legacies – subsided. The mechanics of cross-taking, indulgence, rhetoric, ambition and, especially, finance survived. Interest in crusading history flourished. Traditional enthusiasm could be reignited, as in the defence of central Europe in the 1450s. But the *negocium crucis* was no longer part of religious routine. Its important place in Christian life awarded by the reformers of the thirteenth century had evaporated.

Ironically, in the late Middle Ages, when crusading was marginal, there was little criticism of it, except in the coded attacks on warfare within Europe which culminated in the unedifying wars of the Great Schism. Yet, when crusading had been habitual, despite the official ecclesiastical consensus on its spiritual value, some, perhaps many, regarded the institution as being uncomfortably like any other aspect of European politics: manipulated, partial and corrupt.

Criticism and Decline

There has been much modern debate about the extent and significance of criticism of crusading, some of it ill-conceived, for example searching for 'neutral public opinion', as if opinion could, by definition, be neutral. That criticism existed is unquestioned.[259] What is disputed is the relationship of criticism to the popularity of the institution itself or, more pointedly, of certain crusades rather than others. Advocates of an inclusive definition of crusading have been at pains to argue that crusades against the Hohenstaufen or in Italy were not unpopular, although this appears irrelevant to their argument about legitimacy. Successful recruitment is hardly an accurate barometer of the views of the recruited, given that crusade armies, as any other, were gathered by a mixture of enthusiasm, loyalty and cash: still less is it a gauge of the attitudes of those not recruited.

There is a tendency among these scholars to scrutinize critically the prejudices and ulterior motives of anti-papal critics but to accept more or less at face value the evidence of defenders of the papacy.[260] There seems little point in stopping being a Ghibelline merely to become a Guelph. There is even an implicit strand of theological, confessional apologetics. Such arguments occasionally stretch credulity, as when it is argued that acknowledged hostility to Curial behaviour was offset by what Beryl Smalley described, in a different context, as the 'deep acquiescence' of Christendom towards papal policy.[261] In the political sphere, in which on one level crusading must be placed, it is hard to see such calm acceptance of papal action in the age of Frederick II or Philip IV. Elsewhere, reception of papal directives appears not so much hostile as conservatively discriminating. Over this whole discussion there seems to hang unhistorical assumptions of right or wrong.

Away from partisan polemics, in the operation of crusading in society there is, as has been seen, clear local evidence of the acceptance (a better word than popularity) of the Holy War to the Holy Land as an ideal in the daily lives of western Europeans. This lingered into the sixteenth century.[262] It is hard to equate any other crusading endeavour precisely with that to the Holy Land. Crusades elsewhere had less universal appeal, not because they lacked full legal authority, or even that the privileges offered by the papacy differed. Those Florentines who, in the later thirteenth century, were careful to reserve their donations for the Holy Land, were not alone in resisting an inclusive theory of crusading.[263] Other crusades were not promoted as widely, were ostensibly of secondary importance to successive popes, and remained rhetorically, legally and emotionally in the shadow of the Holy Land.[264]

There is an argument that support for crusading in general declined as the papacy corrupted the ideal by using it as a method to raise money, and diverting it to wars against Christians. Yet, despite vociferous hostility, papal crusades in Italy were sustained with some vigour. Unsurprisingly, many were indiscriminate in enjoying the plenary indulgences. However, some insist that whatever the doctrinal position as interpreted by interested parties, there was no general acceptance of the equality of status of European crusades with those to the Holy Land.[265] Here, too, how contemporary criticism is interpreted is fundamental. But once again, no consensus is discoverable; neutral or disinterested comment is unlikely to be loud. Either way, for those who base themselves on a reading of Canon Law and those who stake their position on the extent of voiced hostility, criticism of crusading lies at the heart of an appreciation of its nature and fate.

There are, however, two problems in using criticism this way, one of method; the other of fact. Until recently, debates about crusading have been largely restricted to high politics, international ecclesiastical elites, upper-class literature and academic disputation; to grand schemes and complex ideology. What this chapter has tried to indicate is that the crusade is to be observed no less vividly in its implementation in practice and in the localities, in parish churches, manor-houses and law courts, as much as in the council chambers, war rooms or studies of the great. In humbler surroundings, the noise of the slanging matches of the polemicists is filtered, their language and ideas less precise. By looking exclusively at the Curial establishment and reactions to it, the nature of the crusade has been distorted, rendering it as cohesive as papal rhetoric desired instead of as fragmented as it appeared to the faithful. Here, for instance, lies the gulf between the inclusive view of crusading and the perceived primacy of the Holy Land. In this context, much of the debate about criticism appears beside the point.

Equally, the practical impact of criticism or lack of it needs recognition. There is little evidence that hostility to papal policy in Italy, as opposed to the policy itself, prevented major eastern crusades after 1250. The critics had singularly little effect, either, on the willingness of the faithful to contribute alms, legacies and donations. Until the 1330s expectations in the West of a new eastern general *passagium* ran high. That none occurred can be attributed initially to tensions between western rulers and the recognized massive logistical problems. The papacy spent much effort in trying to organize smaller expeditions against the Turks throughout the fourteenth century and, up to the 1360s at least, the nobility of the West was willing to take the Cross and prepare for action.[266]

On the other hand, apart from political obstacles such as the Hundred Years War, credibility was a growing problem. There were major initiatives to support then recover the Holy Land by Gregory X in 1274; Nicholas IV after 1291; Clement V at the Council of Vienne (1312); and John XXII (1333). Their efforts received diplomatic approval, especially in the early fourteenth century from the kings of France.[267] But as time went on, and as money raised for the Holy Land was either not spent or diverted elsewhere, a wary caution verging on cynicism was evident, less among the putative crusaders than among the taxpayers, who increasingly adopted the line that money would be forthcoming only when preparations were under way, a potentially self-defeating cycle. Here, it was not critics of crusades who expressed scepticism but potential supporters unwilling to be hoodwinked and disappointed by results.[268] God's displeasure and the world's contempt threatened backsliding crusaders.[269]

One symptom of this frustration and creeping disillusion came in the form of attacks on the Military Orders and plans for their merger, renewal or suppression. Increasingly as the thirteenth century progressed, these Orders had taken over the military and financial arrangements for the routine defence of Outremer. Their failure to secure this inevitably led to suggestions for reform. Most common in the years around 1300 was the idea of a new, united order, which appealed to strategists eager to avoid the bickering of the past and to consolidate income for the *passagium*, as well as to secular rulers keen to assert control over the enterprise: many schemes included proposals for a royal commander to lead the new order.[270] In the view of some, notably Philippe de Mézières at the end of the fourteenth century, the new order should comprise the whole crusade army. Only thus could the necessary finance, discipline and spiritual purity be guaranteed.[271]

In certain cases this unease at past failure turned to rejection and, in the case of the Templars, persecution and abolition (1307–14). A measure of the weakening force of traditional assumptions and rhetoric under the pressure of changed circumstances was the great debate over the legitimacy of the Teutonic Knights' crusade against the newly Christian rulers of Poland-Lithuania at the Council of Constance (1414–18). Although the Knights' defence was generally accepted, they failed to obtain approval from the Council or Pope Martin V (1417–31) for a Holy War against the Poles. During the case, although rejected, the arguments of the Polish spokesmen, in particular Paul Vladimiri, raised fundamental criticisms both of the northern crusade and, by implication, the whole ideal. The conservative replies to these revealed not a set array of accepted doctrine, but a lawyer's thicket of *ad hoc* academic justification and special pleading.[272]

However, any impression of universal decay is misleading. Responses ebbed and flowed unevenly with wide local and national differences. Respect and support for the Hospitallers of Rhodes, unimpeachably active on the front line against Islam, persisted.[273] More widely, revivals of interest in campaigns against the Muslims were achieved in the 1360s, 1390s and the 1450s, not coincidentally in periods when France was not fighting the English. The partisan crusades in Italy ceased after the Great Schism and the antics of John XXIII and Ladislaus of Naples, impervious no longer to the damage that such enterprises had done the reputation of the papacy itself and, perhaps more tellingly, the Curia's capacity to raise money from national churches.[274] The 1417 Concordat between Martin V and the English Church merely recognized a status quo of national fiscal autonomy long practised even over the crusade in both England and France.[275]

Nonetheless, before 1378 criticism of the Italian crusades had not brought them to an end. Any decline in the crusade needs to be seen front by front. There was no unified movement with a life (growth, decline, inaction, etc.) of its own. Campaigning in Italy or the Baltic was not regarded in the same light by participants or promoters as the Holy Land *passagium*. There were few opponents of the crusade to the Holy Land, except when campaigns had gone disastrously wrong, as in the 1140s or 1250. [276] Even then, as with the Shepherds' Crusade in 1251, there was a tendency to blame the organizers or fighters for letting Christendom down, rather than root-and-branch condemnation of the sort approached by Ralph Niger during preparations for the Third Crusade, and proclaimed before the Inquisition by Peter Garcia in 1247.[277] As active crusades against the Muslim occupants of Palestine receded into memory, so Outremer crusading acquired an aura of fame, gilded by countless poems and fictional or semi-fictional narratives.

As crusading became increasingly associated with papal wars in Italy in the fourteenth century, so there was a shift in criticism. Critics of wars within Christendom, even those under the guise of crusades, persisted for as long as those wars continued. It is difficult to maintain that these wars were rended either more or less impossible by such attacks. Advice presented to the Council of Lyon in 1274 had confirmed that there was hostility to 'political' crusades and that a mixture of distraction, indifference and sloth stood in the path of new Holy Land crusade.[278] However, inertia and European wars, not the vitriol of critics, hobbled attempts by Gregory X to orgainize a new *passagium*: and the Italian crusades went on. Nevertheless, to say that criticism was ineffective is not to say that it was marginal, merely that crusading as understood by the Curia was, by the late thirteenth century, impervious to disorganized popular responses. Crusades had become big business for suppliers, shippers, mercantile cities, governments and nobilities as well as the Church. It was not 'deep acquiescence' to papal authority that ensured support for crusading, but indulgences, redemptions, pay, propaganda and secular loyalties to community or lord.

After 1300, by insisting on equating their political aims in Europe with the war against the infidel, popes ran the risk of the reverse, of turning the whole enterprise upside-down by divorcing the crusade from its original function. In view of the clear priorities of funding and organization, papal crusades could be castigated for preventing wars against Islam.[279] This may not have been intentional or even, for popes such as Urban V (1362–70), policy. But it was an evident, indelible effect of their actions.

Another complaint which cut at the heart of the reforms of Innocent III was of the system of vow redemptions; the easy availability, which amounted to the direct sale of indulgences; and the use to which the money was put. Very large sums were raised in this way until the system broke down in the mid-fourteenth century. An unsophisticated law of demand and supply operated. There was inevitable sensitivity to charges of peculation, lent added edge by the sight of mendicant friars collecting substantial sums of money. There were charges that vows were redeemed either for too much (from the poor) or too little (from the rich). [280] There was something unedifying at the sight of one of the richest men in Europe, Richard, earl of Cornwall, being allowed to milk the collected profits from vow redemptions years after he had returned from Outremer.[281]

Across Europe, from rulers as well as ruled, there was a suspicion that the whole exercise could easily become a racket. Grievances concentrated on abuse, rather than the principle. However, there were those from the Fifth Crusade onwards who linked the failure of large crusade expeditions to the East to the practice: God's disapproval was manifest.[282] It is possible that there was resentment from those at the bottom of free society. Although now within the embrace of the crusade indulgences, their material contributions were comparatively negligible. Spiritual equality may have been little compensation for a reinforcement of hierarchical awareness.[283] Yet, Innocent III's extension of the facility to redeem vows operated within an explicitly material context: how best to mobilize men, money and materials. The fate of vow redemptions, the transformation into the sale of indulgences, reinforces a view of crusading as subject to change and diffusion away from its original objective.

Nevertheless, emotional and practical links with the origins of crusading persisted, nowhere more evident than in works on the crusade itself. No crusade sermon was complete without reference to the past, either historical models of behaviour or uplifting anecdotes drawn from a heroic past. Such stories shaped contemporary perception. Writers wishing to influence rulers in organizing a new *passagium* placed their ideas in a historical frame. Every king of France was made actely aware of his crusading pedigree. If any forgot, there was the Office of St Louis to remind him.[284] St Louis remained a supreme model, but Philippe de Mézières, in his *Epistre Lamentable* (1397), was equally content to illustrate his opinions with detailed analysis of the behaviour of Philip II or Richard I.[285] Everywhere the image of Godfrey de Bouillon hovered over the imagination of the later Middle Ages, in drama, song, tapestry and literature.

Apparently practical men of affairs, such as Marino Sanudo or Emmanueli Piloti, were well versed in crusade history and legend or, in the case of Godfrey de Bouillon and Peter the Hermit, the potent mixture of both.[286] The longevity of the crusade was here a self-perpetuating process of recall and reinvention. The use of history was a fundamental part of defining what crusading was and could be again, lending shape and coherence to otherwise distinct events. This is elaborately displayed in Sanudo's *Secreta Fidelium Crucis*, where the longest book of three is a history of the crusade and Outremer, beginning with the 'commotio mirabilis' of 1095–96. Sanudo's reliance for his early narrative on Jacques de Vitry who, in turn, depended on William of Tyre, kept a distinctive twelfth-century interpretive tradition alive, his book being widely disseminated through the courts of fourteenth-century western Europe to an apparently appreciative audience.[287] Perceptions shaped reality, stories of earlier campaigns setting strategic examples to be followed or rejected. The libraries of Europe were stuffed with crusade narratives, advice, propaganda and fantasies. This historical glue was neither natural nor accidental but carefully manufactured by those with direct material or moral interest in the enterprises.

The constant reiteration of the past moulded the attitudes even of those on the front line against Islam. Marino Sanudo is one example of this. Another is Philippe de Mézières, chancellor of Cyprus, pilgrim, crusader and veteran propagandist for a new crusade order of Chivalry, the Order of the Passion. He confessed that as a young man in Picardy he had been inspired by stories of Christian heroism in Palestine.[288] His writings, notably the massive *Songe du Vieil Pèlerin* (1389) and his *Epistre Lamentable*, written after the news of the Nicopolis disaster had reached Paris in December 1396, display a combination of pragmatism and sentimentality, a mixture of experience and wishful thinking typical of much that was composed on the later medieval Eastern Question. In the *Songe*, Mézières on the one hand urged Charles VI of France to read about the exploits of Godfrey de Bouillon, while on the other carefully apportioning responsibility for the collapse of Philip VI's crusade schemes in the 1330s.[289]

Mézières was not in position to distinguish between the past of legend and the past of history. Nobody was, but this was not necessarily as much of an impediment as it may seem to a modern audience. Whereas a writer such as Sanudo, although similarly unknowingly handicapped, adopted the pose of a sober, massively erudite expert, Mézières employed an insistently allegorical style which allowed him to criticize without overt offence. Beneath his rhetorical panoply, Mézières dealt sensibly if optimistically with the salient issues affecting responses to Islam: strategy; diplomacy; organization; morale and attitudes. For all the extravagance and obscurantism of his approach, Mézières was much less of a fantasist or crackpot than some apparently more sober writers, such as John Torzelo in 1439 or Jean Germain in 1452, who saw the destruction of the Turk and the recapture of Jerusalem as a matter of weeks and months. [290]

The grip of the past was evident in the optimism born of an insidiously romantic belief in linking the threat of the Ottomans with the old grievance against the Mamluk rulers of Palestine. Even observant fifteenth-century critics such as Piloti and the Burgundian Bertrandon de la Broquière abided by the conventions of 'recovery' literature familiar since the late thirteenth century. While the Ottomans were the vital danger, the dream of Jerusalem may have helped focus the spiritual, moral and redemptive aspects of war against the Infidel. [291] More generally, talk of the recovery of Jerusalem became the small change of diplomatic parleys or the glitter to top gaudy bombast, as in Charles VIII's protestations when invading Italy in 1494 or Francis I's attempt to impose an Italian peace in 1515. [292] Humanists even took up the theme. In 1498, the Roman poet laureate, celebrating the coronation of Louis XII of France, associated the new King with the reconquest of Jerusalem. Humanist propaganda produced an odd mix of the medieval and

classical, Louis XII being promised a Roman triumph if he freed the
Holy Land and Constantinople and a greeting by Apollo.[293]
    The atmosphere as well as the apparatus of crusading infected the
language in which battles against the Turks were described. Jean
d'Auton's account of the attack on Lesbos in 1501 is embroidered with
a lay crusade sermon by the French King's lieutenant, complete with
promise of papal indulgences, eternal life, temporal glory, renown and
immortal honour.[294] The grip of the past was welcome and strong.
From first to last, history and historiography, event and commentary
were inseparable and self-referential, at least until the sixteenth century
when, it is worth noting, none of the debates or decrees of the Fifth
Lateran Council (1512–17), discussing an *expeditio* against the Turks,
mentioned Jerusalem, nor did its crusade canons much rely on *Ad
Liberandam*.[295]

Survival of popular interest in the Holy Land, as opposed to Italy or
elsewhere, is attested by a wide variety of sources. Propagandists were
joined by poets, such as the versatile courtier and musician Philippe de
Vitry in the mid-fourteenth century.[296] Where politics denied them,
would-be crusaders, with Mézières (1346), Marshal Boucicaut and the
count of Eu (1388/9), along with hundreds, possibly thousands of others over more than two centuries after 1291, became Holy Land pilgrims (in the case of Boucicaut, one not unwilling to serve the Ottoman
Sultan, either).[297] Even those with Lollard scruples against papal crusades in Christendom joined expeditions against the Infidel, went on
pilgrimage to the East and considered joining Mézières's Order of the
Passion for the recovery of Jerusalem.[298]
    A certain amount of material concern for the Holy Land was concen-
trated on the surviving eastern Mediterranean Military Order, the
Hospitallers in Rhodes, whose commanderies across Christendom
provided, in annual dues (responsions) sent east, a tangible link between western farms and the battle against Islam. Fourteenth-century
Orders of chivalry from Cyprus to Naples to Aragon paid at least formal recognition to the primacy of the war in the East as a goal of
endeavour.[299] In early fourteenth-century Paris, there was a *confrarie* of
the Holy Cross founded by St Louis himself and a new *confrarie* of the
Holy Sepulchre, catering for bourgeois who had or hoped to take the
Cross, which acted as a charity to care for Holy Land pilgrims.[300] These
latter were accorded special consideration and financial assistance by
the Lincoln guild of Tailors. Two Norfolk guilds founded in 1384,

St Christopher's at Norwich and Assumption of the Virgin Mary at Wiggenhall, began their meetings with prayers for the recovery of the Holy Land.[301]

Something of the nature and extent of such social commitment is witnessed in wills. Fourteenth-century monarchs and nobles were still in the habit of leaving notionally huge sums to the crusade, up to tens of thousands of *livres*. Lower down the social scale, a crusade legacy tended to be one of the largest bequests by a testator. This was true not only for such as Clement V or the last four Captian kings of France, but also for Guillaume de Villeneuve, from the Carcassonne region, who left a mere 10 *livres tournois*.[302] Some bequests were tiny. In 1349 Agnes le Horir, widow of a Southampton burgess, left 3*d*; Matha de la Roque, wife of a Bordeaux *bourgeois*, 20 sous in 1334.[303] The general motive was summed up in the will of Philip VI of France: 'for love of Our Lord and the salvation of our soul'.[304] Specifically, money was left to redeem unfulfilled crusade vows or, as with John Bron of Beverley in 1347 or Hugh, seigneur of Montmorot in 1315, to send proxies on the next *passagium*.[305] Occasionally, an individual tone creeps in. Louis X of France went beyond the usual formulae in confessing to have the crusade 'plus a cuer' and two women from Bordeaux, Agnes del Bosquat (who left 52 *livres bordelais* in 1311) and Matha de la Roque, twenty years later, gave money 'pour venger le mort de nostre senhor Dius Jhesu-Christ'.[306] As with those buying indulgences, the social embrace was wide: men and women; kings, nobles, seigneurs, lords, knights, gentry, clerics and bourgeois; more or less anyone with property to bestow.

Such evidence cannot be taken quantitavely to measure the extent of popularity, as most wills are lost and most that survive, especially as the fourteenth century progressed, did not include Holy Land or *passagium* bequests. Qualitatively, however, such wills show the tenacity of the ideal of the recovery of the Holy Land in the hearts and around the hearths of western Europe, a hope inspired and maintained by a Church and a hierarchy wedded to a habit of mind and frame of behaviour at once noble and fulfilling, even when not realized. As a social custom, crusading became as much about social esteem, self-respect and spiritual insurance as about carnage amongst the enemies of God, although it was about that too. That is why the phenomenon lasted; and that is why it died away. The supreme irony is that the crusading melted into a political, fiscal and ecclesiastical charade at precisely the time of greatest need of western Europe in the face of Ottoman attacks from the 1440s to the

1560s. What defeated crusading was not Islam, but the politics of Christendom and the Christian Reformation. What had been invented and manipulated by a clerical elite and supported by the self-serving ethics of a lay aristocracy ceased to inspire ready confidence and understanding when those structures of authority toppled or changed. Initially one way of justifying occasional religious wars which was later deliberately woven into the fabric of a papally ordered Christian society, the crusade did not exist independent of the forces, circumstances, institutions and persons who sustained its edifice of belief and aspiration. Without the acceptance of that value-system, crusading became the preserve of the confessional sectarian and the antiquarians with whom the crusades took on new life, or, rather, lives.

3

PROTEUS UNBOUND:
CRUSADING HISTORIOGRAPHY

'Since the creation of the world, what has been more miraculous ex-
cepting the mystery of the Cross, than what has happened in modern times
in this journey of our Jerusalemites?'[1] Ever since this extravagant conceit of
Robert of Rheims, failed abbot and popular historian of the First Crusade, written some time before 1108, appreciation of the significance,
nature, even course of such expeditions and of the importance of the
attendant religious, social, political and fiscal mechanisms has depended on interpreters, not witnesses. Most medieval written primary
sources were exercises in interpreting reality, not describing it. Even
before the transmuting interests of modern historians operate, the
record of the past is slanted. Thus perceptions of the First Crusade were
created by the historians it inspired as much as by the experiences of
those who campaigned. The actions of the latter were set in a precise,
explicable context by the former. Not for the last time, the deeds of soldiers were explained to them by non-combatants. The sources, charters as well as chronicles, tend to be self-conscious attempts to explain
actions and events according to the intellectual fashions of the time.
The First Crusade united observers in astonishment, admiration and
awe. Robert of Rheims and his contemporaries interpreted the years
1095–99 in terms of wide forces of human history, divine providence,
and their own prejudices. So Guibert of Nogent, as for many since, depicted crusading as the *Gesta Dei Per Francos*, the 'other Jerusalemites'
being firmly relegated to subsidary status.[2] The main narratives of the
First Crusade were compiled by historians who imposed their own
vision on events, illustrating their didactic interpretations with the

primary evidence of eye-witnesses mixed with their own imaginings. Even supposed eye-witness accounts were carefully contrived.

This set a pattern for the subsequent near-millennium of observation and study of crusading, influencing not only the interpretation of evidence but its very nature. Few subjects have been so vulnerable or, alternatively, attractive to the presumptions of commentators and scholars (and their audiences). Those writing when crusading Holy War was a feature of western European society, roughly from the eleventh to the sixteenth centuries, were part of the phenomenon itself, not just its historiography. The literary explosion prompted by the First Crusade helped establish historical writing as an acceptable, even important exercise for the intellectual elites of the medieval West.[3] It also determined succeeding perceptions of this Holy War. By forging together knowledge and interpretation, contemporary historians played as significant a role in defining the activity as promoters or participants: often they were the same people.[4] It is a central argument of this book that much of the record of crusading is self-referential, not objective, impartial or necessarily concerned with accuracy or truth. Perceptions of reality – i.e. histories – were born from a fusion of events with the interests of those who identified in those events actions that could serve their own purposes, political, pastoral or polemic.

In the eighteenth century, David Hume remarked that 'the crusades . . . engrossed the attention of Europe and have ever since engrossed the curiosity of mankind'.[5] Once the arid traditional uniformity of official church pronouncements gave way to strategic imperatives and open debate in the sixteenth century, each generation has fashioned its own crusades.

The Sixteenth Century: Continuity and Change

In the sixteenth century the crusade was inevitably a subject of concern and controversy. Since the fall of Constantinople in 1453, the Ottoman advance seemed to many to be forcing Christendom, as Pius II put it, into a narrow angle of Europe.[6] Humanists and traditionalists united in alarm for culture and religion. Sporadic intense activity and propaganda by an often unjustly maligned papal Curia were matched by almost incessant ululations of those who likened the loss of Constantinople and Romania to the triumph of a new barbarism over a fallen Greece. With the front-line of the religious conflict established across central Europe and the Adriatic, there was fresh immediacy to calls for Holy War. Even Henry VI of England was told in 1459 that Turks on the Danube were a direct threat to the Rhine, and hence to English interests.[7]

One consequence was, for many near the front-line, to shift the emphasis from a war of religion to a war of territory. Obviously such a stance appealed to George Podiebrad, the Hussite King of Bohemia (1457–71), for whom papal militarism was anathema.[8] But it was also a growing theme of tracts by orthodox but critical Catholics, disenchanted by past Holy Wars yet anxious lest there were no concerted resistance to the Ottomans. In Germany, some saw a new role for the Holy Roman Emperor as defender of Europe as much as Defender of the Faith.[9] The conciliarist Juan de Segovia went even further in the later fifteenth century. Presaging Erasmus and Luther in his critique of Holy War, he accepted the legitimacy of resisting Muslim invasion of Christian lands while condemning wars fought against Muslims for religious motives.[10] The proximity of Turkish armies and fleets made such distinctions possible.

The secularization of Holy War in the sixteenth century was, paradoxically, both a major cause of the disintegration of crusading as an ideal, and a bridge over which much of the inspiration and enthusiasm for war against the infidel could reach those confessionally opposed to traditional crusading, such as the Lutheran Ulrich von Hutten in the 1520s or the Huguenot François de la Noue in the 1580s.[11] A range of polemic and response was therefore available when Christendom's defences were severely tried by Suleiman the Magnificent (1520–66). However, with the Ottomans once again threatening to engulf Europe, ideological crusading was rejected by Protestants, while political crusading was compromised by an increasing tendency of western powers, such as France and England, to see the Turk as an ally against more immediate foes, the Habsburgs.

The return of the Muslim threat to dominate the crusade debate in the fifteenth century was frequently obscured by layers of academic artifice, rhetorical posturing and political sycophancy, whether in humanist Florence, disorganized Germany, lustrous Burgundy or acquisitive France. With the conquests in the East of Selim I (1512–20) and the rapid advance of Suleiman at Rhodes (1522), Mohács (1526) and Vienna (1529), and the subsequent maintenance of Ottoman power at

Buda and the middle Danube, such traditional measures of resistance and counter-attack were inevitably rehearsed, but increasingly found materially and intellectually wanting. Although the physical threat, and the need for a united German military effort encouraged *de facto* Habsburg recognition of Protestants by the early 1530s, attitudes were still conditioned by religion, and thus old-fashioned remedies and rhetoric were challenged.[12] The twin pillars of formal crusading, papal authority and the Church's power to grant indulgences, which had sparked Luther's rebellion in 1517, came under hostile scrutiny, from within the Catholic fold as well as from Protestants. Common to both was an emphasis on Christian humanism and fear of the Turks. The motives of individual Christian warriors, the acceptability of their deeds to God and the evidence of His reaction in terms of victory or defeat were of concern alike to Erasmian humanists and Lutheran polemicists.

In 1532, Matthias Kretz, a German Catholic preacher, well versed in crusade history, explicitly rejected honour, glory, material gain, anger or vengeance as motives for Christian warriors against Islam: 'such motives are Turkish'.[13] They were also those of crusaders from at least Bernard of Clairvaux onwards. Erasmus claimed in 1530 that he was in favour of a successful Holy War against the Turks, but wondered what good it would do unless a Christian example was held up to them as well. He advocated conversion, an extension of the kingdom of Christ rather than the kingdom of the Pope and cardinals. He criticized crusading used as a blind for other policies, describing papal indulgences as shameless. Uninterested in the panoply of dogma and poking fun at the administrative complexity, Erasmus, in his implicit rejection of Christian Holy War, went further than many Protestants in condemning the temporal aspects of crusading.[14] Luther, for example, although initially arguing for non-resistance as the Turks were instruments of God's chastisement, by 1541 had conceded a need for a defensive, secular campaign to defend Germany and Christianity.[15]

Strong conservative elements persisted in official Catholic circles. Pronouncements and policies remained hidebound by precedent, practice and tradition. The crusading bulls of Leo X (1513–21), Pius V (1566–72) or Gregory XIII (1572–85) looked back to a united western Church and the active crusading of two and three centuries before.[16] But increasingly there were doubts expressed. Paul III (1534–49) tried to get crusading indulgence bulls abolished or, at least, restricted, by the Council of Trent. Significantly, his efforts were thwarted by Spanish opposition as, by mid-century, the crusade and its attendant financial machinery of the *cruzada* had become a limb of Habsburg policy.[17] A hostile piece of English doggerel of 1589 talked of:

> ... the Spanish Nation
> That in a Bravado
> Spent many a Crusado
> In setting forth an Armado
> England to Invado.[18]

It was only in 1567, fifty years after Luther's theses had been pinned up in Wittenberg, that Pius V abolished the sale of indulgences. But it is notable that the role indulgences were given was minimal in Catholic tracts on fighting the Turk, from the German *Türkenbüchlein* of the 1510s to the 1540s to the advice of the Savoyard diplomat and crusade enthusiast Réné de Lucinge in the 1580s.[19] This *de facto* abandonment of the indulgence was part of the secularization of crusading common across religous divisions and of the equally mutual concentration on inner piety common to reformers, Catholic as well as Protestant.

Unsurprisingly, there was some disarray at Rome. Apart from concerted rhetoric, notably from Leo X, aimed at encouraging a new Turkish crusade, other targets occasionally intruded. While in general maintaining fifteenth-century resistance to crusades within Christendom, a crusade to bring Henry VIII of England to heel was mooted in the 1530s, and Julius III (1550–55), both before and after becoming pope, toyed with expeditions against the Protestant Schmalkaldic League and Henry II of France. There are distinct crusade overtones to attempts to unsettle and unseat Elizabeth I, including the Armada and the Irish rebellion in 1600. Julius II (1503–13), on the other hand, had issued crusade indulgences to his supporters in Italy (for which he was lampooned in Erasmus's *Julius Exclusus*) and to Henry VIII's armies invading France in 1512. More eccentrically, Paul IV (1555–59) waved the menace of a crusade against the Habsburgs Charles V and Philip II.[20]

Such manoeuvrings exposed what was obvious from the thirteenth century. Except, perhaps, when applied to the expansion of Christianity, in the Atlantic and the Americas, crusade rhetoric or ideology had not developed far since Innocent III and, essentially based not on Scriptural but Patristic theology, looked awkward in the face of sixteenth-century attacks founded on the New Testament. Parallel to this was the elaboration of secular international laws of war that, in the hands of theorists such as Gentili (1552–1608) or Grotius (1583–1645), discounted religion as a sufficient just cause.[21] Thus intellectual fashion combined with political realities to place the war with the Ottomans in a temporal frame. This process was mirrored by the growth in an ecumenical concept of Europe and common Christendom witnessed by Protestant English prayers for the survival of Malta in 1565, authorized by, among others, the fanatical anti-Catholic Bishop Jewell of Salisbury, and Londoners dancing in the streets at the news of Lepanto in 1571, a victory celebrated in verse by the Calvinist-trained James VI of Scotland who, for years after, hankered after the leadership of a Christian League against the Turk.[22]

Such ecumenism was largely impossible during the crisis of the early Reformation, out of which came the first academic studies of medieval crusade texts. The libraries of the great, rich and pious had long been full of crusade writings, a popularity nurtured by nostalgia and wishful thinking, yet testament to a living cultural tradition and aspiration. Manuscript collections of crusade texts continued to be produced. When a long compendium of narratives and advice was presented to Henry VIII, mostly celebrating the deeds of the king's crusading ancestors, the context was explicit, if optimistic: 'the passage of an army and hoste of pilgrymes by your highness blessedly to be purposed and conducted ayenst infideles for the recouery of the Holy Lande'.[23] Early printers, such as Caxton, Wynkyn de Worde and Pynson, also satisfied this market. However, from the 1520s the printing press served more partisan causes, as with the *Turkenbüchlein*, often highly polemic Catholic and Protestant pamphlets on competing means to resist the Ottomans in central Europe.[24] Thereafter, as the religious schism widened and solidified, attitudes and interpretations were recruited to the ideological debate. This prompted a new scrutiny of crusade history as well as possible crusading futures.

Whereas the revived or fresh appeals to action of generations around 1500 were part of a lively and accepted tradition, now, on both sides of the theological divide, crusading was studied from fractured perspectives. Catholic apologists, while continuing to promote versions of traditional crusading, again toyed with the equation of infidel and heretic. It has been argued for Ignatius Loyola, founder of the Jesuits, that aspects of spirituality associated with crusading were translated into internal purification and external 'reconquest' of Protestants.[25] After the 1520s, identifying Protestants with Turks became a familiar theme in Catholic discourse, prompting renewed interest in medieval accounts of crusading. François Moschus of Armentières edited Jacques de Vitry's *Historia Orientalis* in 1597. In his Preface to Readers, he drew a clear parallel between wars against Islam and those against 'Lutherans and other Evangelical pseudo-prophets' before embarking on a long comparison between the religion of Luther and of Mohammed. Moschus had searched for manuscripts of the *Historia Orientalis*, pressing scholarship into the service of controversy, a tactic familar to subsequent generations and, not least, Moschus's confessional opponents.[26]

It may be ironic, but not surprising, that much of the impetus for studying the crusades as a distinct historical phenomenon came from Protestants. Their dismissal of the legal and theological foundations of the exercise did not mean that they condemned the whole idea of armed conflict with infidels. In his *History of the Turks* (1566), the English martyrologist John Foxe had no doubts that the Muslims were 'the enemies of Christ' and praised the heroic defence of Rhodes by the Hospitallers in 1522. What concerned him was the sustained failure of the crusades ('viages'), which he could by no means attribute to lack of courage, effort or preparation. He identified two causes. One was entirely in keeping with the conclusions of most medieval commentators, namely the sins of the Christians whose evil living hardly merited God's support. The other reason, Foxe claimed, was 'the impure idolatry and profanations' of the Roman Church. 'We war against the Turk with our works, masses, traditions and ceremonies: But we fight not against him with Christ. . . . He that bringeth St George or St Denis, as patrons, to the field . . . leaveth Christ, no doubt, at home.' The recurrent theme in his description of the crusades was the increasing defilement of pure religion by popes and their allies. To this he attributed the failures of the thirteenth century, the rise of the Ottomans, the disasters of Nicopolis (1396) and Varna (1444) and the loss of Constantinople (1453). He was predictably scathing about the attacks on the Albigensians and Waldensians by the 'pope's crossed soldiers'. In the tradition of Erasmus and the humanists as much as of Luther, Foxe's account contained most of the elements which were to sustain the Protestant critique of crusading for a century: the laudable desire to fight the infidel had been corrupted by Roman Catholicism.[27]

Foxe was hardly scholarly in his approach. Far more considered and subtle was the analysis of Foxe's younger contemporary, the German scholar Matthew Dresser (1536–1607). A Lutheran, Dresser held a number of chairs of classical languages, rhetoric and history in northern Germany as well as being the official historiographer to the Elector of Saxony. In his academic circle the editing of medieval texts was flourishing as part of the determination of the reformed churches to claim continuity with at least parts of the medieval past. One such editor, Reinier Reineck (1541–95), asked Dresser to contribute a commentary on the causes of the 'Holy War' for a critical edition of an anonymous compendium of crusade texts which he called the *Chronicon Hierosolymitanum* (1584).[28] ('Holy War' was the standard academic description, as in Joannes Herold's *De bello sacro* of 1549; the German vernacular called it war, *zug*, hence *kreuzzug*, war of the Cross.)[29]

Dresser focused more clearly than Foxe on the crusading paradox of the failure of a good cause. He argued that simply because Frederick Barbarossa drowned on crusade (1190), there was no reason to doubt his pious intent. The bulk of his commentary was an erudite excursus demonstrating that the Holy Wars were blighted by papal lust for terrestrial power. Popes had put their trust in earthly Jerusalem, whereas God wanted His people to aspire to heavenly Jerusalem. However, Dresser distinguished between the deceit, greed and corruption of the papacy and the piety and honesty of the crusaders themselves, a distinction rendering the attack on the papacy more telling. The First Crusaders were likened, in classic humanist manner, to the Argonauts, praised for their faith, yearning for the Holy Sepulchre and wish to expel the infidel. Their only failing was simplicity in obeying a duplicitous pope and profane monks. This suggestion, that crusaders were ignorant and misled rather than mischievous, became – and remains – familiar to students of the crusade. His analysis allowed Dresser to conclude that the only thing wrong with resistance to the Turks was papal interference. Just as Foxe attributed the successful defence of Vienna in 1529 to the presence of some good German Protestants, so Dresser ascribed the collapse of Hungary in the years before to papal and episcopal control. An army free from clerical direction and composed of pious, honest and virtuous (i.e. Protestant) soldiers would attract the fortune that had so palpably eluded the crusades. In the midst of Protestant diatribe some prominent features of crusading historiography were assayed: the clash of temporal and spiritual motives; papal self-interest; superstition and popular piety.

The academic context of Dresser's commentary included the first even remotely critical editors of crusade texts, among whom Dresser's coadjutor, Reineck, was prominent. Comparing his texts with others, such as William of Tyre or Robert of Rheims, his vision broadened by his knowledge of the Byzantine writers, Reineck produced a number of editions of crusade sources, including Albert of Aachen. Like Dresser, Reineck demonstrated a clear, unashamed bias towards the great deeds of Germans. The spirit of nationalism, hatched after the First Crusade, dogged medieval scholarship down to the present century. Nevertheless, the desire to praise national heroes, no less than the urge to vilify religious opponents, while distorting judgement, stimulated enquiry.

This was very evident in the work of one the greatest editors of crusade texts, the Frenchman Jacques Bongars (1554–1612). Bongars was not primarily an academic but a Huguenot diplomat working for Henry of Navarre, later Henry IV of France. However, from his student days he had turned to history, as a young man researching in libraries in Rome. As a diplomat he travelled throughout Europe, from England to Constantinople and especially in Germany, where he acted as Henry of Navarre's agent to the Lutheran princes, including the duke of Brunswick, a patron of Dresser and Reineck. Bongars's connection with the Lutheran scholars may have been direct. He had studied at Jena shortly before Dresser became a professor there, and when he compiled his edition of crusade chronicles the only one he was content to reprint rather than re-edit was Reineck's Albert of Aachen.

Bongars's widely circulated *Gesta Dei Per Francos* (1611)[30] was massive, comprising more than 1,500 pages. Among the texts edited are the main sources for the First Crusade: the *Gesta Francorum*, Robert of Rheims, Baldric of Dol, Raymond of Aguilers, Albert of Aachen, Fulcher of Chartres and Guibert de Nogent. In addition he included the histories by William of Tyre and Jacques de Vitry and Oliver of Paderborn's account of the Fifth Crusade. In the second part he edited, from a bewildering variety of variant manuscripts, Sanudo's *Secreta Fidelium Crucis* (final redaction 1321) and Pierre Dubois's *De recuperatione Terrae sanctae* (1306). In scope and detail of scholarship, Bongars's *Gesta Dei Per Francos* was a stupendous achievement, based on meticulous scrutiny of variant manuscripts wherever he could get access to them, from Rome to Cambridge.[31]

Aside from the scholarly effort, one arresting feature of Bongars's work was the sight of a Calvinist devoting his energies to the study of events inspired by doctrines he rejected. Calvin had described the Turks as 'perpetual enemies of Christianity' and, after initially flirting with opposition to anti-Muslim violence, had been careful to distinguish between legitimate resistance and papal self-interest, while persisting in seeing the Turkish threat in predominantly theological terms.[32] Bongars was able, therefore, to describe Holy War simultaneously as 'most dangerous and most glorious'.[33] Even though they shared an intellectual *milieu,* Bongars's purpose was far removed from Dresser's. While acknowledging elements of impiety, superstition and shame, the Frenchman shied away from Protestant polemic, remarking that such things were the common experience of mankind, history being 'a mirror of human life'. Instead, the introductory prayer for peace and title indicated a path away from religious controversy. In line with both Lutheran and Calvinist orthodoxy, the prayer called on princes to implement God's commands, while the title presented the crusades as God's deeds done by Frenchmen. Bongars was openly chauvinist and royalist. The first part of the *Gesta Dei* was dedicated to the Most Christian King of France, Louis XIII, son of Bongars's old patron, Henry IV, namesake and descendant of Louis IX. Of all princely houses, Bongars proclaimed, the kings of France had the closest concern with the Holy War. Thus in a new secular cult of kingship was the Calvinist reconciled to crusading.

The changed religious and political circumstances of the sixteenth century allowed for responses to the crusades beyond either religion or politics. Although not aggressively emerging until two centuries later, a romantic view of crusading evoking an escapist glamour or simplicity of a lost age ran parallel to confessional or national posturing. William Shakespeare could see in the crusades an appropriately ennobling, if frustrating – and historically not entirely inaccurate – ambition to lend to the English Henry IV (*c.*1597). Torquato Tasso's *Gerusalemme Liberata* (1580) reinvented the First Crusade as a romantic tale of chivalry, love and magic within the more familar story of Godfrey de Bouillon. Tasso was internationally popular, republished and translated with regularity and enthusiasm. His approach, appealing to rose-tinted images of valour, loyalty, honour and love, was to have a long history. Tasso was not alone. One of his contemporaries, the French writer Pierre de Bourdeille, seigneur de Brantôme, in his anecdotal *Recueil Des Dames,* taking his cue from the stories (of twelfth-century origin) of the indiscretions of Eleanor of Aquitaine on the Second Crusade, claimed that many women joined the 'guerre sainte' in search of amorous adventure; 'arms and love lie well together'.[34] For Brantôme, here and elsewhere, the crusades appeared amusing, alien, possibly absurd, certainly quaint, a bit of the past that was being remoulded into good stories, entertaining rather than uplifting or admonitory. This secular image of unreality was the obverse of the secular reality imposed by Ottoman threat and religious feuding.

Not all commentators were trapped into partisan special pleading or fanciful romancing. It is of infinite regret that Francis Bacon failed to complete his *Advertisement touching the Holy Warre* (1622).[35] In it, he planned to investigate the views of all sides in the form of a dialogue between a moderate divine; Catholic and Protestant zealots; a soldier; a courtier and a 'politique'. In the completed fragment, Bacon dispassionately, and occasionally with humour, exposes a wide range of opinion, including the traditional Catholic defence of war fought for religion; nostalgia for war fought for a noble cause and an end to internecine Christian conflict; stern Protestant denial of the justice of religious warfare; even to the cynical dismissal of the whole idea: 'the Philosopher's Stone and an Holy war were but the *rendez vous* of cracked brains that wore their feather in their head instead of their hat'.[36] As notable as the objective scrutiny of conflicting ideas and the scope of examples from Urban II to the Incas was the sense conveyed by Bacon that Christian war against the Turk was a current concern. Bacon was examining this from different perspectives, even if merely as an intellectual exercise (although his former employer James I was an enthusiast for war against the Turks). Above all, however, the *Advertisement* shows how far the nature of the debate had changed in the previous hundred years. The touchstone seemed no longer faith, but prudence; not religion, but law.

The Development of Modern Views

Traditional crusading was no longer an active part of what Gibbon was to call the 'World's Debate'. Distance from the age of certainty was growing. Commentary became increasingly self-regarding, as witnessed by Jean-Aimes de Chavigny's *Discours parenetique sur les choses turques* (1606), which surveyed sixteenth-century crusade plans.[37] Writers felt free to impose different current concerns on studying Holy War, which, despite the continued Turkish problem, was of diminishing practical relevance. While Bongars and his fellow-editors supplied a textual, and hence factual basis for more obviously literary histories of crusading, they also bequeathed some tenacious themes of interpretation: religious, intellectual or moral disapproval on the one hand; admiration for reasons of national, rather than religious pride on the other.

These two legacies were well illustrated in the seventeenth century by the contrasting works of the Anglican divine Thomas Fuller (1608–61) and the French Jesuit Louis Maimbourg (1610–86). Fuller's *History of the Holy Warre* (1639) resounded with moderate Protestant criticism both of the theology and actions of the crusaders. Fuller's awareness of the danger of the Turks and willingness to acknowledge the role of Catholic powers in protecting Protestant countries added bite to his attacks on miracles, pilgrimages, the behaviour of crusade leaders, the role of the clergy, papal policies, the wickedness, the treachery and the sheer wastefulness of the enterprise. Some natural causes for failure, such as a hostile climate, were adduced, but Fuller's criticisms were fundamental. The whole endeavour was folly: 'it being better husbandry to save a whole cloth in Europe than to win a rag in Asia'. Moreover, 'superstition not only tainted the rind, but rotted the core of this whole action. Indeed most of the pottage of that age tasted of this wild gourd.'[38] For perhaps the first time a tone of lofty condescension rather than anger enters the discussion. Fuller, while providing a detailed account up to the defence of Rhodes by the Hospitallers, clearly wished to distance himself from the emotions and culture of the crusades.

Louis Maimbourg's *History of the Crusades* (1675), aiming, like Fuller, at an educated general readership, was very different. A Jesuit and a scourge of the Jansenists, Maimbourg was nevertheless a strident Gallican. His *History of the Crusades* was introduced by a wildly exaggerated paean of sycophantic praise to Louis XIV, the whole work being shot through with national and royal bias. Yet Maimbourg's reading embraced Robert of Rheims, Guibert of Nogent, Suger of St Denis, William of Tyre, Nicetas Choniates, Matthew Paris and Joinville. The conception of the crusade was the grandest. It was a vast, important 'famous enterprise', full of 'heroic actions . . . scarcely to be out-done' (except by Louis XIV). 'One shall with difficulty meet with anything more memorable' than this 'noble and agreeable' subject involving 'the Great Concerns and the Principal Estates of Europe and Asia', a cosmic view which was also to have a long future.

Maimbourg's narrative was not bombast alone. By bringing his story into the seventeenth century, he was able to relate it to resurgent fears of the Ottomans and schemes to combat them in eastern Europe. Key elements in Maimbourg's treatment were vicarious triumphalism, an attention to narrative sources over a long period, a strident national pride and an undogmatic appreciation of temporal causation. As his English translator and fellow-*dévot* of monarchy, John Nalson, remarked, Maimbourg 'hath the least of that foolish Bigotry, which never fails to render any Profession of Religion ridiculous'. As with Fuller, Maimbourg was very popular, both in France and abroad.[39] It is ironic that a work by a Jesuit should set a seal on the secularization of the study of crusading, rendering it a vehicle for profane rather than sacred debate.

The traditions of Fuller and Maimbourg – scholarly, judgemental and patriotic – persisted into the eighteenth century. In a dissertation presented at Nuremberg in 1709, Georg Christoph Müller attacked the papacy for 'ambition, greed, tyranny and treachery', in particular for diverting crusades to Italy and Sicily, against the Albigensians and Frederick II. Müller's thesis, based on a wide variety of the major western chronicles, defined a crusade as a military campaign authorized by the Pope to recover the Holy Land on which soldiers bore the sign of the Cross and received plenary indulgences, this despite an etymological discussion on the words used in his sources for expeditions embracing objectives other than the Holy Land (e.g. *passagium, expeditio, iter, via, acquisitio, bellum, cruciata*, etc.). Müller also numbered the crusades, a habit of inescapable convenience that has helped writers and hindered understanding ever since. His five were 1096, 1147, 1190, 1217–29 (an idea by no means abandoned by modern scholars) and 1248, although he admitted that others included eight in the canon.[40]

Against this dry scholarship could be placed J. D. Schoeplin's *De Sacris Galliae Regum in Orientem Expeditionibus* (*The Holy Wars of the Kings of France in the East*), published at Strasbourg in 1726. As its title suggests, this praised the role of the French, especially their kings, in what the author regarded as wonderful events. Although trading in hyperbole, Schoeplin had done some research which he displayed, unusually, in footnotes. Although, like Müller, assuming the terminal dates 1095–1291, in common with Fuller and Maimbourg, he did not ignore the contemporary survivors of the crusades, the Knights of Malta, to whose support, Schoeplin urged, all Christian princes should rally.[41]

The strongest impression left by the eighteenth century is very different from these traditional versions. Four of the most influential writers of the period, Diderot, Voltaire, Gibbon and Hume, all considered the crusades, arriving at similar conclusions. They were at once appalled and intrigued by the ignorant and violent fanaticism involved in what David Hume imperishably described as 'the most signal and most durable monument of human folly that has yet appeared in any age or nation'.[42] For Gibbon, as for Diderot and Voltaire, rational disdain was a cloak for profound anti-clericalism. There were different nuances. While Hume unequivocally dismissed superstition and militarism, in Diderot's entry on the crusades in the *Encyclopaedia*, the Olympian tone was tinged with frank astonishment at the quest for 'a piece of rock not worth a single drop of blood', which he ascribed to a form of emotional or intellectual 'vertigo'. For Diderot, crusades were 'wars undertaken by Christians either for the recovery of the Holy Places or for the extirpation of heresy and paganism'. Crusaders were moved by 'imbecility and false zeal' or political self-interest, sustained by intolerance, ignorance, violence and the Church. Diderot thought the consequences of the crusades dire: the Inquisition, vast loss of life, the impoverishment of the nobility, decline in agriculture, a dearth of bullion, the collapse of ecclesiastical discipline and an increase in monastic wealth (not seen as a particularly good thing).[43] Such attention, however superficial, to the long-term effects of the crusades became a central obsession of subsequent writers, suited to any King Charles's head, religious, philosophical, political, racial, imperial, economic or cultural.

Voltaire adopted a more favourable interpretation not of the crusade *per se* but of the individuals caught up in it. His *History of the Crusades*, which he later incorporated into the *Essay on the Manners and Spirit of Nations* (1756, but already in English translation in 1753) was altogether more scholarly than Diderot's piece. His use, for example, of Anna Comnena and Joinville led him to praise the heroes of each: the Byzantine Emperor Alexius I appeared as 'moderate and sagacious', while for Louis IX was reserved the extravagant accolade: 'it is impossible for man to attain to a more sublime degree of virtue'. Frederick Barbarossa was applauded for the care with which he prepared for the Third Crusade; Saladin received a striking encomium: 'at once a good man, a hero and a philosopher'; and, rather pointedly, Frederick II's conduct on crusade in 1228–29 was described as 'a model of the most perfect policy'. The enterprise as a whole, however, was wasteful and pointless, the only tangible reward for western Europe being, in Voltaire's opinion, the freedoms that impoverished nobles were forced to grant 'divers boroughs'.[44]

In his chapters on the crusades in the *Decline and Fall of the Roman Empire* (1776–88), which derived many attitudes directly from Voltaire,

Gibbon presented heroism not as a function of individuals but as a cultural feature of the medieval West which, although suborned by the Church, gave hope for the future. Within the crusade movement lurked an active energy which was ultimately to cast off the shackles of the 'savage fanaticism' (i.e. religious enthusiasm) Gibbon identified as 'the principal cause of the crusades'. This concept of harnessed barbarian energy is a theme touched on by Friedrich Schiller, who equated crusading with the age of migrations. On individuals and their motives, Gibbon's misanthropy, by turns amused and contemptuous, forbade the generosity of Voltaire. Saladin was a fanatic 'in a fanatic age', a 'royal saint' and so a Muslim counterpart to Louis IX, promoter and victim of 'this holy madness', whose crusade vow was 'the result of enthusiasm and sickness'.[45]

From the lofty eminence of his reason, Gibbon inevitably criticized the crusades but was markedly even-handed in his condemnation of their excesses as compared with the harshness of Islam or the decadence of Byzantium. Some credit was even allowed. The loss of life and wealth among the nobility undermined 'the Gothic edifice', witnessed by charters of freedom to tenants as well as boroughs. In spite of themselves, the crusades were, in a limited area, a potential force for change, if not progress. Although in general the crusades 'checked rather than forwarded the maturity of Europe' and led to no discernible cultural or intellectual fertilization with Muslims or Greeks, nevertheless, following Joseph de Guignes's *Histoire des Huns* (1756–58), Gibbon suggested they opened western eyes to new horizons of trade, manufacture and technology.[46]

To the earlier themes of religious or rational disapproval and national pride, by the nineteenth century were added the cultural progress and political ascent of the West. The removal of the Turk as a physical menace allowed less acerbic reactions to the crusade. Exotic Mediterranean tourism and a passion for Orientalism stripped views of crusading of any sense of abiding conflict or hostility. Contempt replaced fear. This threw the emphasis of many accounts on to the motives and inspiration of the crusaders themselves rather than on the clash with the infidel. This self-regarding trend suited the growing dominance of Europe in politics, trade, science and industry. The Muslim enemy became a curiosity and the past was rearranged to match current self-images of superiority. Gibbon's positive forces could be celebrated even in stories of defeat. This recasting of history was stimulated by events, such as

Napoleon's campaign in Egypt and Syria in 1798, and culminated in the absurd (but successful) posturing of western powers at the Versailles Peace Conference in 1919 when the French claimed a mandate in Syria because of their medieval claims. As Emir Faisal acidly asked: 'Would you kindly tell me just which one of us won the crusades?'[47] The failure of the crusades was submerged in a prolonged orgy of self-congratulation at the heroism and adventure of the crusaders, win, or, as more often, lose. Almost as Gibbon wrote, crusading began to cease to be a dirty word.

This historic reappraisal was gilded by a new admiration and sentimental nostalgia for virtues which had seemed so ludicrous and repellent to the Enlightenment. The nineteenth century may appear a century of enthusiastic mixtures of emotion and reason: romanticism, nationalism, imperialism, colonialism, liberalism, socialism. Many of these touched crusade historiography directly; none more than medievalism. For perhaps the first time, writers in the early nineteenth century made the effort of imagination to examine the Middle Ages on their own terms, without condescension. Often these attempts were unsuccessful, sentimental, sometimes downright absurd, but the removal of disdain was a prerequisite for serious academic study.[48]

This was not always immediately apparent in studies of the crusades by medieval enthusiasts, but it was noticed by one of the first genuinely critical textual scholars, the German Heinrich von Sybel (1817–95), who commented approvingly on the positive attitude adopted towards the Middle Ages by a pioneer of the eastern sources, Frederick Wilken (1777–1840), in his *History of the Crusades* (1807–32).[49] However, Sybel accurately observed that Wilken's work was vitiated by uncritical scrutiny of the trustworthiness of his texts. Wilken was a scholar: for other, more sentimental medievalists, such objections were compounded. A new revivalist cult of chivalry became fashionable across post-French Revolutionary Europe, providing a moral and cultural buttress for an *ancien régime* that was losing much of its social and political exclusivity, integrity and legitimacy. Inevitably, in chivalry's wake the crusades received close attention.

Not all of this was flattering. The novelist Sir Walter Scott (1771–1832) admired chivalry for its perceived truth, faith, honour, selflessness and gallantry, but was no friend of the crusades. In novels such as *The Talisman* (1825), set in Palestine during the Third Crusade, and *Ivanhoe* (1819), chivalrous heroes are contrasted with devious and intolerant Templars, some of the most sympathetic characters being Saracens and

Jews. Such anxieties were not unique to Scott. Charles Mills (1788–1826) was a prominent figure in the literary medieval revival through works such as his *History of Chivalry* (1825). Yet his popular *History of the Crusades* (1820, already into a fourth edition by 1828) was distinctly equivocal. The bravery and stamina of crusaders 'awe and command our imagination', while their material self-sacrifice 'throws an air of sublime devotedness round [their] exploits and forbids us from censuring with severity the madness of the enterprise'. However, whereas chivalry, as an ethical and religious force, 'was a circumstance beneficial to the world', the crusades 'encouraged the most horrible violences of fanaticism'. Positively Gibbonian in his criticism, Mills retained a cynical view of papal motives and even dismissed Gibbon's and Voltaire's notion that the crusades had encouraged freedom.[50]

Yet Mills's position was not always clear. The crusades may have 'cast a baleful influence' on chivalry, but the two were inseparable, crusaders merely lacking the 'polish' and the 'soft collar of the gentle affections' displayed by knights-errant. It is hard to see how far Mills's disapproval reached when he talked of Louis IX's 'fierceness of piety and chivalry'. There was the ringing condemnation that the crusade 'retarded the march of civilisation, thickened the clouds of ignorance and superstition and encouraged intolerance, cruelty and fierceness', being 'iniquitous and unjust'. Yet there was also sympathy for 'the deluded fanatic and the noble adventurer in arms'. In a moment of unusual, if sententious relativism, Mills could even write: 'the crusades were not a greater reproach to virtue and wisdom than most of those contests which in every age of the world pride and ambition have given rise to'.[51] Here sympathy is hardly sneaking, expressing a contradiction inherent in the views of a man who could write that 'the mixture of the apostle and the soldier was an union which reason abhors' and, six years later, accept election to the Military Order of the Knights of Malta.[52]

Mills stood on the cusp between disapproval and devotion. Others were more prepared, in the words of one of Mills's readers, to 'continue the illusion' which invested crusaders with boundless virtues of loyalty, generosity and love. A tide of Gothicism swept aside qualifications, especially in the popularizing texts such as Kenelm Digby's *Broad Sword of Honour* (1828–29). Some unease remained. In his *History of Chivalry and the Crusades* (1830), Henry Stebbings pondered the 'grand but erring spirit of enthusiasm to which chivalry and the crusades owed their existence'.[53] Increasingly, however, Catholic and Protestant apologists, imaginative travellers and popular historians gave crusaders and

crusading the benefit of any doubts, their approval often cloaked in fanciful empathy or a pseudo-academic pretence to avoid anachronistic
value-judgements of the sort they accused their eighteenth-century
predecessors of having made. Yet these nineteenth-century enthusiasts
were in no way objective or dispassionate. Nowhere was this more obvious than in France.

The most substantial literary contribution to the study of the crusades in the early nineteenth century was by Joseph François Michaud
(1767–1839), in two works, the *Histoire des croisades* (from 1817; revised
after 1831; sixth edition 1841; ninth 1856) and the companion volume
of texts, including translations, the *Bibliothèque des croisades* (1829).
Their traditionally uncritical antiquarianism reflected the preoccupations of author and audience. Michaud was a monarchist, anti-revolu-
tionary, nationalist and Christian who scorned the condescension of
the *philosophes*. He was also the last crusades scholar of what might be
called the age of innocence, before Leopold von Ranke (1795–1886)
and his disciples subjected the past to critical textual analysis. There
were many historians after Michaud who ignored the techniques of the
nineteenth-century German seminars, but they can hardly lay claim to
serious scholarship, even if they were – and are – widely read.

Michaud, like his predecessors, was a collector of information which
he fashioned more according to his own purposes than to the evidence
itself. He summed up his attitude by describing the crusades as 'heroic
victories . . . astonishing triumphs which made the Muslims believe
that the Franks were a race superior to other men'. Such a message had
obvious appeal in France across political divides. However, Michaud
was partisan, his popularity coinciding with that of the restored Bourbon, then Orleanist, monarchy. Crusader heroism was edifying, explicitly Christian, a product of 'religious and martial enthusiasm'.[54] So
far, so traditional. Even in defeat, Michaud optimistically insisted, the
crusades sapped the spirit of Islam, although he conceded that the un-
dermining of Byzantium had materially assisted the advance of the Ottomans, a theme revisited with unmatched elegance in this century by
Steven Runciman. Particular praise was heaped on crusade leaders, not
least Louis VII and, of course, Louis IX. Michaud's enthusiasm was
further directed towards what became a dominant feature of French
crusade historiography. 'The victorious Christian law began a new destiny in those far away lands from which it had first come to us.'[55]

Michaud's emphasis upon the material consequences of the crusades
had a specific and popular slant. 'The vast and mysterious work of the

holy wars . . . had as their goal the conquest and civilisation of Asia.'
The crusaders established, in Michaud's phrase, 'Christian colonies'.[56]
This sense of the physical and political expansion of Europe, especially
of France, possessed especial resonance in a period when the collapse
of Ottoman power, the introverted feebleness of Asiatic powers and the
opening-up of Africa found Europeans once again imposing their culture on far distant lands. If crusaders were regarded as proto-colonists
at a time when colonies were increasingly respectable, the crusades
themselves attracted greater lustre, especially in France, complacent in
the tradition of *Gesta Dei Per Francos*. The first room in the Musée des
Colonies in Paris was given over to Syria and Cyprus at the time of the
crusades, just as Louis Philippe (King of the French 1830–48) devoted
rooms at Versailles to commemorating French crusade involvement.[57]
It was increasingly difficult to argue that crusading hindered the march
of progress. Colonialism was a symptom of European economic and
political hegemony, but was praised by its apologists in terms of cultural ascendancy. It became almost axiomatic that the crusades had
played some part in this triumph of western progress, identified variously and indiscriminately as a defensive shield against infidel hordes,
a softening and humanising of the primitive military barbarism of the
Dark Ages, or a conduit for the acceptance of the material and intellectual riches of the East.

Thus to romantic nostalgia was added supremacist ideology, a
double dose of fantasy that produced results unexpected, bizarre and
sinister. Crusading became popularly admired, even if the excesses of
violence aroused flickers of disapproval. As Elizabeth Siberry has noticed, enthusiasts ranged from Sir William Hillary, an English Knight
of Malta, proposer of a new crusade in 1840 and founder of the Royal
Lifeboat Institution, to Richard Hollins Murray, inventor of road-
safety cats' eyes.[58] From being a disreputable example of excess, crusading became synonymous with fighting good causes, primarily
religious or moral, throughout the western world, including North
America. In Britain, for example, innumerable evangelical and temper-
ance organizations appropriated the name for themselves and new
crusad-ing hymns were composed, most famously 'Onward Christian
Soldiers', words by the High-Church antiquarian Sabine Baring-Gould
(1834–1924); famously set to music by Sir Arthur Sullivan (1842–1900),
who also composed an opera *Ivanhoe*.[59] The historical crusades were
fashionable across Europe as subjects or settings for novels, poetry,
paintings, sculpture, plays and operas. These often compensated for his-

torical inaccuracy with lavish bad taste. In 1864 John Wisden chose to pad out the first edition of his *Cricketers' Almanack* with a list of the dates of the eight main crusades. In all this there could be an element of pantomime, never far from the elbows of nineteenth-century medieval enthusiasts or entrepreneurs. A number of extravagant entertainments loosely but openly based on the crusades were performed at Astley's Amphitheatre, near Westminster Bridge, London, in the early decades of the century.[60] In its way more absurd, during the 1895 celebrations at Clermont to mark the eight-hundredth anniversary of Urban II's speech, was the sight of the commemorative procession headed by a leading local antiquarian in the guise of Godfrey de Bouillon, complete with chain mail and pince-nez.

This enthusiasm rendered scholarly investigation both respectable and important. In one famous instance the influence was malign and criminal. To satisfy the desire of the parvenu aristocracy of the Orleanist monarchy of the 1840s in France, an imaginative rogue, Eugène-Henri Courtois, a crooked genealogist, Paul le Tellier, and a future Inspector-General of the French archives, Eugène de Stadler, set up a profitable business in forged documents which purported to demonstrate the crusading antecedents of anxious new nobles. Only exposed in 1956, and even then in the teeth of Establishment disapproval, Courtois and his accomplices satisfied a market created by snobbery, wilful gullibility and admiration for the crusades to produce one of the most successful academic forgeries ever.[61] They even supplied scholarly needs. In 1841, H. Géraud published a paper noting that Richard I's mercenary captain, Mercadier, had not accompanied the King on the Third Crusade. Within a few months a letter had been 'discovered' showing that Mercadier had indeed been with Richard at Acre, which the unsuspecting Géraud duly published in 1843 as evidence that his earlier comment had been mistaken. The letter was a Courtois forgery.[62]

The Courtois affair depended on more than criminal greed and the vanity of social climbers. Within the French academic community, with its close links with court and nobility, there was an evident desire for these documents to be genuine. Whatever else Michaud had done, he had based the popularity of crusade history on a textual and documentary basis to parallel its romantic appeal. However, in the very year that the Courtois forgeries began to appear on the market, it was pointed out that Michaud, in his own way, had been just as gullible as those who flocked to prove their ancestry with bogus charters.

The Modern Age

The historiography of the crusades was placed on a different footing with the publication in 1841 of Heinrich von Sybel's *History of the First Crusade,* his first book. Sybel, a pupil of Ranke, as a young man followed closely his mentor's path of objective textual analysis, only later subordinating his skills to a fervent Prussian nationalism. The essential fact Sybel wished to convey in the *First Crusade* was one he owed to Ranke himself, who in 1837 had suggested that William of Tyre could not be used as an original source for the First Crusade as his account was demonstrably based on those of Albert of Aachen, Raymond of Aguilers and the *Gesta Francorum.* Sybel developed this by analysing all available sources, letters as well as chronicles, establishing their dates, examining their contents and determining their interrelationships. Sybel revealed a number of different contemporary traditions represented by the extant writers. Demolishing almost all previous historians since the twelfth century who had based their accounts on William of Tyre (i.e. Jacques de Vitry onwards), he demonstrated that it was not enough – and indeed made no sense – to cobble together existing, conflicting records to form one cohesive narrative. The key to understanding sources, Sybel argued, was appreciation of the process by which memories of actual events were transmitted through contemporary stories and later legends. This was and remains an essential insight. From the beginning, the crusades, rather like the Norman Conquest, were an invention of writers at various removes from the action.[63]

Sybel was not immune to medieval enthusiasm. He viewed the crusades as 'one of the greatest revolutions that has ever taken place in the history of the human race', comparable with the Persian Wars, the Germanic invasions, the Reformation and the French Revolution. His significance may be measured by contrasting his systematic criticism of texts and Michaud's almost entirely descriptive presentation. The German's analysis was a qualitative leap in subtlety. His demonstration of the flaws in previous accounts of the First Crusade in relying on William of Tyre led directly to H. Hagenmeyer's *Peter the Hermit* (1879), which established an orthodoxy on the origins and course of the First Crusade not seriously challenged until the 1980s.[64] The foundation of the new approach was what Sybel called critical method, the lack of which condemned in his eyes all earlier writers. From the 1840s, the study of the crusades was placed on a sounder intellectual basis, grounded on critical editing rather than simple transcription of sources.

In France, Michaud's work was continued but improved in the great series of editions in the *Recueil des historiens des croisades* (1841–1906), which included all the main western as well as Arabic and eastern Christian chronicle sources. Elsewhere, the Frenchmen Riant, Mas Latrie, Rey, Kohler, Delaville le Roulx and Schlumberger and the Austrian Röhricht, as well as the German Hagenmeyer, set new scholarly standards in the discovery, appraisal and editing of old and new sources, thereby transforming both content and interpretation of the subject.[65]

Their labours did not, however, have the decisive effect on crusade historiography that at first sight would have seemed inevitable. Old habits died hard. In less austere academic circles even the most digestible fruits of Teutonic scholarship could be wished away at the turn of a phrase. Fifteen years after Hagenmeyer's *Peter the Hermit*, and half a century after Sybel, an English history of the Latin Kingdom of Jerusalem, T. A. Archer and C. L. Kingsford, *The Crusades* (1894), could seriously protest:

> there is little in the legend of Peter the Hermit which may not very well be true, and the story as it stands is more plausible than if we had to assume that tradition had transferred the credit of the First Crusade from a pope to a simple hermit . . . Such is Albert of Aix's narrative and, despite some taint of legend it is no doubt true in the main.

The whole work was littered with sophistry (and indeed snobbery), despite a spurious patina of learning evinced in illustrations of seals and artefacts, and familiar references to original texts. There was no genuine scholarship.[66]

Such travesties, bad even on their own terms in their disregard for contemporary scholarship, were not, however, the most surprising feature of the post-Rankean world. There will always be a market for the glib, opinionated and lightly researched, especially when, as often, allied to contemporary obsessions, such as modern conflicts in the Middle East and the Balkans or western ignorance and fear of Islam. More intriguing was the phenomenon of serious works of scholarship, packed with 'critical method', which nevertheless displayed almost precisely the same patterns of prejudice as the histories of former, less rigorous days. The sirens of nationalism, colonialism, sentimentality, moral outrage and religious and confessional enthusiasm were – and are – still heard.

In the nineteenth century many European nations were establishing or re-establishing a sense of identity and pride in a corporate past as a guarantee for a common future. The crusades provided one of the mines from which such national myths could be quarried. In France, for monarchist, Bonapartist and republican alike, the crusades offered a proud memory of Frenchness in an uncertain world, especially with national interests once again embracing Muslim countries of the Mediterranean. For Germans the crusade offered a more directly propagandist dividend. With politicians and academics (including Sybel) pushing for German unification and international power, past heroics of national leaders had obvious appeal. Frederick Barbarossa became a folk-hero to such an extent that between 1874 and 1879 German archaeologists were seriously engaged in trying to discover his bones in excavations at Tyre until the nonsense was stopped by an academic barrage from H. G. Prutz. In the same year as Röhricht's pioneering history of the Latin kingdom was published (1898), Kaiser Wilhelm II made a pretentious, highly posturing visit to Jerusalem and Damascus, during which he associated himself with the mantle of pilgrim and holy warrior as well as, rather confusingly, the reputation of Saladin. A London newspaper, in a reference to the British travel agent through whom the Kaiser arranged his journey, ridiculed him as 'Cook's crusader'.[67] Nonetheless, scholarship and nationalism remained closely linked: in Germany the *Monumenta Germaniae Historicae* and in Britain the Rolls Series (i.e. *The Chronicles and Memorials of Great Britain and Ireland during the Middle Ages*) were dedicated to editing specifically national texts: both included some important sources for the crusades.

Twentieth-century annexation of the crusades has tended to be overtly, usually malignly political. Propagandists of the Second and Third Reichs exploited the memory of the Teutonic Knights' gory activities in the Baltic. Hindenberg's victory over the Russians in East Prussia in 1914 was given the name Tannenberg and portrayed as revenge for the Knights' defeat in 1410. The Nazis admired, and Himmler's SS sought to imitate what they saw as the Knights' powerful mix of violence, discipline, racism and nationalism. In Spain the tradition of the *reconquista* infected political rhetoric. During the Spanish Civil War (1936–39), members of the pro-Republican International Brigade saw themselves as fighting a crusade, in the sense of an ideological war, against fascism, while Franco's fascists portrayed their revolt against the republican government as the 'crusade of Spain', a Holy War against godless leftists and democrats. After Franco's victory, this political revival spilled over into the writing of history by reinforcing, even reimposing a historiographical fashion which conveniently interpreted Spanish medieval history as the rise of Christian Spain to expel the infidel, a process finding its culmination in the capture of Granada and unification of Spain by Ferdinand and Isabella in 1492 (and, by analogy and association, the capture of Madrid by Franco in 1939).[68]

If the excesses of nationalist interpretations of the crusade belong primarily to political propaganda and cheap journalism, the identification of the crusades as harbingers of colonialism retained a hold on academic perceptions, especially in France. At least since the seventeenth century, the French have assumed a role of cultural imperialism, and the importance of territorial colonies to successive French governments from Napoleon III to de Gaulle needs no elaboration. As already noticed, French triumphalism over the crusades, however ludicrous, had direct political repercussions at the Treaty of Versailles. Thereafter, during the period of the French mandate in the Lebanon and Syria, certain French historians sought to identify the virtues of French/Frankish dominion and argued for the existence in the crusader conquests of a unique Franco-Syrian civilization, a view most forcefully promoted by Louis Madelin in 1917 in his description of supposedly beneficent and benevolent Frankish rule in the Levant.[69] The lengthiest exposition of this concept of 'French colonies' was Réné Grousset's *Histoire des croisades* (1934–36), in which he talked of 'la France du Levant' and associated the country of Tripoli with Maronite appeals for French protection in 1860 and 1919. Grousset ended the work with a revealing comment: 'The Templars held on only to the islet of Ruad (until 1303) south of Tortosa through which one day – in 1914 – the "Franks" were to set foot once again in Syria.'[70] This tradition remained influential. In 1953 Jean Richard wrote of 'Frankish colonies', the kingdom of Jerusalem as 'one of the aspects of the early twelfth century rise of Europe' and of a 'Frankish, perhaps even French, state in the East', 'the first attempt by Franks of the West to found colonies'.[71]

Since 1945 colonialism as a political or cultural enterprise has fallen, perhaps justifiably, into disrepute. Confidence in western European superiority is less widely voiced than before. Yet as an interpretation of the crusades it has by no means disappeared. On the contrary, it has been lent a new dimension through the work of modern Israeli scholars, most notably the French-educated Joshua Prawer. The Israelis have brought to their studies of the crusades, especially the Latin settlements, a fresh perspective and a unique sense of place. For Prawer, as for his French predecessors, 'it is justified to regard the Crusader kingdom as the first European colonial society'. However, so far from being the enriching symbiotic phenomenon of Madelin, Latin rule is characterized by Prawer as 'non-integration, or more exactly *Apartheid*'.[72] Whether relations between Israelis and Palestinians will prove equally discrete cannot be prophesied, but it is clear that the experience of living in Palestine and Israel has exerted a profound influence on the historical interpretations of Prawer and his disciples, as well as provoking sharpened perceptions of the region's past.

It is not only political colonialism that has declined in the twentieth century. Attitudes to war and religion have changed in the face of events. It is now less easy to share the admiration of Ernest Barker in his brilliant essay on the crusades for the eleventh edition of the *Encyclopaedia Britannica* (1910–11):

> it would be treason to the majesty of man's incessant struggle towards an ideal good, if one were to deny that in and through the Crusades men strove for righteousness' sake to extend the kingdom of God upon earth . . . . Humanity is the richer for the memory of those millions of men, who followed the pillar of cloud and fire in the sure and certain hope of an eternal reward . . . nor can we but give thanks for their memory.[73]

Such sentimental praise of medieval chivalry died in the mud of the Western Front, but only after a struggle. Deluded but prominent members of the Anglican hierarchy portrayed hostilities with Germany as a Holy War. Escapist but explicit crusading rhetoric and imagery were deployed to aid recruitment and sustain the bereaved. It entirely fits the mood of 1914 that a later editor of the *Gesta Francorum* equated the visions experienced by crusaders with the Angels of Mons.[74] The crusader theme in 1914–18 was picked up by poets, writers, even cartoonists. Lloyd George described the war, with characteristic style and opportunism, as 'the great crusade'. As a synonym for a good cause pursued by military means, the crusade also found favour during the Second World War, particularly with the otherwise academically unremarkable Dwight D. Eisenhower, who saw the war as a personal crusade, describing the D-Day landings of 6 June 1944 as 'a great crusade', and giving his war memoirs the title *Crusade in Europe*.[75] Especial resonance inevitably surrounded the campaigns in Palestine and Syria in 1917–18 by the British General Edmund Allenby, during which both Jerusalem and Damascus were captured from the Turks. Hardly surprisingly, one veteran of the campaign, Vivian Gilbert, penned *The Romance of the Last Crusade – with Allenby to Jerusalem* and a contemporary account of the fall of Jerusalem in 1917 was described by its author, H. Pirie-Gordon, as 'the final continuation of William of Tyre'.[76]

If the mirage of personal combat and chivalry was, *pace* Henry Newbolt, cut to pieces by the Gatling gun and its heirs, the many devastating twentieth-century wars in the name of just causes and the peculiar viciousness of conflicts founded on ideology or religion have rendered approval of the crusades at best contingent.[77] One of the less credible statements of a customarily unbelievable politican was the comment of the Polish leader General Wojcieck Jaruzelski in 1981: 'Thank goodness we do not live in medieval times, when people fought wars over ideas.'[78] Ideological and religious violence not only remains to plague the world, it has even spawned a new theology in the Christian–Marxist theories of Liberation Theology. Contemporary experience of racist, nationalist and anti-semitic pogroms on an almost industrial scale in the context of religious or ideological conflict has rendered justifications of force hard to accept with equanimity. The cautious reaction of the papacy to South American Liberation Theology, especially in relation to the use of violence, is, perhaps, more than a little tinged with this unease. At least for the Curia, this time the genie is to remain in the bottle. Nonetheless, in recent conflicts between Christian and Muslim in the Lebanon or the Balkans, some Christian voices have been publicly and privately raised in calling for vigorous, even military responses to renascent Islam.[79]

It was to a world in which civilization had gone almost as far as man's ingenuity permitted in destroying itself that Steven Runciman addressed his chilling conclusion to his magnificent three-volume *History of the Crusades* (1951–54): 'the Holy War itself was nothing more than a long act of intolerance in the name of God, which is the sin against the Holy Ghost'.[80] Later twentieth-century historians cannot avoid intellectual and personal constraints similar to those of their predecessors. Religion and war, ideology and violence, civilization and barbarism, cultural exchange or domination, attract as passionate interest now as they have done for centuries past. Modern disapproval, like past enthusiasm, is as much a product of our times as of the crusades. So, too, is modern respect for ideas which, as Riley-Smith insists, may not be shared but can be understood on their own terms. Despite concern for a wider range of evidence and themes than were recognized by previous generations, a modern scholar, no less than those who have gone before, will, in Mayer's words, 'see the crusades filtered through the material of his own mind'.[81] There may be more attention paid to the record of charters or government archives, to piety, law, the anthropology of frontiers, the mentalities of groups and individuals, but interpretation is still screened sympathy, another form of judgement.

Although there are few, if any, ideological or emotional orthodoxies among modern crusade historians, some aspects of crusade historiography betray close links with the past. The theme of waste is common to Fuller in the mid-seventeenth century and to Professor Mayer in the late twentieth. Runciman's devastating description of the events of 1204, the more remarkable for being published in 1954 ('there was never a greater crime against humanity than the Fourth Crusade'),[82] is in lineal descent from Gibbon, as his conviction that the crusaders' destruction of Byzantine power permitted the successes of the Ottomans is shared with Michaud. When Simon Lloyd writes that the 'effects of the crusading movement were almost limitless' as well as being 'one of the most important components, and defining characteristics, of late medieval culture', he is in the tradition of the vision of Archer and Kingsford who saw the crusades as the 'central drama [of the Middle Ages] to which all other incidents were in some degree subordinate'.[83] Like Charles Mills, Professor Riley-Smith is a Knight of Malta.[84]

As research has expanded, so it has been enriched and enlivened by such personal preoccupations and presumptions. Individual insights are the stuff of history. There can be no unified opinion of the crusades. Evidence and the process of writing history forbid it. The shape of the subject, no less than the interpretation of detail, are conditioned by the vantage-point from which it is viewed. Here, too, modern scholars are the successors of those who wrote in the months and years after Jerusalem was captured in July 1099. Over fifty years ago J. L. La Monte lamented that 'one of the real problems in the historical study of the crusades is the remarkably bad history that they have called forth . . . With the possible exception of Renaissance Florence probably no field has been the subject of so much worthless pseudo-historical trash.'[85] This is far less true today, populist hacks apart. Crusade scholarship now confronts the prejudices not only of modern observers but more crucially of the sources themselves: yet both are united by the common habit of creating the crusade in their own image. Nonetheless, although it may be regretted that the great paladins of crusade historiography have more cautious heirs, at least the latter try to offer conclusions which have, as their mainspring, a principle which may be summed up by a slight adaptation of a remark of the greatest crusader historian of all, William of Tyre: 'the writer of history, by virtue of his office, must commit to letters not such events as he himself might desire, but such as the evidence affords'.[86]

If historical perceptions of the crusade are today fragmented, not united, prosaic rather than epic, in one central respect they follow their predecessors. They paint their canvases in contemporary colours. For almost a millennium writers concerned with the Holy Wars which originated in the first campaign to Jerusalem have demonstrated that there are few absolutes in interpreting a past which, as often as not, is the construct of the present. The invention of the crusades began in 1095: it has not ended yet.

NOTES

Introduction

1. H. E. Mayer, *Geschichte der Kreuzzüge* (Stuttgart 1965; trans. J. Gillingham, Oxford 1972), esp. pp. 281–6.
2. J. S. C. Riley-Smith, *What Were the Crusades?* (London 1977, 2nd edn 1992).
3. Mayer, *The Crusades*, new edn of Eng. trans. (Oxford 1988), p. 312.
4. *Grand Larousse encyclopédique*, iii (Paris 1960), p. 667.
5. N. Housley, *The Later Crusades* (Oxford 1992), pp. 2–6. For another recent 'pluralist' view, E.-D. Hehl, 'Was ist eigentlich ein Kreuzzug?', *Historische Zeitschrift*, cclix (1994), 297–336.
6. H. E. Mayer's review of Riley-Smith, *What Were the Crusades?*, *Speculum* (1978), pp. 841–2.
7. J. Riley-Smith, 'The Crusading Movement and Historians', *Oxford Illustrated History of the Crusades*, ed. J. Riley-Smith (Oxford 1995), p. 9; C. J. Tyerman, 'The Holy Land and the Crusades of the Thirteenth and Fourteenth Centuries', *Crusade and Settlement*, ed. P. Edbury (Cardiff 1985), pp. 105–12.
8. Housley, *Later Crusades*, pp. 3–4.
9. Mayer, *Crusades*, p. 313.
10. N. Housley, 'The Crusading Movement 1274–1700', *Illustrated History of the Crusades*, pp. 268, 270, 274, 277.
11. To take two incidences noted recently by Riley-Smith, 'The State of Mind of Crusaders', *Illustrated History of the Crusades*, pp. 80, 82. For the most recent restatement of the idea of a self-conscious, definite crusade movement in the twelfth century, see J. Riley-Smith, *The First Crusaders 1095–1131* (Cambridge 1997), which even resorts to describing some events as 'Crusades', rather than crusades.

1 Were there any Crusades in the Twelfth Century?

1. Guibert of Nogent, *Gesta Dei Per Francos, Recueil des Historiens des Croisades*, ed. *Académie des Inscriptions et Belles Lettres* (Paris 1841–1906) *Documents Occidentaux* (henceforth *RHC Occ.*), iv, p. 124.

2. Robert of Rheims, *Historia Iherosolimitana, RHC Occ.*, iii, p. 723; J. Riley-Smith, *The First Crusade and the Idea of Crusading* (London 1986), ch. 6.

3. H. W. C. Davis, 'Henry of Blois and Brian FitzCount', *English Historical Review* (henceforth *EHR*), xxv (1910), pp. 301–3.

4. *Patrologia cursus completus. Series Latina* (henceforth *PL*), ed. J. P. Migne (1844–64), 180, cols. 1064–6. E. Caspar, 'Die Kreuzzugsbullen Eugens III', *Neues Archiv der Gesellschaft für ältere Deutsche Geschichtskunde*, 45 (1924), pp. 300–5 and, in general, pp. 285–305; for an English translation, L. and J. Riley-Smith, *The Crusades; Idea and Reality* (London 1981), pp. 57–9.

5. Bernard of Clairvaux, *Opera*, ed. J. Leclercq *et al.* (Rome 1957–77), vols. vii, viii, *Epistolae*, nos 256, 288, 363–5, 371, 380, 467–9. *Letters of St Bernard of Clairvaux*, trans. B. S. James (London 1953), nos 391–6, 398–401, 408, 410; J. Bédier, *Les chansons de croisade* (Paris 1909), pp. 8–11 *(Chevalier, Mult Estes Guariz*, esp. 1.4: 'Ki li vut fait tels deshenors').

6. For *Quantum praedecessores*, see n. 4 above; cf. J. G. Rowe's comment that the bull was 'a shot in the dark', 'Origins of the Second Crusade', *The Second Crusade and the Cistercians*, ed. M. Gervers (New York 1992), p. 86; in general see G. Constable, 'The Second Crusade as seen by contemporaries', *Traditio*, ix (1953), esp. pp. 247–65.

7. J. Gilchrist, 'The Erdmann Thesis and the Canon Law 1083–1141', *Crusade and Settlement*, pp. 37–45; J. Gilchrist, 'The Papacy and war against the "Saracens" 795–1216', *The International History Review*, 10 (1988), pp. 174–97; cf. a different recent view, H. E. J. Cowdrey, 'Canon Law and the First Crusade', *Horns of Hattin*, ed. B. Z. Kedar (Jerusalem 1992), pp. 41–8. For a more general similar perspective, C. Morris, *The Papal Monarchy* (Oxford 1989), pp. 277–80.

8. Cf. J. A. Brundage, 'St. Bernard and the Jurists', *Second Crusade and Cistercians*, pp. 29–30; Riley-Smith, *First Crusade*, esp. pp. 150–2.

9. Constable, 'Second Crusade', pp. 241–4; G. Constable, 'Medieval Charters as a Source for the History of the Crusades', *Crusade and Settlement*, pp. 73–89; G. Constable, 'The Financing of the Crusades in the Twelfth Century', *Outremer: Studies in the History of the Crusading Kingdom of Jerusalem Presented to Joshua Prawer*, ed. B. Z. Kedar, H. E. Mayer and R. C. Smail (Jerusalem 1982), pp. 64–88. Cf. M. Bull, *Knightly Piety and the Lay Response to the First Crusade* (Oxford 1993), esp. chs. 4, 6.

10. Odo of Deuil, *De Profectione Ludovici VII in Orientem*, ed. V. G. Berry (New York 1948), pp. 2–3; *Receuil des historiens des Gaules et de la France* (henceforth *RHGF*), ed. M. Bouquet *et al.* (Paris 1738–1904), xv, p. 488; Constable, 'Second Crusade', pp. 216–44.

11. J. Riley-Smith, 'Death on the First Crusade', *The End of Strife*, ed. D. M. Loades (London 1984); Riley-Smith, *First Crusade*, esp. pp. 91–100, 112–19; cf. the Iberian experiences during the Second Crusade of Duodechlin of Lahnstein, *M[onumenta] G[ermaniae] H[istorica], S[criptores]* (henceforth *MGHS*) (Hanover, etc. 1826–), xvii, p. 28; *De Expugnatione Scalabis, Portugaliae Monumenta Historia, Scriptores*, i (Lisbon 1856), pp. 94–5. Perhaps miracles were more a feature of successful campaigns: martyrs were common to all sorts, Constable, 'Second Crusade', pp. 221–2.

12. Radulfus Glaber, *Historiae Libri Quinque*, ed. J. France (Oxford 1989), pp. 82–5; Gratian, *Decretum*, ed. A. Friedberg, *Corpus Iuris Canonici*, i (Leipzig 1879), Causa XXIII: Quest. V, c. xlvi; Quest. VIII, c. vii.

13. Compare Robert of Flanders ('his memory will live for ever') with the deserters Stephen of Blois or the Grandmesnil brothers: Henry of Huntingdon, *Historia Anglorum*, ed. T. Arnold, Rolls Series (henceforth RS) (London 1879), p. 238; Orderic Vitalis, *Ecclesiastical History*, ed. M. Chibnall (Oxford 1969–80), v, pp. 98, 106, 268, 324; vi, p. 18.

14. C. W. David, *Robert Curthose* (Cambridge, Mass. 1920), p. 179 and n. 17; Robert of Torigni, *Chronicle, Chronicles of the reigns of Stephen, Henry II and Richard I*, ed. R. Howlett, iv, RS (London 1889), pp. 85–6.

15. P. Edbury, 'Looking Back at the Second Crusade', *Second Crusade and Cistercians*, pp. 163–9; cf. tone and content of *Audita tremendi* (below, n. 32) with *Quantum praedecessores*.

16. Orderic Vitalis, v, p. 168; Petrus Tudebodus, *Imitatus et Continuatus Historia Peregrinorum*, *RHC Occ.*, iii, pp. 218–19; Ralph of Caen, *Gesta Tancredi*, *RHC Occ.*, iii, p. 689; Albert of Aachen, *Historia Hierosolymitana*, *RHC Occ.*, iv, pp. 410; Baldric of Dol, *Historia Jerosolimitana*, *RHC Occ.*, iv, pp. 49 n. 12; 71 n. 7; 102 n. 8.

17. *PL*, 162, cols. 144–5, no. 135; Orderic Vitalis, vi, p. 158.

18. Orderic Vitalis, vi, p. 162.

19. Suger, *Vie de Louis le Gros*, ed. H. Waquet (Paris 1929), pp. 78–9; *Letters of Peter the Venerable*, ed. G. Constable (Cambridge, Mass. 1967), i, p. 409; *Letters of St. Bernard*, no. 391, p. 461; Bernard, *Opera*, iii, p. 215.

20. Bede, *Ecclesiastical History*, ed. B. Colgrave and R. A. B. Mynors (Oxford 1967), esp. Bks II, III; Gilchrist, 'Papacy and war', pp. 179–83; P. D. King, *Charlemagne: Translated Sources* (Lancaster, 1987), *Annals* and *Revised Annals of the Kingdom of the Franks, passim*; cf. p. 85 for papal absolution in the war against Tassilo of Bavaria. For contemporary Carolingian acceptance of church militancy, see the Veronese poem of the late eighth century on Pippin of Italy's victory over the Avars, verses 4 and 13, and Ernoldus Nigellus's pre-840 poem *In Honorem Hludovici Pii* regarding the Frankish conquest of the Frisians and Saxons, ll. 275, 281–4, P. Godman, *Poetry of the Carolingian Renaissance* (Oxford 1985), pp. 188–91; 254–5. But cf. Alcuin's essentially pacifist response to the sack of Lindisfarne in 793 (Godman, *Poetry*, pp. 126–39).

21. For Lucius II, see the references in J. Kelly, *The Oxford Dictionary of the Popes* (Oxford 1986), p. 172; H. Zimmermann, *Papstregesten 911–1024* (1969), no. 34, p. 14 and no. 35, p. 15; Liutprand of Cremona, *Historia Ottonis, Opera*, ed. J. Becker, *Monumenta Germanica Historica* (henceforth *MGH*) (Hanover and Leipzig 1915), pp. 166–7; Gilchrist, 'Papacy and war', p. 179 *et seq.*

22. Ralph of Bethlehem: William of Tyre, *Historia Rerum in Partibus Transmarinis Gestarum*, *RHC Occ.*, i–2, p. 162; B. Hamilton, *The Latin Church in the Crusader States* (London 1980), pp. 117–18, 123, 125, 130–1, 157, 164–5; Rainald von Dassel: R. Munz, *Frederick Barbarossa* (London 1969), esp. p. 95 and refs.; Hubert Walter: *Itinerarium peregrinorum et gesta regis Ricardi*, ed. W. Stubbs, RS (London 1864), p. 116; Boniface of Savoy: Matthew Paris, *Chronica Majora*, ed. H. R. Luard, 7 vols, RS (London 1872–83),

v, pp. 121–2; Bishop Despenser: R. B. Dobson, *The Peasants' Revolt* (London 1970), pp. 236–8, 259–61.

23. Gilchrist, 'Papacy and war', pp. 174–9.

24. Morris, *Papal Monarchy*, pp. 277–80.

25. *Anglo-Saxon Chronicle*, sub anno 1128, *English Historical Documents*, ii, ed. D. C. Douglas (London 1953), p. 195; William of Tyre, *Historia, RHC Occ.*, i–2, p. 40 ; *Gesta Ambaziensium Dominorum, Chroniques d'Anjou*, ed. P. Machegay and A. Salmon (Paris 1856), p. 205 (cf. Fulk's visit of 1120 which was, apparently, explicitly penitential, Orderic Vitalis, vi, p. 310). Cf. Calixtus II's authorization of a crusade and the Venetian response in 1122–24; J. Riley-Smith, 'The Venetian Crusade of 1122–24', *I communi italiani nel regno di Gerusalemme*, ed. B. Kedar (Genoa 1986), pp. 337–50.

26. On papal policy in the twelfth century, E. -D. Hehl, *Kirche und Krieg im 12 Jahrhundert* (Stuttgart 1980) and Morris, *Papal Monarchy*. More specifically, R. C. Smail, 'Latin Syria and the west 1149–1187', *Transactions of the Royal Historical Society* (henceforth *TRHS*), 5th ser., 19 (1969), pp. 1–20.

27. S. Runciman, *History of the Crusades* (Cambridge 1951–54), ii, pp. 46–9 (p. 48: 'The interests of Christendom as a whole were to be sacrificed to the interests of Frankish adventurers'); J. G. Rowe, 'Paschal II, Bohemond of Antioch and the Byzantine Empire', *Bulletin of the John Rylands Library*, xlix (1966), pp. 165–202; Orderic Vitalis, vi, pp. 68–73; Suger, *Vie de Louis le Gros*, pp. 44–51.

28. E. Vacandard, *Vie de Saint Bernard, Abbé de Clairvaux*, 2 vols (Paris 1895), ii, pp. 439–46. *RhGF*, xv, p. 457, no. 65.

29. *Letters of John of Salisbury*, ed. W. J. Miller and C. N. L. Brooke, ii (Oxford 1979), p. 632, no. 287; C. J. Tyerman, *England and the Crusades* (Chicago 1988), pp. 37–8; E. Siberry, *Criticism of Crusading* (Oxford 1985), esp. pp. 190–2 (cf. pp. 77–80).

30. On the early development of these legends, see M. Bennett, 'First crusaders' images of Muslims: the influence of vernacular poetry', *Forum for Modern Languages Studies*, 22, no. 2 (1986), pp. 101–22; for a different emphasis, N. Daniel, *Heroes and Saracens* (Edinburgh 1984), *passim*. Robert of Normandy even had false legends – such as his refusal of the crown of Jerusalem and his splitting of a Muslim emir into two – concocted during his lifetime, e.g. pre-1125 (Robert died in 1134), William of Malmesbury, *Gesta regum Anglorum*, ed. W. Stubbs, 2 vols, RS (London 1887–89), ii, pp. 433, 460, 461.

31. Morris, *Papal Monarchy*, pp. 277–8.

32. *PL*, 180, cols 1064–6; 200, cols 384–6, 599–601, 1294–6; Smail, 'Latin Syria and the west', p. 18; R. Hiestand (ed.), *Papsturkunden für Templer und Johanniter, Abhandlungen des Akademie der Wissenschaften in Göttingen*, lxxvii (1972) nos 165, 175; for *Audita tremendi* (29 Oct. 1187), Roger of Howden, *Gesta regis Henrici Secundi*, ed. W. Stubbs, 2 vols, RS (London 1867), ii, pp. 15–19 and A. Chroust (ed.), 'Historia de expeditione Friderici imperatoris', *MGHS* (Berlin 1928), v, pp. 6–10.

33. P. Jaffé, *Regesta Pontificum Romanorum*, ii (Leipzig 1886), p. 296, no. 12684.

34. Tyerman, *England and the Crusades*, ch. 2, esp. pp. 40–5.

35. *RhGF*, xv, pp. 681–2; cf. Gelasius II's idea of indulgences commensurate with material contributions from non-participants towards the siege of Saragossa, 10 Dec. 1118, *PL*, 163, col. 508, no. 25.

36. *MGH, Epistolarum*, v (Berlin 1898), p. 601; vii (Berlin 1921), pp. 126–7.

37. On this aspect of the Council of Pisa, see N. Housley, 'Crusades against Christians', *Crusade and Settlement*, p. 23.

38. Suger, *Vie de Louis le Gros*, pp. 174–6; Guibert of Nogent, *Autobiographie*, ed. E. -R. Labande (Paris 1981), p. 410; Orderic Vitalis, vi, pp. 258–9.

39. Henry of Huntingdon, *Historia Anglorum*, pp. 262–3; cf. his account of the speeches by the leaders of both sides before the battle of Lincoln (1141), each of which appealed to a just cause and God's active favour, although without mention of indulgences, Henry of Huntingdon, *Historia Anglorum*, pp. 268–73. For a similar account of the bishop of the Orkneys, John of Hexham, in Simeon of Durham, *Opera*, ed. T. Arnold, *RS* (London 1885), ii, p. 293.

40. Housley, 'Crusades against Christians', pp. 24–6.

41. Bernard, *Epistolae*, no. 467; *Letters of St Bernard*, no. 394.

42. Caffaro, *Annales Ianuenses*, ed. L. T. Belgrano, *Fonti per la Storia d'Italia*, ii (Rome 1890), pp. 33–5; *Ystoria captionis Almarie et Turtuose*, in Belgrano, *Fonti*, pp. 79–89; Constable, 'Second Crusade', pp. 226–35.

43. P. Linehan, 'The Synod of Segovia (1166)', *Bulletin of Medieval Canon Law*, x (1980), p. 42.

44. *PL*, 163, col. 515 for Lorenzo of Verona's account of recruitment for the Balearic campaign; for Calixtus's letter of 2 April 1123, D. Mansilla, *La documentación pontífica hasta Innocencio III* (Rome 1955), no. 62; the 1123 Lateran decree: J. D. Mansi, *Sacrorum Conciliorum Collectio*, xxi, col. 284; for Gelasius II's letter of 1118, *PL*, 163, col. 508, no. 25; H. E. J. Cowdrey, 'The Mahdia campaign of 1087', *EHR*, 92 (1977), pp. 1–29; *De Expugnatione Scalabis*, pp. 94–5; *De Expugnatione Lyxbonensis*, ed. C. W. David (New York 1936), p. 175. In general, R. A. Fletcher, 'Reconquest and crusade in Spain *c.* 1050–1150', *TRHS*, 37(1987), pp. 31–47; Bull, *Knightly Piety*, ch. 2.

45. Geoffrey of Monmouth, *Historia Regum Britanniae*, ed. A. Griscom and R. Ellis Jones (London 1929), pp. 437–8; L. Thorpe's translation, *History of the Kings of Britain* (London 1966), p. 216 infers, almost certainly correctly, that 'professione insigniti' implies the sign of the Cross.

46. *De Expugnatione Lyxbonensis*. The author has been identified as a prominent Anglo-Norman priest on the expedition, Raol, by H. Livermore, 'The "Conquest of Lisbon" and its author', *Portuguese Studies*, vi (1990), 1–16.

47. *De Expugnatione Lyxbonensis*, pp. 70–85 (p. 78 for the quotation which is a play on words from a letter of St Jerome to Paulinus).

48. *De Expugnatione Lyxbonensis*, pp. 78–82 (the patristic references were almost certainly not taken directly from the originals); Gilchrist, 'Papacy and war', pp. 189–90; Cowdrey, 'Canon Law and the First Crusade', *passim*.

49. *De Expugnatione Lyxbonensis*, p. 83.

50. *De Expugnatione Lyxbonensis*, pp. 126–7, 146–59; Gilchrist, 'Papacy and war', p. 182 and n. 43 for references and quotations.

51. Cf. the renewed absolution for the crusaders at Constantinople in the winter of 1203–04 and the arguments employed by the clergy then, Geoffrey

de Villehardouin, *De la Conquête de Constantinople*, ed. P. Paris (Paris 1838), pp. 71–2.

52. *De Expugnatione Lyxbonensis*, pp. 134–5; pp. 104–11 for Glanvill's speech; pp. 104–5 for the resistance of the Veils; *passim* for hostile comments on the actions and motives of the Flemish and Rhinelanders.

53. Odo of Deuil, *De Profectione, passim.*

54. *De Expugnatione Lyxbonensis*, p. 122–3 for the 'trial of the sword; pp. 114–25 for the challenge and the Muslim reply; pp. 130–2 for Muslim taunting.

55. Bédier, *Chansons de croisade*, p. 10.

56. H.-D. Kahl, 'Crusade Eschatology as seen by St Bernard in the Years 1146–8', *Second Crusade and Cistercians*, pp. 35–47, esp. pp. 42–3.

57. E.g. the unemotional account, by the priest Duodechlin of Lahnstein, of the capture of Lisbon by a 'navali expeditione'. Miracles only appeared as *post hoc* signs of divine approval, *MGHS*, xvii, pp. 27–8.

58. P. Jaffé, *Monumenta Corbeiensia* (Berlin 1864), p. 126, no. 48; *RhGF*, xv, pp. 495–6.

59. Gilchrist, 'Erdmann Thesis', *passim* and esp. n. 63.

60. Housley, 'Crusades against Christians', p. 31.

61. Housley, 'Crusades against Christians', p. 31. Housley's argument stressing continuity and fusion of forms supports my contentions, but he maintains a misleading typology which sets 'crusade' and 'ecclesiastical warfare' at odds, in need of 'juridical fusion' by Innocent III. My argument is that Innocent III transformed one sort of ecclesiastical warfare into what could be described as juridical crusading.

62. Orderic Vitalis, vi, p. 310.

63. On the contrast with secular knighthood, A. Grabois, '*Militia* and *Malitia*: The Bernardine Vision of Chivalry', *Second Crusade and Cistercians*, pp. 49–56; in general, M. Barber, *The New Knighthood* (Cambridge 1993).

64. 'It is not from the accident of war but from the disposition of the heart that either peril or victory is alloted to the Christian', St Bernard, *De Laude Novae Militiae, Opera*, iii, p. 215; trans. L. and J. Riley-Smith, *The Crusades*, pp. 102–3.

65. Caspar, 'Kreuzzugsbullen', pp. 300–5; *PL*, 180, cols 1064–6.

66. For the confusion of a panel of clerics facing a claim to crusader immunity in 1106–07, *PL*, 162, cols 176–7 and below p. 133, n. 84.

67. J. S. C. Riley-Smith, 'Peace never established: the case of the Kingdom of Jerusalem', *TRHS*, 5th ser., xxviii (1978), pp. 87–8, 94–5 and n. 47, p. 102; cf. Riley-Smith, 'Venetian Crusade'. William of Tyre, *Historia, RHC Occ.*, i–1, p. 549 is silent on the Doge's status, the implication being that he was simply a pilgrim; Albert of Aachen, *Historia Hierosolymitana, RHC Occ.*, iv, pp. 595–7, 600–1, 632–4; K. Jordan, *Henry the Lion*, trans. P. S. Falla (Oxford 1986), pp. 150–4.

68. Odo of Deuil, *De Profectione*, pp. 8–11, 14–19; A. Grabois, 'The Crusade of Louis VII: A Reconsideration', *Crusade and Settlement*, pp. 94–104; cf. the distinctly non-martial tone of the reference to Louis's crusade in the Second Crusade song *Chevalier, Mult Estes Guariz*, Bédier, *Chansons de croisade*, p. 8.

69. Constable, 'Medieval Charters', p. 77; for the relevant discussion on the invisibility of crusading in charters, pp. 74–7 and, generally, pp. 73–89; cf.

Constable's other article on crusade charters, 'The Financing of the Crusades', *Outremer*, pp. 64–88 which suffers from the same evidential problem.

70. Fulcher of Chartres, *Historia Iherosolymitana, RHC Occ.*, iii, p. 329.
71. M. Markowski, 'Crucesignatus: its origins and early usage', *Journal of Medieval History*, 10 (1984), pp. 157–65; for bearing the Cross against the Moors of the Balearic islands and Spain, Lorenzo of Verona, *De Bello Balearico, PL*, 163, col. 515; Mansilla, *La documentación pontíficia*, no. 62 and above, n. 36.
72. H. Hagenmeyer, *Die Kreuzzugsbriefe aus den Jahren 1088–1100* (Innsbruck 1902), p. 142.
73. *Gesta Francorum et aliorum Hierosolimitanorum*, ed. R. Hill (London 1962), p. 7.
74. Mansi, *Collectio*, xxi, col. 284; *PL*, 180, cols 1065, 1320; 200, cols 599–601, 1294–96; Howden, *Gesta Henrici*, ii, pp. 18–19.
75. *Libellus de Vita et Miraculis S. Godrici Heremitae de Finchale*, ed. J. Stevenson, Surtees Society (1847), pp. 33–4, 52–7; cf. William of Newburgh's account of Godric's visit to Jerusalem barefoot and in poverty, *Historia rerum Anglicarum*, ed. R. Howlett, *Chronicles of the reigns of Stephen, Henry II and Richard* I, i, RS (London 1884), p. 149.
76. Orderic Vitalis, vi, p. 379.
77. *Chartes de St. Julien de Tours*, ed. L. J. Denis, 2 vols (Le Mans 1912, 1913), i, pp. 87–8, no. 67.
78. J. A. Brundage, 'Crucesignari: the rite for taking the Cross in England', *Traditio*, xxii (1966), pp. 289–310; Odo of Deuil, *De Profectione*, pp. 8–11; *Vita Godrici*, p. 33 (where the Cross was given by a priest); *Chronica de Gestis Consulum Andegavorum, Chroniques d'Anjou*, p. 152; *Chartes de St Julien de Tours*, i, no. 67.
79. Brundage, 'Crucesignari', *passim*; K. Pennington, 'The rite for taking the Cross in the twelfth century', *Traditio*, xxx (1974), pp. 429–35.
80. See above, n. 61; M. Clanchy, *From Memory to Written Record* (London 1979), esp. pp. 244–8 for crosses.
81. Pennington, 'Rite', p. 433, late twelfth-century, possibly Italian; cf. similarly wide protective powers in the so-called Bari Pontifical, p. 432; for a fourteenth-century example, A. Franz, *Die Kirchlichen Benediktionen im Mittelalter*, ii (Freiburg-im-Breisgau, 1909), p. 284.
82. See the examples in Brundage, 'Crucesignari' and Pennington 'Rite'. As Pennington notes (p. 431), the differences, even when not great, suggest 'an *ad hoc* basis, without having many established models on which to rely . . . . Perhaps the crusade was not considered to be more than an ephemeral ecclesiastical institution, and the liturgical texts reflect this attitude.'
83. In general, see the classic survey, J. A. Brundage, *Medieval Canon Law and the Crusader* (Madison 1969).
84. *PL*, 162, nos 168–70, 173, cols 170–4, 176–7; for Urban II and the application of the Truce of God provisions, Riley-Smith, *First Crusade*, pp. 22, 26, and refs; and Bull, *Knightly Piety*, pp. 21–69.
85. *Epistolae Pontificum Romanorum ineditae*, ed. S. Löwenfeld (Leipzig 1885), no. 199, pp. 103–4; Howden, *Gesta Henrici*, ii, 15–19.
86. Glanvill, *Tractatus de legibus et consuetudinibus regni Angliae*, ed. G. D. G. Hall (London 1965), pp. 16–17, 151; for the distinctions drawn between pilgrimages and crusades, Henry de Bracton, *De legibus et consuetudinibus Angliae*,

ed. T. Twiss, 6 vols, RS (London 1878–83), v, pp. 159–65 (although as Professor Thorne has shown, Bracton was almost certainly not the author); John de Longueville, *Modus Tenendi Curias (c.1307), The Court Baron*, ed. F. W. Maitland and W. P. Baildon, Selden Society (London 1891), p. 82; cf. Jean de Joinville's reference (*c.*1290s) to the 'pèlerinaige de la croix', *Histoire de St Louis*, ed. N. de Wailly (Paris 1868), p. 2.

87. *Councils and Synods with other Documents relating to the English Church*, gen. ed. F. W. Powicke (Oxford 1964 and 1981), I-ii, pp. 1028–9, for the crusader's term of three years.

88. *In quantis pressuris*, 29 June 1166, Hiestand, *Papsturkunden für Templer und Johanniter*, no. 53; *Pipe Roll 3 Richard I*, ed. D. M. Stenton (London 1926), pp. 33 (where, in line with the 1188 ordinances, Richard of Clare pleads for a moratorium for his debts 'ad terminum crucesignatorum'), 76. In general, it may be noted that most of the evidence used by Brundage, *Medieval Canon Law and the Crusader*, to show how privileges worked comes from the Public Record Office, i.e. the archives of secular, not ecclesiastical, government.

89. *Recueil des chartes de l'abbaye de Cluny*, ed. A. Bruel, v (Paris 1894), no. 3737, p. 87; *Cartulaire de l'abbaye cardinale de la Trinité de Vendôme*, ed. C. Metais (Paris 1893–97), ii, no. 402, pp. 157–8; *Annales Herbipolensis, MGHS*, ed. G. H. Pertz, xvi (Hanover 1858), p. 3.

90. For two recent regional studies of this, C. B. Bouchard, *Sword, Miter and Cloister: Nobility and the Church in Burgundy 980–1198* (Ithaca, 1987); Bull, *Knightly Piety*.

91. C. Morris, *The Discovery of the Individual 1050–1200* (London 1972), esp. pp. 96–107; Brundage, 'St Bernard', *Second Crusade and Cistercians*, pp. 29–30; for possible Cistercian influence on popular crusade songs on the theme of love, M. Switten, 'Singing the Second Crusade', *Second Crusade and Cistercians*, pp. 67–76.

92. Walter Map, *De Nugis Curialium*, ed. M. R. James, C. N. L. Brooke and R. A. B. Mynors (Oxford 1983); W. L. Warren, *Henry II* (London 1973), ch. 8; Chrétien de Troyes, *Arthurian Romances*, trans. D. D. R. Owen (London 1987).

93. *De Expugnatione, Lyxbonensis*, pp. 56–7; 104–5; *De Itinere Frisonum, Quinti belli sacri scriptores minores*, ed. R. Röhricht (Geneva 1879), pp. 59, 69; *Gesta Crucegerorum Rhenanorum*, Röhricht, *De Itinere*, p. 30; Ralph of Diceto, *Ymagines Historiarum, Opera Historica*, ed. W. Stubbs, 2 vols, RS (London 1876), ii, p. 65; Tyerman, *England and the Crusades*, pp. 69–79, 182–3.

94. Ralph of Diceto, *Ymagines*, ii, p. 65; William of Newburgh, *Historia*, pp. 308–24; Tyerman, *England and the Crusades*, esp. pp. 71–4 and refs; generally, C. J. Tyerman, 'Who went on Crusades to the Holy Land?', *Horns of Hattin*, pp. 1–26. Such patterns of recruitment operated alongside the primary recruiting agency of lordship.

95. There were elements of this by the Second Crusade (cf. St Bernard's appeal to 'the mighty men of valour', *Letters of St Bernard*, no. 391; Bédier, *Chanson de croisade*, pp. 8–11). The implication is plain in Fitzcount's or Orderic Vitalis's admiration of the First Crusaders and their essentially chivalric rather than their spiritual reputations (e.g. Raimbold Croton). Yet the

parallel strand of renunciation or substitution of chivalry remained; cf. the remarks of Josserand de Brançion during St Louis's first crusade: 'Lord . . . take me out of these wars among Christians', Joinville, *Histoire de St Louis*, p. 99.

96. Peter of Blois, *Passio Reginaldi principis olim Antiocheni*, PL, 207, cols 957–76; M. Markowski, 'Peter of Blois and the Conception of the Third Crusade', *Horns of Hattin*, pp. 261–9; R. W. Southern, 'Peter of Blois and the Third Crusade', *Studies in Medieval History presented to R. H. C. Davis*, ed. H. Mayr-Harting and R. I. Moore (London 1985), pp. 207–18; cf. Riley-Smith's comments, *Bulletin of the Institute of Historical Research* (1990), p. 233.

97. *PL*, 207, col. 974; cf. B. Hamilton, 'The Elephant of Christ: Reynald of Châtillon', *Studies in Church History*, 15, ed. D. Basker (Oxford 1978), pp. 97–108; for Saladin's use of the nickname, Abou Chamah, *Le Livre des deux Jardins, RHC Documents orientaux*, iv, p. 233.

98. Bédier, *Chansons de croisade*, pp. 34 and 70 for two songs c. 1189 associated with the Third Crusade (and, more generally, pp. 67–73); cf. the tone of the slightly earlier *Chanson d'Antioche*, ed. S. Duparc-Quioc (Paris 1977–78); C. Morris, 'Propaganda for War: The dissemination of the crusading ideal in the twelfth century', *Studies in Church History*, 20, ed. W. Shiels (Oxford 1983), pp. 79–101; *Ordinatio de predicatione S. Crucis in Angliae, Quinti belli scriptores*, ed. R. Röhricht, ii, pp. 1–26; Tyerman, *England and the Crusades*, pp. 160–6 and refs; P. Cole, *The Preaching of the Crusades to the Holy Land 1095–1270* (Cambridge, Mass. 1991), esp. chs V–VII; above, pp. 62–74, 76–83.

99. *Councils and Synods*, I–ii, pp. 1028–9; Bédier, *Chansons de croisade*, p. 45 *(Bien me Deusse Targier*, verses III, IV).

100. *Pipe Roll 1 Richard I*, ed. J. Hunter (London 1844), p. 20; *Pipe Roll 3 Richard I*, pp. 28, 33, 58, 76; cf. Markowski, 'Crucesignatus', *passim*.

101. Bédier, *Chansons de croisade*, p. 21 (l. 36 of *Vos qui ameis de vraie amor*) and p. 45 (verse III of *Bien me Deusse Targier*); Villehardouin, *Conquête*, p. 1 ('Tuit cil qui se croiseroient'); Robert of Clari, *La Conquête de Constantinople*, ed. P. Lauer (Paris 1924), p. 4 *(croisiés*).

102. *La chanson de la croisade contre les Albigeois*, ed. P. Meyer (Paris 1875–79), ll. 393, 409, 2450; above, pp. 49–55.

103. Markowski, 'Crucesignatus', pp. 160–1.

104. *Annales S. Iacobi Leodicensis, MGHS*, xvi, p. 641.

105. E.g. look at the English *Ordinatio* of 1216, *passim* above, n. 98, where there is only one First Crusade *exemplum*, and none about the period 1099–1187, or the *exempla* of Jacques de Vitry, G. Frenken, *Die Exempla des Jacob von Vitry* (Munich 1914), nos lxxii, xcvi and p. 149: the anecdote about Jocelin I of Edessa's beard is hardly crusading, no. lxxi; T. F. Crane, *The Exempla of Jacques de Vitry*, Folk Lore Society (London 1890), nos lxxxv, lxxxix, cxix, cxxii, clxiii, ccxi, cccxii; nos cxxiv and cxxi are timeless; only nos xxxvi and xc, both concerning Templars, are clearly about events pre-1187, perhaps an intentional comment on what Jacques saw as the Order's decadence (no. xc). Tyerman, *England and the Crusades*, pp. 163–5 and refs; Cole, *Preaching of the Crusades*, pp. 115, 123–5, 131–3, 195,

197–9; F. C. Tubach, *Index Exemplarum* (Helsinki 1969), nos 238, 1041, 1043, 1044, 1390–5, 2497, 3087, 3088, 3802, 3804, 4005, 4114–17, 4538, 4722–4, 5199.

106. *PL*, 207, col. 969; William of Tyre, *Historia, RHC Occ.*, i–2, pp. 796, 802; Hamilton, 'Elephant of Christ', *passim*, where the point is missed by assuming, wrongly, that all who lived and fought in Frankish Outremer were crusaders, cf. Riley-Smith, 'Peace never established', pp. 87–8, 102.

2 Definition and Diffusion

1. For the background to Innocent III's 1215 decree *Omnis utriusque sexus* enjoining annual Confession, see A. Murray, 'Confession before 1215', *TRHS*, 6th ser., iii (1993), pp. 51–81.
2. For the Inquisition, see H. C. Lea, A *History of the Inquisition* (London 1900–01).
3. For these developments, Brundage, *Medieval Law and the Crusader*; M. Purcell, *Papal Crusading Policy 1244–91* (Leiden 1975); Mayer, *Crusades*, pp. 196–7; Riley-Smith, *The Crusades*, esp. chs 6, 7; S. Lloyd, 'The Crusading Movement 1096–1274', *Illustrated History of the Crusades*, pp. 34–65; Riley-Smith, *What Were the Crusades?*; Tyerman, *England and the Crusades*, chs. 3, 4, 7, 8; S. Lloyd, *English Society and the Crusade 1216–1307* (Oxford 1988) esp. chs. 1, 2. J. Richard, '1187, Point de départ pour une nouvelle forme de la croisade', *Horns of Hattin*, pp. 250–60. For the development of the financial and administrative structures, W. R. Lunt, *Papal Revenues in the Middle Ages* (New York 1965).
4. *De profectione Danorum in Hierosolymam, Scriptores Minores Historiae Danicae medii aevi*, ed. M. C. Gertz (reprint, Copenhagen 1970), ii, 457–92.
5. *Albert von Beham und Regesten Pabst Innocenz IV*, ed. C. Höfler (Stuttgart 1847) pp. 16–17.
6. For Lincoln 1217, T. Wright, *Political Songs of England* (Camden Society 1839), pp. 22–3; for Lewes and Evesham 1264–65, William of Rishanger, *Chronicle*, ed. J. O. Halliwell (Camden Society 1840), pp. 31, 46; for the Russian Crusade of 1240–42, E. Christiansen, *Northern Crusades* (London 1980), pp. 126–30; for southern France, in general M. Roquebert, *L'Epopée Cathare* (Paris 1970–86); for papal wars in Italy, N. Housley, *The Italian Crusades* (Oxford 1982); J. V. A. Fine, *The Bosnian Church* (London 1975), pp. 137–55 for Bosnia. For the rest, the general works of Mayer, Riley-Smith, etc.
7. *Registrum Episcopatus Aberdonensis* (Spalding & Maitland Clubs, 1845), ii, 15; quoted in A. Macquarrie, *Scotland and the Crusades 1095–1560* (Edinburgh 1985), p. 41.
8. E. Riant, *Pèlerinages des Scandinaves en Terre Sainte* (Paris 1865), p. 398.
9. Marino Sanudo Torsello's works in J. Bongars, *Gesta Dei per Francos* (Hanau 1611), ii, 293, 305; F. Kunstmann, 'Studien über Marino Sanudo',

Abhandlungen der historische Classe der Königliche bayerischen Akademic der Wissenschaften, vii (1855), esp. pp. 766–7, 770, 772–3, 784–6, 799, 803, 809; C. J. Tyerman, 'The Holy Land and the Crusades', *Crusade and Settlement*, pp. 103–12; C. J. Tyerman, 'Marino Sanudo Torsello and the Lost Crusade', *TRHS*, 5th ser., 32 (1982), pp. 57–73.

10. Matthew Paris, *Chronica majora*, ed. H. R. Luard, RS (London 1872–84), iii, 287–8, 373–4; iv, 9, 133–4; v, 67, 73–4, 201; for his moderating his attack on the Friars and vow redemptions, *Historia Anglorum*, ed. F. Madden, RS (London 1866–69), iii, 51–2; C. Tyerman, 'Some English Evidence of Attitudes to Crusading in the Thirteenth Century', *Thirteenth Century England*, i, ed. P. R. Coss and S. D. Lloyd (Woodbridge 1986), pp. 168–74, esp. pp. 169–70.

11. Matthew Paris, *Chronica majora*, iii, 373; iv, 175; v, 150–4.

12. Henry of Livonia, *Chronicon Livoniae*, ed. L. Arbusow and A. Bauer (Hanover 1955), pp. 12 (and n. 8), 20, 23, 29, 31, 34, 37, 50, 57, 100, 141; for Marian association, pp. 92, 132; and Christiansen, *Northern Crusades*, pp. 90–1.

13. In general, H. Roscher, *Papst Innocenz III und die Kreuzzüge* (Göttingen 1969) and n. 3 above; E. T. Kennan, ' Innocent III and the first Political Crusade', *Traditio*, 27 (1971); E. T. Kennan, 'Innocent III, Gregory IX and Political Crusades; A Study in the Disintegration of Papal Power', *Reform and Authority in the Medieval and Reformation Church*, ed. G. F. Lytle (Washington 1981), pp. 15–35. For *Quia Maior*, G. Tangl, *Studien zum Register Innocenz III* (Weimar 1929), pp. 88–97; for *Ad Liberandam*, N. P. Tanner, *Decrees of the Ecumenical Councils* (London and Washington 1990), pp. 267–71.

14. Mayer, *Crusades*, pp. 23–37; 293–5 (n. 15); and pp. 312–13 (n. 108) for a general discussion of indulgences and main references. For a translation of *Quia Maior*, L. and J. Riley-Smith, *The Crusades*, pp. 119–24.

15. Cf. a number of anecdotes of Caesarius of Heisterbach of the early thirteenth century discussed by P. Throop, *Criticism of the Crusade* (Amsterdam 1940), p. 91.

16. For the development of this policy in practice, Lloyd, *English Society and the Crusade*, pp. 17–21.

17. *The Letters of Pope Innocent III (1198–1216) concerning England and Wales*, ed. C. R. and M. G. Cheney (Oxford 1976), nos 171–2.

18. Lloyd, *English Society and the Crusade*, pp. 51–2 and refs; Tyerman, *England and the Crusades*, p. 159; *Councils and Synods with Other Documents relating to the English Church*, gen. ed. F. M. Powicke , ii, 175.

19. Tanner, *Decrees of the Ecumenical Councils*, pp. 267–71; 297–301; 309–14; 350; John XXII, *Lettres communes*, ed. G. Mollat (Paris 1904–47), nos 61324–7, pp. 233–4.

20. Clement VI, *Lettres closes, patentes et curiales se rapportant à la France*, ed. E. Déprez *et al.* (Paris 1901–61), no. 433 (cf. Gregory XI's 'customary indulgences' against the Turks in 1373, *Lettres sécrètes et curiales intéréssant les pays autres que la France*, ed. G. Mollat (Paris 1962–65), nos 1610–13, 1744, 1940); Clement VI, *Lettres closes, patentes et curiales intéréssant les pays autres que la France*, ed. E. Déprez and G. Mollat (Paris 1960–61), no. 847. For the privilege of choosing a confessor, see the 1352 grant to Henry of Grosmont, *Calender of Papal Registers*, ed. W. T. Bliss *et al.* (London 1893–1960), iii, 459. For

other variants on the Innocentan theme, N. Housley, *The Avignon Papacy and the Crusades* (Oxford 1986), Appendix III, pp. 310–11.

21. Mayer, *Crusades*, pp. 312–13.

22. Tanner, *Decrees of the Ecumenical Councils*, pp. 234, 295–6.

23. Housley, *Later Crusades*, pp. 308–12; J. Muldoon, *Popes, Lawyers and Infidels* (Liverpool 1979); Riley-Smith, *The Crusades*, p. 237.

24. F. H. Russell, *The Just War in the Middle Ages* (Cambridge 1975), p. 196 and, in general, pp. 195–212; Brundage, *Canon Law and the Crusader*, p. 82.

25. Etienne de Bourbon, *Anecdotes historiques, légendes et apologues*, ed. A. Lecoy de la Marche (Paris 1877), pp. 36–7 for an anecdote that depended for its effect on the existence of the forty-day term; Hostiensis, *Suma Aurea* (Venice 1574), pp. 1141–2; Russell, *Just War*, p. 205.

26. Russell, *Just War*, pp. 210–11.

27. Honoré Bonet, *Tree of Battles*, ed. G. W. Coopland (Liverpool 1949), Pt IV, ch. ii; pp. 126–8. For comment on the lack of a Canon Law treatise *De crucesignatis*, Brundage, *Canon Law and the Crusader*, p. 190.

28. On taking the Cross, see above, pp. 78–83; on vows, Brundage, *Canon Law and the Crusader*, pp. 30–114; M. Villey, 'L' idée de la croisade chez les juristes du môyen age', *Relazioni del X Congresso internazionale di scienzo storiche*, iii (1955), pp. 581–8; Russell, *Just War*, pp. 125 and n. 128; 208, 288–9. On the power of the vow in a public context to resolve clashes of obligation, see Robert Curzon's opinion, discussed by J. W. Baldwin, *Masters, Princes and Merchants: The Social Views of Peter the Chanter and his Circle* (Princeton 1970), i, 211; ii, 148–8.

29. J. Brundage, 'The crusader's wife: a canonistic quandary', *Studia Gratiana*, xii (1967), 425–41.

30. Russell, *Just War*, p. 210.

31. Russell, *Just War*, pp. 129–30 for Hostiensis's categories of war and, in general, pp. 74–6 and ch. 5.

32. See the general accounts by Mayer and Riley-Smith, Christiansen on the north and Housley on the later crusades. Some useful information is in the uneven *History of the Crusades*, gen. ed. K. M. Setton, 5 vols to date (Madison, Wiconsin 1969–). On the legal extensions of the crusade, Muldoon, *Popes, lawyers and Infidels*.

33. Alexander IV, *Registres*, ed. C. Bourel de la Roncière *et al.* (Paris 1902–53), nos 1578, 3063–9; for comparable privileges of Innocent IV, *Registres*, ed. E. Berger (Paris 1884–1921), nos 4000, 4088–90, 4092; *Regesta pontificum romanorum inde ab anno post Christum natum 1198 ad annum 1304*, ed. A. Potthast (Berlin 1874–75), nos 11657, 11803.

34. Clement V, *Regestum editum cura et studio monarchorum Ordinis S. Benedicti* (Rome 1885–92), no. 7893.

35. The initiative for the forty-day term appears to have come from the papal legates, but was understood, for example by the count of Champagne, as having an origin in secular custom; S. Reynolds, *Fiefs and Vassals* (Oxford 1994), pp. 308–9 and n. 246 & refs; H. A. Schumacher, *Die Stedinger* (Bremen 1865), pp. 51–76; Kennan, 'Innocent III, Gregory IX and political Crusades', p. 26; C. T. Maier, *Preaching the Crusades* (Cambridge 1994), pp. 52–6 for a recent review of the Stedinger episode and pp. 167–9 for the

war against the Drenther; Fine, *Bosnian Church*, pp. 137–55. On the Hussites, Housley, *Later Crusades*, pp. 249–59; F. G. Heyman, *History of the Crusades*, ed. Setton, iii, 586–646; G. A. Holmes, 'Cardinal Beaufort and the Crusades against the Hussites', *EHR*, 88 (1973), 721–50.

36. For positive accounts of papal wars, especially in Italy, after 1254 see the works by Housley: *Italian Crusades; Avignon Papacy and the Crusades*, esp. pp. 74–81 and chs. 3, 4; *Later Crusades*, ch. 8. For an older narrative, J. R. Strayer, 'The Political Crusades of the Thirteenth Century', *History of the Crusades*, ed. Setton ii, 343–75; for contrasting perspectives, Tyerman, 'Holy Land and the Crusades', pp. 105–12; Mayer, *Crusades*, pp. 312–13 & refs.

37. Maier, *Preaching the Crusades, passim*; A. Gottlob, *Die Kreuzzugssteuern des 13 Jahrhundert* (Heiligenstadt 1892), pp. 94–116; Lunt, *Papal Revenues;* W. R. Lunt, *Financial Relations of the Papacy with England* (Cambridge, Mass. 1939–62).

38. J. Larner, *The Lords of the Romagna* (London 1965), p. 38.

39. As in M. H. Keen, 'Chaucer's Knight, the English Aristocracy and the Crusade', *English Court Culture in the Later Middle Ages*, ed. V. J. Scattergood and J.W. Sherborne (London 1983), p. 46; the sentiments are those of Mayer, *Crusades* (1st edn 1972), pp. 281–6; against this are Riley-Smith, *What Were the Crusades?*, esp. p. 74 and Housley, e.g. *Italian Crusades*, p. 3.

40. Tyerman, 'Holy Land and the Crusades', pp. 105–7.

41. Innocent IV, *Registres*, nos 30, 162, 2050, 2229, 2230, 2931, 3054, 3860, 4097, 4333, 5109, 5556, 6212, 6322, 6845, 7312, 7792, 7793, 7881, 7946.

42. Maier, *Preaching the Crusades*, pp. 88–9.

43. Eudes Rigaud, *Regestum visitati num archiepisopi Rothomagensis*, ed. E. Bonnin (Roven 1852), p. 733.

44. Tyerman, *England and the Crusades*, pp. 144–6.

45. *Die Schriften des Kölner Domscholasters späteren Bischofs von Paderborn und Kardinal-Bischofs von S. Sabina Oliverus*, ed. H. Hoogeweg (Tübingen 1894), p. 316; Maier, *Preaching the Crusades*, pp. 67, 138, 141 and refs.

46. Richard of S. Germano, *Chronica, MGHS*, xix, 349 for Frederick II's appropriation of vow redemptions.

47. Menko, *Chronicon, MGHS*, xxiii, 540.

48. Tyerman, *England and the Crusades*, pp. 111–23.

49. M. Barber, 'The Crusade of the Shepherds in 1251', *Proceedings of the 10th Annual Meeting of the Western Society for French History*, ed. J. F. Sweet (Lawrence 1984), pp. 1–23; G. Dickson, 'The advent of the *pastores* (1251)', *Revue Belge de philologie et d'histoire*, lxvi (1988), 249–67.

50. Gregory IX; *Registres*, ed. L. Auvray (Paris 1890–1955), nos 3363, 3633, 4027; Matthew Paris, *Chronica majora*, iii, 620; *Annals of Burton, Annales Monastici*, ed. H. R. Luard, RS (1864–69), i, 265–7; 360–3; *Calendar of Papal Registers*, i, 234; *Documents of the Baronial Movement of Reform and Rebellion*, selected by R. F. Treharne, ed. I. J. Sanders (Oxford 1973), pp. 278–9; *Lois et coutumes de la ville de Lille*, ed. E. B. J. Brun-Lavainne and J. Roisin (Lille 1842), pp. 308–9.

51. G. Villani, *Cronica*, ed. F. Gherardi Dragomanni (Milan 1848), iii, 331–2 (Bk II, ch. 99.)

52. D. Queller, *The Fourth Crusade* (Philadelphia 1977), pp. 63–4, 69, 71 and refs; Housley, *Italian Crusades*, p. 37 and refs, pp. 84–6 and refs; Throop,

Criticism of the Crusade, p. 112; Christiansen, *Northern Crusades*, p. 146; Jean de Joinville, *Histoire de St. Louis*, ed. N. de Wailly (Paris 1868), pp. 261–2; William Rishanger, *Chronica*, ed. H. T. Riley, RS (London 1865), pp. 66–8; Thomas Wykes, *Chronicon, Annales Monastici*, iv, 237–40; Tyerman, 'Holy Land and the Crusades', pp. 105–6.

53. C. J. Tyerman, 'Some English evidence of attitudes to crusading', pp. 170–1; Housley, *Italian Crusades*, pp. 111–13.

54. Tyerman, 'Holy Land and the Crusades', p. 107 and n. 20, p. 111.

55. E. Baluze, *Miscellaneorum*, i (Paris 1678), pp. 165–95.

56. Tyerman, *England and the Crusades*, pp. 333–40; E. Siberry, 'Criticism of crusading in fourteenth-century England', *Crusade and Settlement*, pp. 127–8.

57. Thomas Walsingham, *Historia Anglicana*, ed. H. T. Riley, RS (London 1863–64), ii, 88–9.

58. Tyerman, *England and the Crusades*, pp. 257–8 and refs. Cf. the arrival of the July 1333 bulls at Albi and Lodève in southern France in March and August 1334, Bibliothèque Nationale Collection MSS Doat, fols 157v–175r, 186r–188r.

59. J. M. Powell, *Anatomy of a Crusade 1213–1221* (Philadelphia 1986), pp. 97–102; for a translation of a letter of the master of the Temple mentioning the anticipation of Frederick's arrival, E. Peters, *Christian Society and the Crusades 1198–1229* (Philadelphia 1971), pp. 140–1 (and p. 105 for an example of Pelagius using his financial muscle).

60. On these latter, Housley, *Later Crusades*, pp. 102–4.

61. On Louis IX, W. C. Jordan, *Louis IX and the Challenge of the Crusade* (Princeton, 1979); J. Richard, *Saint Louis: Crusader King of France* (Cambridge 1992).

62. Siberry, 'Criticism of crusading in fourteenth-century England'; A. Luttrell, 'Chaucer's Knight and the Mediterranean', *Library of Mediterranean History*, i (1994), pp. 127–60.

63. Housley, *Later Crusades*, esp. p. 260.

64. Roger of Howden, *Gesta Henrici Secundi*, attrib. Benedict of Peterborough, ed. W. Stubbs, RS (London 1867), i, 276; Ralph of Coggeshall, *Chronicon Anglicanum*, ed. J. Stevenson, RS (London 1875), p. 151.

65. E.g. Layettes du Trésor des Chartes, ed. A. Teulet *et al.*, ii (Paris 1866), no. 1789 (Languedoc); C. Kohler, 'Documents inédits concernant l'Orient Latin et les croisades', *Revue de l'Orient Latin*, vii (1900), 11–14 (Constantinople); Henry of Livonia *ut supra* (Baltic); Housley, *Italian Crusades*, p. 164 (Italy).

66. *Layettes du Trésor des Chartes*, ii, no. 5295.

67. See below pp. 76–7.

68. Housley, *Avignon Papacy and the Crusades*, p. 1.

69. See above pp. 27–8.

70. F. Godefroy, *Dictionnaire de l'ancien langue française*, ii (Paris 1883), p. 378 *et seq.*; *Anglo-Norman Dictionary*, ed. W. Rothwell *et al.* (London 1992), p. 124; cf. as e.g. *Chronique d'Ernoul et de Bernard le Trésorier*, ed. M. L. de Mas Latrie (Paris 1871), pp. 21, 25, 125, 126, 248, 262, 340, 348, 349, 401, 403, 410, 414, 416 (410 for *croiserie*); 'Dialogue between Henry de Lacy and Walter Bibblesworth on the Crusade', *Reliquae Antiquae*, ed. T. Wright and

J. O. Halliwell, i (London 1841). For use of *croisé* and *voyage*, Olivier de la Marche, *Mémoires*, ed. H. Beaune and J. d'Arbraumont (Paris 1883–88), ii, 339, 381; cf C. Du Fresne Du Cange, *Glossarium Latinitatis* (Niort 1883–87), iii, 625–30.

71. E.g. 'fach de la crozada' (1332/3), *Inventaire sommaire des archives communales de Périgueux antérieures de 1792*, ed. M. Hardy (Périgueux 1894), p. 72 (CC52); Dante, *Paradiso*, xv. ll. 139–48 referred to the Second Crusade as a *crociata*. For papal use, see below, pp. 54–5.

72. Hostiensis, *Summa Aurea*, pp. 1141–2.

73. Bernard Gui, *De secta illorum qui se dicunt esse de ordine apostolorum* in *Manuel de l' Inquisiteur*, ed. and trans. G. Mollat (Paris 1964), ii, 104.

74. C. J. Tyerman, 'What's in a name? The identity of the crusade in the twelfth and thirteenth centuries', forthcoming.

75. Sanudo, *Secreta Fidelium Crucis*, Bongars, *Gesta Dei*, pp. 153–5, 160–1, 166, 168, 196–7, 199, 202–19, 223–4; p. 219 for *crucesignatio*.

76. *Recueil des historiens des croisades, Documents Arméniens*, ii (Paris 1906), pp. 365–517. The same variety was shown in Jean Miélot's translation of the 1450s; cf. the two texts on pp. 368, 402, 411, 414, 415, 416, 446, 463–4, 464, 497, 516. Similar flexibility was shown in the Latin and French versions of Hayton's 1307 *Flowers of the History of the East, RHC Arm.*, ii, 113, 117, 221, 236, 247, 248, 255, 258, 340, 350, 359.

77. Henry Knighton, *Chronicon*, ed. J. R. Lumby, RS (London 1895), ii, 198–203. Thomas Basin, *Historiarum de rebus a Carolo Septimo*, ed. J. Quicherat (Paris 1855–59), i, 289–91. *Sanctum opus* and *peregrinatio* are similarly used interchangeably by Pope Pius II in a letter to John, duke of Bourbon in 1463, L. d' Achéry, *Spicilegium sive collectio veterum aliquot scriptorum* (Paris 1723), iii, 824. J. Germain, *Discours du Voyage d' Oultremer,* ed. C. Shéfer, *Revue de l'Orient Latin,* iii (1895), 325, 339.

78. *Chronique de Mathieu d' Escouchy*, ed. G. du Fresne de Beaucourt (Paris 1863–64), pp. 160–2 *et seq.*, 366–7.

79. For the 1390 expedition, Jehan Cabaret d'Orville, *La Chronique de bon duc Loys de Bourbon*, ed. A.-M. Chazaud (Paris 1876), pp. 219–58; *Chronique du religieux de St Denys*, ed. L. Bellaguet, ii (Paris 1840), esp. pp. 428–9, 487–522. The *Chronographia Regum Francorum*, ed. H. Moranvillé (Paris 1891–97), iii, 139 does call those massacred after Nicopolis as 'crudeliter martirizati sunt', but they are nowhere called crusaders or pilgrims by the author. The irony is that those fighting the Infidel may not have taken the Cross while those who fought Christians, e.g. in 1383, had.

80. *Chronique de Mathieu d' Escouchy*, p. 204, the vow of Philippe de Viefvil; *pace* Housley, *Later Crusades*, p. 395.

81. Jean de Joinvlle, *Histoire de St. Louis,* ed. N. de Wailly (Paris 1868), pp. 2, 262, Philippe de Beaumanoir, *Les Coutumes de Beauvoisis*, ed. Le Comte Beugnot (Paris 1842), ii, 503.

82. Joinville, *Histoire*, p. 25.

83. Joinville, *Histoire*, pp. 2, 25, 39, 260, 261–2.

84. *Layettes du Trésor des Chartes*, no. 1789.

85. *Chronique d' Ernoul*, p. 416; cf. pp. 12, 21, 25, 125, 126, 248, 262, 301, 340, 348, 401, 403 (for Curzon's preaching), 410, 414, 423, 435, 453, 458.

86. Rutebeuf, *La desputizons dou croisié et dou descroisié*, in *Onze poèmes concernant la croisade*, ed. J. Bastin and E. Faral (Paris 1946), pp. 84–94.

87. Walsingham, *Historia Anglicana*, ii, 88–9.

88. *Calendar of State Papers, Venetian* (1509–19), ii, 63–4, no. 169.

89. Du Cange, *Glossarium*, iii, 629.

90. See, for example, the references to Wyclif's commentary on Matthew 24 and Knighton's account of the 1383 crusade, *The English Works of John Wyclif*, ed. F. D. Matthew (London 1880), p. 491; *Register of Henry Chichele*, ed. E. F. Jacob, iv (Oxford 1947), pp. 101–2; *Register of Thomas Langley*, ed. R. L. Storey (Durham 1956–70), no. 794. For the lateness of the word's appearance in Anglo-Irish sources, see R. E. Latham, *Revised Medieval Latin Word-List* (London 1965), p. 123.

91. Housley, *Italian Crusades*, p. 119.

92. *Calendar of Papal Registers*, iv, 294–5; Lunt, *Financial Relations of the Papacy with England*, ii, 549.

93. Wyclif, *Polemical Works in Latin*, ed. R. Buddensieg (London 1883), ii, 582.

94. E. Charrière (ed.), *Négociations de la France dans le Levant*, i (Paris 1848), pp. 28, 35, 43, 53–4; M. J. Heath, *Crusading Commonplaces: La Noue, Lucinge and Rhetoric* (Geneva 1985), p. 79.

95. J. Goni Gaztambide, *Historia de la Bula de la Cruzada en Espana* (Vitoria 1958).

96. *Oeuvres de Georges Chastellain*, ed. Kervyn de Lettenhove, iii (Brussels 1864), p. 69: sub anno 1454, heading of ch. xiii. Elswhere 'voiage' seemed to have been preferred, e.g. pp. 75–6.

97. Tyerman, *England and the Crusades*, pp. 319, 335.

98. F. Bacon, *Advertisement Touching on Holy Warre* in *The Works of Francis Bacon*, ed. J. Spedding *et al.*, vii (London 1859), p. 25.

99. See the entry on 'Crusade', with refs., in the *Oxford English Dictionary*, 2nd edn (Oxford 1989), iv, pp. 85–6.

100. Roger of Howden, *Gesta Henrici*, ii, 30–3; Gervase of Canterbury, *Historical Works*, ed. W. Stubbs, RS (London 1879–80), i, 409–10; Ralph of Diceto, *Ymagines Historiarum*, ed. W. Stubbs, Rolls Series (London 1876), ii, 51; *Councils and Synods*, i, pt 2, 1025–9; Rigord, *Gesta Philippi Augusti, Oeuvres de Rigord et de Guillaume le Breton*, ed. F. Delaborde, i, 84–5, 88; Tyerman, *England and the Crusades*, pp. 59–64, 75–8; Brundage, *Canon Law and the Crusader*, pp. 160–87 and *passim*; and above, pp. 24, 27–8, 35–41.

101. *Curia Regis Rolls of the Reigns of Richard I, John and Henry III* (London 1922–79), viii, 324.

102. *Coutumiers de Normandie*, ed. E.-J. Tardif (Rouen 1881–1903), i, 37; Glanvill, *Tractatus de legibus et consuetudinibus regni Angliae*, ed. G. D. G. Hall (London 1965), pp. 16–17, 151.

103. *Coutumiers de Normandie*, iii, p. 91.

104. *Coutumiers de Normandie*, ii, 64–6; chs. XLIV, XC, XCIV, XCVIII; Henry de Bracton (*sic.*), *De legibus et consuetudinibus Angliae*, ed. T. Twiss, RS (London 1878–83), v, 159–69; *Coutumes de Beauvoisis*, i, 160; *Coutume de Touraine Anjou*, ed. P. Viollet, *Les Etablissements de St. Louis* (Paris 1881–86), iii, c. lxxvii.

105. *Établissements et coutumes, assises et arrêts de l'échiquier de Normandie au treizième siècle,* ed. M. A. J. Marnier (Paris 1839), pp. 133–4.
106. Roger of Howden, *Gesta Henrici,* ii, 18–19.
107. Tyerman, *England and the Crusades,* p. 219 and refs.
108. *Receuil des actes de Philippe Auguste,* ed. H.-F. Delaborde *et al.* (Paris 1916–79), i, no. 228.
109. Tanner, *Decrees of the Ecumenical Councils,* p. 269.
110. *Receuil des actes de Philippe Auguste,* no. 1360.
111. Matthew Paris, *Chronica majora,* iv, 521.
112. Tyerman, *England and the Crusades,* p. 219 and n. 143; *Summa de legibus Normannie in curis laicali,* ch. XLIV in *Coutumiers de Normandie,* ii.
113. *Coutumes de Beauvoisis,* i, 160; *Coutumes de Beauvaisis,* trans. F. R. P. Akehurst (Philadelphia, 1992), pp. 318–19.
114. *Curia Regis Rolls,* viii, 23–4.
115. *Établissments de l'échiquier de Normandie,* pp. 171, 201.
116. *Ordonnances des rois de France de troisième race* (Paris 1723–1849), v, 161; xi, 250.
117. *Layettes du Trésor des Chartes,* ii, no. 3560; Gregory X, *Registres,* ed. J. Guiraud *et al.* (Paris 1892–1906), Appendix II, p. 391, no. 1017.
118. *Rolls of Justices, Lincolnshire 1218–19 and Worcestershire 1221,* ed. D. M. Stenton (London 1934), p. 150, no. 324.
119. *Établissements de l'échiquier de Normandie,* pp. 177–8.
120. *Curia Regis Rolls,* iii, 193; *Rolls of Justices, Lincolnshire 1218–19 and Worcestershire 1221,* p. 641, no. 1428; *Summa de legibus Normannie in curia laicali, Coutumiers de Normandie,* ii, 64–6.
121. *Les Olim ou Registres des Arrêts rendus par la cour du roi,* ed. Le Comte Beugnot (Paris 1839–48), i, 854.
122. *Summa de legibus Normannie in curia laicali, Coutumiers de Normandie,* ii, 64–6.
123. Tyerman, *England and the Crusades,* p. 221 and n. 157 and refs.
124. Pierre de Fontaines, *Conseil,* ed. M. A. J. Marnier (Paris 1846), p. 167.
125. Tyerman, *England and the Crusades,* p. 219 and n. 144 and refs; *Coutumes de Beauvoisis,* ii, 50.
126. *Les Établissements de St. Louis,* ed. P. Viollet (Paris 1881–86), ii, 145–6.
127. Bracton, *De legibus,* v, 159–65; Pierre de Fontaines, *Conseil,* p. 172.
128. *Coutumes de Beauvoisis,* i, 139, 160; cf. Akehurst, *Coutumes de Beauvaisis,* ch. viii, 265.
129. *Coutumiers de Normandie,* iii, 33 and lxix n. 1.
130. *Établissements de l'échiquier de Normandie,* pp. 139–40, 153–4, 183; *Coutumes de Beauvoisis,* ii, 503.
131. *Coutumes de Normandie,* ii, 64–6, 215–16, 225–6, chs. xliv, xc, xciv.
132. *Register of Eudes of Rouen,* ed. S. Brown and J. O'Sullivan (London 1964), p. 594.
133. *Ordonnances des rois de France,* iii, 60; viii, 39.
134. C. J. Tyerman, 'Philip VI and the recovery of the Holy Land, *English Historical Review,* c (1985), pp. 41–2.
135. *The Mirror of Justices,* ed. W. J. Whittaker and F. W. Maitland (Selden Society 7, 1893), p. 84.
136. *Le Grand Coutumier de France,* ed. E. Laboulay and R. Dareste (Paris 1868), pp. 435–6.

137. Matthew 16:24. For a general discussion of Urban's speech, J. Riley-Smith, *The First Crusade and the Idea of Crusading* (London 1986), ch. I; cf. Mayer, *Crusades*, pp. 8–10.

138. E. O. Blake and C. Morris, 'A hermit goes to war: Peter and the origins of the First Crusade', *Studies in Church History*, xxi (1984).

139. Jacques de Vitry, *Historia Occidentalis*, ed. J. F. Hinnebusch (Fribourg 1972), pp. 89–90, 94–102, esp. 90, 95.

140. Maier, *Preaching the Crusades, passim.* Cf. D. D'Avray, *The Preaching of the Friars* (Oxford 1985).

141. E.g. Fulcher of Chartres's omission of Jerusalem in his version: see Riley-Smith's comment, *First Crusade*, p. 167 n. 21; cf. H. E. J. Cowdrey, 'Pope Urban II's preaching of the First Crusade', *History*, lv (1970).

142. Günther of Pairis, *Historia Constantinopolitana*, ed. Comte Riant, *Exuviae sacrae Constantinopolitanae*, i (Geneva 1877), pp. 60–6; Günther of Pairis, *Solymarius, Archives de l'Orient Latin*, i (1881), 555–61; F. R. Swietek, 'Günther of Pairis and the "Historia Constantinopolitana"', *Speculum* (1978), pp. 49–79. For Robert of Rheims's influence on Frederick I and his crusade, see the famous illustration of the emperor as crusader, being presented with a copy of the *Historia* by the provost of Schäftlarn, Biblioteca Apostolica Vaticana, MS Vat. Lat. 2001, fol. lr.

143. Alan of Lille, 'Sermon de cruci domini', *Textes inédits*, ed. M. T. d'Alverny, *Études de philosophie mediévale*, lii (Paris 1965), 281–2; Baldwin, *Masters, Princes and Merchants.*

144. *Historia Iherosolimitana, RHC Occ.*, iii.

145. Jacques de Vitry, *Lettres*, ed. R. B. C. Huygens (Leiden 1960), pp. 135, 139; cf. William of Tyre, *Historia*, Bk V, ch. 10. For these and other parallels I am indebted to the research of Ms Jessalyn Bird of The Queen's College, Oxford. Jacques de Vitry, *Historia Orientalis*, ed. J. Bongars, *Gesta Dei*, i, 1047–1127; Oliver of Paderborn, *Historia Damiatina*, ed. H. Hoogeweg, *Die Schriften des kölner Domscholasters* (Tübingen 1894), trans E. Peters, *Christian Society and the Crusades* (Philadelphia 1971), pp. 48–139. For William of Tyre's sources, P. W. Edbury and J. G. Rowe, *William of Tyre* (Cambridge 1988), esp. pp. 44–58.

146. J. J. van Moolenbroek, 'Signs in the heavens in Gröningen and Friesland: Oliver of Cologne and crusading propaganda', *Journal of Medieval History*, xiii (1987), 251–72; Jacques de Vitry, *Historia Occidentalis* (ed. Hinnebusch), pp. 89–90, 94–102.

147. Riley-Smith, *First Crusade*, pp. 30–5 and, generally, ch. 2; Cowdrey, 'Urban II's preaching', pp. 183–4; R. Somerville, 'The Council of Clermont and the First Crusade', *Studia Gratiana*, xx (1976); Anselm, *Opera Omnia*, ed. F. S. Schmitt (Edinburgh 1938–61), iv, 85–6, no. 195; Tyerman, *England and the Crusades*, pp. 16, 19, 154; Blake and Morris, 'A hermit goes to war'; *Vita Sancti Roberti de Arbrissello* in Migne, *PL*, clxii, cols 1017–58.

148. S. Runciman, *History of the Crusades* (Cambridge 1951–54), i, 122; Ekkehard of Aura, *Historia Hierosolymita, RHC Occ.*, v, 18–19; *Gesta Francorum*, ed. R. Hill (London 1962), p. 7.

149. Tyerman, *England and the Crusades*, pp. 30–1 and refs.

150. *De Expugnatione Lyxbonensis*, p. 72; cf. P. W. Edbury, 'Preaching the Crusade in Wales', *England and Germany in the High Middle Ages*, ed. A. Haverkamp and H. Vollrath (Oxford 1996), pp. 230–1.

151. Roger of Howden, *Gesta Henrici*, i, 275.

152. Tyerman, *England and the Crusades*, pp. 50–3 and refs.

153. Tyerman, *England and the Crusades*, pp. 59–61, 161–2; E. N. Johnson, 'The Crusades of Frederick Barbarossa and Henry VI', *History of the Crusades*, ed. Setton, ii, 90.

154. Jacques de Vitry, *Historia Occidentalis*, p. 101; Maier, *Preaching the Crusades*, esp. pp. 136–45; Throop, *Criticism of the Crusade*, pp. 82–94, 182, 184, 198–9, 287–8; E. Siberry, *Criticism of Crusading* (Oxford 1985), pp. 150–5.

155. Günther of Pairis, *Historia*, p. 61.

156. Matthew Paris, *Chronica majora*, iv, 488–9.

157. See the list of sermons of Jacques de Vitry, Philip the Chancellor, Eudes of Châteauroux, Gilbert of Tournai, Humbert of Romans and Frederigo Visconti in Maier, *Preaching the Crusades*, pp. 170–2 and refs. This impression must be tempered, however, by evidence that passages relevant for crusading were contained in many contemporary sermons whose titles do not highlight that purpose.

158. Maier, *Preaching the Crusades*, p. 112 and refs. to D'Avray and Cole. Cf. pertinent remarks by Mayer, *Crusades*, p. 197.

159. E.g. Jacques de Vitry, *Exempla*, ed. T. F. Crane (London 1890), pp. 55–6, nos cxxi, cxxii. For recruiting, Tyerman, *England and the Crusades*, pp. 167–86; Lloyd, *English Society and the Crusade*, esp. chs 3, 4, 5, and Lloyd in *Illustrated History of the Crusades*, ed. Riley-Smith, pp. 48–54.

160. *Regesto del cardinale Ugolino d'Ostia*, ed. G. Levi (Rome 1890), no. cv.

161. Levi, *Regesto*, in computation of the total of knights contracted 'exceptis illis qui amore Dei crucem receperunt, quorum numerum ignoramus'.

162. Roger of Wendover, *Flores Historiarum*, ed. H. G. Hewlett, RS (London 1886–89), ii, 323.

163. Humbert of Romans, *De predicatione Sanctae crucis* (Nuremburg 1495), ch. 1; for a summary, Maier, *Preaching the Crusades*, pp. 114–16.

164. Jacques de Vitry, *Lettres*, esp. nos I, II.

165. See Mayer's pointed discussion of this, *Crusades*, pp. 320–1.

166. Tyerman, *England and the Crusades*, pp. 156–60; Edbury, 'Preaching the Crusade in Wales', *passim*.

167. Gerald of Wales, *Journey Through Wales*, trans. L. Thorpe (London 1978), p. 75; Gerald of Wales, *Opera Omnia*, ed. J. Brewer, RS (London 1861–91), i, 74; Gerald of Wales, *De rebus a se gestis*, trans. H. E. Butler, *The Autobiography of Giraldus Cambrensis* (London 1937), p. 99.

168. J. P. Pitra, ed., *Analecta Novissima* (Paris 1885–88), ii, 428 ('Sermo and crucesignatos vel crucesignandos'); Humbert of Romans, *De Praedicatione*, ch. 28.

169. H. Finke, *Acta Aragonensia* (Berlin and Leipzig 1908–66), i, 459–60, no. 308; Tyerman, 'Philip VI and the recovery of the Holy Land', p. 30 and n. 7.

170. Joinville, *Histoire de St. Louis*, p. 260.

171. Tyerman, 'Philip VI and the recovery of the Holy Land', p. 27 and n. 5.

172. Matthew Paris, *Chronica majora*, v, 281–2.

173. Gerald of Wales, *Autobiography*, pp. 99–101; *Opera*, i, 75–6; *Journey through Wales*, pp. 141, 186–6; *De Expugnatione Lyxbonensis*, p. 71; *Barling's Chronicle*, ed. W. Stubbs, *Chronicles of Edward I and II*, RS (London 1883), ii, cxvi.

174. E.g. Maier, *Preaching the Crusades*, pp. 114, 120–2.

175. Günther of Pairis, *Historia*, pp. 61–6; Swietek, 'Günther of Pairis', p. 58.

176. Günther of Pairis, *Historia*, p. 66; Gerald of Wales, *Journey through Wales*, p. 114; Gerald of Wales, *Opera*, vi, 55; Jacques de Vitry, *Lettres*, p. 77.

177. Humbert of Romans, *De praedicatione*, ch. 1; cf. Gerald of Wales's sermon at Haverfordwest in 1188 and the English Preaching *Ordinacio* (see n. 178).

178. Gerald of Wales, *Autobiography*, pp. 99–101; Gerald of Wales, *Opera*, i, 75–6; *Ordinacio de predicatione Sancti Crucis in Angliae*, ed. R. Röhricht, *Quinti Belli Sacri Scriptores Minores*, Société de l'Orient Latin, ii (Geneva 1879), pp. 18–26; Bibliothèque Nationale MS Latin 3293, fol. 249r cols i, ii; Laurentian Library, Florence, MS Leopoldina-Gaddiana no. 116, fol. 76r col. ii–fol. 77v col. i. In general, Cole, *Preaching of the Crusades*; C. Morris 'Propaganda for War: The Dissemination of the Crusading Ideal', *Studies in Church History*, ed. W. Shiels (Oxford 1983).

179. H. Martin, *Le métier de Prédicateur en France septentrionale à la fin du môyen age 1350–1520* (Paris 1988), p. 550.

180. On Mézières in general see N. Iorga, *Philippe de Mézières et la croisade au XIVe siècle* (Paris 1896).

181. Cf. F. C. Tubach, *Index Exemplorum* (Helsinki 1969), nos 238, 1043–4, 1390–5, 2497, 3087–8, 3802, 3804, 4005, 4114–17, 4538, 4722–4, 5199.

182. Purcell, *Papal Crusading Policy*, p. 64; Mayer, *Crusades*, p. 321.

183. *Historical Papers from Northern Registers*, ed. J. Raine, RS (London 1873), pp. 93–6.

184. See the list in Maier, *Preaching the Crusades*, pp. 170–2 and n. 157 above for cautionary comment.

185. Cf. Bibliothèque Nationale MS Latin 3293 fol. 249r col. i with fol. 142v col. i.

186. Giles de Muisis, *Chronicon majus*, ed. J. J. Smet, *Receuil des Chroniques de Flandres*, ii (Brussels 1841), p. 216.

187. *Chronique parisienne anonyme de 1316 à 1339*, ed. A. Hellot, *Mémoires de la société de l'histoire de Paris et de l'Île de France*, xi (1184), p. 30; generally on this, Tyerman, *England and the Crusades*, pp. 159, 168; C. J. Tyerman, 'The French and the Crusade 1313–1336' (unpublished D. Phil. Thesis, University of Oxford 1981), pp. 55–6, 139.

188. The phrase used by Pierre Roger; see n. 185 above.

189. Matthew Paris, *Chronica majora*, iv, 1; *Register of Eudes of Rouen*, p. 658. Tyerman, *England and the Crusades*, p. 429, n. 99; Lloyd, *English Society and the Crusade*, pp. 77–8.

190. *Curia Regis Rolls*, xii, 12, no. 69.

191. *Historic Manuscripts Commission, Fifth Report*, Appendix (London 1872), p. 462.

192. *Archives de l'Hôtel Dieu de Paris*, ed. L. Brièle (Paris 1894), pp. 87–8, no. 203.

193. Jacques de Vitry, *Lettres*, p. 77.

194. C. J. Tyerman, 'Who Went on Crusade to the Holy Land?', *Horns of Hattin*, p. 19 and refs.; Tyerman, *England and the Crusades*, pp. 61, 63.

195. J. A. Brundage, 'The crusader's wife: a canonistic quandary', *Studia Gratiana*, xii (1967), 425–41; J. A. Brundage, 'The crusader's wife revisited', *Studia Gratiana*, xiv (1967), 241–52.

196. Tyerman, *England and the Crusades*, pp. 209–11.

197. *Analecta Novissima*, ii, 426; Brundage, *Canon Law and the Crusader*, p. 154.

198. *Layettes du Trésor des Chartes*, iv (Paris 1902), no. 5519.

199. The will of Elizabeth de Burgh, Lady Clare, *Testamenta Vestuta*, ed. H. Nicolas (London 1836), I, 56–9, p. 57; she left 100 marks for five armed men to serve God and destroy the enemies in the Holy Land.

200. J. Sumption, *The Albigensian Crusade* (London 1978), p. 113; T. Belperon, *La croisade contre les Albigeois* (Paris 1959), p. 202; *Siege of Carlaverock*, ed. N. H. Nicolas (London 1828), pp. 52–4 for an instance of the black crosses in 1300; cf. Tyerman, *England and the Crusades*, pp. 331, 343.

201. Lea, *History of the Inquisition*, i, 462, 466–71; ii, Appendix X for examples of crosses imposed in the 1240s; Y. Dossat, *Les crises de l'inquisition Toulousaine au xiiie siècle (1233–73)* (Bordeaux 1959), pp. 108, 110–12, 172–3, 180–1, 211, 214, 252–60 (for lists and statistics), 264–5; Bernard Gui, *Practica inquisitionis heretice pravitatis*, ed. C. Douais (Paris 1886), pp. 3, 6, 11–13, 36–8, 50–3, 89–90, 98–101. I am indebted to Dr Peter Biller for references and discussion on these points.

202. *Leet Jurisdiction in the City of Norwich*, ed. W. Hudson, Selden Society (London 1892), pp. xlii–xliii, 77 and n. 5.

203. Purcell, *Papal Crusading Policy*, p. 70; *Chronicle of Andres*, sub anno 1212, Achéry, *Spicilegium*, ii, 852; Housley, *Italian Crusades*, pp. 136–7; Tyerman, *England and the Crusades*, p. 139, 147–8; *Flores Historiarum*, ed. H. R. Luard, RS (London 1890), ii, 495; cf. the depiction of a praying knight, British Library Royal MS 2A xxii fol. 220.

204. For the Baltic design of 1147, *Annales Stadenses, MGHS*, xvi, 327.

205. *Register of Thomas Langley*, no. 796 (silk); *Testamenta Vetusta*, ed. Nicolas, i, 148 (brass); *Registrum Abbatiae Johannis Whethamstede*, ed. H. T. Riley, RS (London 1872–73), ii, 191–2 (iron).

206. For these and other examples see Tyerman, *England and the Crusades*, pp. 36, 49–50, 59–60, 134, 139, 141, 148–9, 327–9, 337, 360, 368.

207. Housley, *Italian Crusades*, p. 137 (and n. 116 where the contemporary contrast with the red crosses for the Holy Land is shown).

208. *Weltchrönik der Monchs Albert*, ed. R. Sprandel, *MGH* (Munich 1994), p. 312, sub anno 1410; for Paul Vladimiri's *Articuli contra cruciferos* (1416), Christiansen, *Northern Crusades*, pp. 228–9.

209. Tyerman, *England and the Crusades*, pp. 141, 148–9; cf. the use of crosses as emblems in the Hundred Years War by the English (red) and French (white), *Letters and Papers illustrative of the Wars of the English in France during the reign of Henry VI*, ed. J. Stevenson, RS (London 1861), i, pp. 41, 46, 424.

210. 'Propositum eundi ultra mare sine voto, non obligat nisi cruces accipiat', Monaldus OFM, *Summa* (c.1254×74) quoted by Villey, 'L'idée de la croisade', p. 581. In general see Brundage, *Canon Law and the Crusader*. Compare Hostiensis's comment on just wars 'sine crucis signaculo', Russell, *Just War*, p. 206.

211. *RHF, Documents orientaux*, ii, 458, 463, 464, 467 for references in the *Eracles* continuation of William of Tyre describing French subsidised contingents arriving at Acre in the 1270s.

212. See n. 79 above.

213. Above, n. 80; Achéry, *Spicilegium*, iii, 795–6 for Frederick III's letter to Charles VII in 1454 about the Turkish danger which referred to past French kings taking the Cross.

214. Lodovico Crivelli, *De expeditione Pii II adversus Turcos*, ed. G. Zimolo (Bologna n. d.), p. 94.

215. Sanudo, *Secreta*, Bk II, iv, c. xix, Bongars, *Gesta Dei*, ii, 74–5; cf. Bk II, iv, cc. xxiii, xxvii, pp. 81–2, 90–2. Cf. the not dissimilar proposal by the author of the *Collectio de Scandalis Ecclesiae* (*c*.1274), probably the Franciscan preacher Gilbert of Tournai, ed. A. Stroick, *Archivium Franciscanum Historicum*, xxiv (1931), p. 40.

216. Villey, 'L' ideé de la croisade', pp. 568, 581.

217. Above, pp. 49–53, 61; L. T. Belgrano, 'Une charte nolis de S. Louis', *Archives de l'Orient Latin*, ii (1884), 233–5.

218. For the Varangeville priest, *Register of Eudes of Rouen*, p. 594.

219. J. A. Brundage, 'Cruce signari: the rite for taking the cross in England', *Traditio*, xxii (1966), 306–7; *Summa de legibus Normannie in curia laicali*, ch. xc, *Coutumiers de Normandie*, pp. 215–16.

220. *Literae Cantuariensis*, ed. J. Brigstocke Sheppard, RS (London 1887–89), iii, 239, no. 1051. For Godric, above, ch. 1, pp. 21–2.

221. Lunt, *Papal Revenues*, ii, 518; C. Kohler, 'Documents inédits concernant l'Orient Latin et les croisades', no. ix, *Revue de l'Orient Latin*, viii, pp. 33–4; J. A. Brundage, 'A note on the attestation of crusaders' vows', *Catholic Historical Review*, lii (1966–67), 236–9; Bibliothèque Nationale MS Collection Bourgogne, vol. 72, fol. 72r.

222. For these and the examples in the next paragraph, see Brundage, *Canon Law and the Crusader*; Brundage, 'A note on attestation'; J. A. Brundage, 'Cruce signari', 289–310; K. Pennington, 'The rite of taking the cross in the twelfth century', *Traditio*, xxx (1974), 429–35; A. Franz, *Die Kirchlichen Benediktionen im Mittelalter*, ii (Freiburg-im-Breisgau 1909), esp. pp. 284, 307; M. Andrieu, *Le Pontifical Romain au môyen age* (Vatican 1940), ii, 418–20; iii, 30, 52, 64, 83, 104, 118, 131, 160, 187, 200, 212, 228, 243, 264, 276, 317, 330, 541–3; Purcell, *Papal Crusading Policy*, pp. 200–1.

223. Brundage, 'Cruce signari', p. 307 (trans. Riley-Smith, *The Crusades: Idea and Reality*, p. 137).

224. Andrieu, *Pontifical Romain*, iii, 30, 228, 243, 330; Purcell, *Papal Crusading Policy*, p. 200.

225. Brundage, 'A note on attestation', p. 238 n. 10.

226. Andrieu, *Pontifical Romain*, ii, 27, 418–20.

227. Pennington, 'Rite', pp. 432–3; Brundage, 'Cruce signari', pp. 306–7 (trans. Riley-Smith, *The Crusades*, p. 139); Purcell, *Papal Crusading Policy*, pp. 200–1.

228. Laurentian Library, Florence MS Leopoldina-Gaddiana no. 116, fol. 76r col. i.

229. H. Finke, *Acta Aragonensia* (Berlin and Leipzig 1908–66), i, 225, no. 147.

230. *Register of Walter Giffard, Archbishop of York 1266–79*, ed. W. Brown, Surtees Society cix (Edinburgh 1904), pp. 279–86.

231. Bibliothèque Nationale MS Latin 3293, fol. 249, fols i, ii.

232. Philippe de Mézières, *Epistre lamentable et consolatoire*, ed. K. de Letten hove, *Oeuvres de Froissart*, xvi (Brussels 1872), p. 475; Achéry, *Spicilegium*, iii, 795–6.

233. Housley, *Italian Crusades*, p. 137; Walsingham, *Historia Anglicana*, ii, 88–9; cf. the use of the *vexillum crucis* at Lisbon in 1147, *De Expugnatione Lyxbonensis*, p. 156–7 and n. 1.

234. Etienne de Bourbon, *Anecdotes historiques* (n. 25 above), pp. 36–8, 89–90, 140, 154, 171–4.

235. Eudes de Châteauroux, *Sermones, Analecta Novissima*, ii, pp. 328–33, Sermon XV.

236. For a recent discussion of these issues, Maier, *Preaching the Crusades*, pp. 118–20 and refs.

237. Joinville, *Histoire de St. Louis*, p. 39.

238. *Analecta Novissima*, ii, 332 (from Sermon XIV).

239. Joinville, *Histoire de St. Louis*, pp. 98–9.

240. For a recent survey, M. Routledge, 'Songs', *Illustrated History of the Crusades*, pp. 91–111.

241. *Livre des faits du bon messire Jean le Maingre dit Bouciquaut*, ed. J. A. C. Buchon, *Les Chroniques de Sire Jean Froissart*, iii (Paris 1840), pt 1, ch. xxi, pp. 589–90.

242. Emmanuele Piloti, *De modo, progressu, ordine ac diligenti providentia habendis in passagio Christianorum pro conquesta Terrae Sanctae*, ed. Baron de Reiffenberg, *Monuments pour servir à l'histoire des provinces de Namur etc.*, iv (Brussels 1846), p. 320.

243. B. Z. Kedar and S. Schein, 'Un projet de "passage particulier" proposé par l'Ordre de l'Hôpital', *Bibliothèque de l'Ecole des Chartes*, cxxxvii (1979), 221.

244. L. de Mas Latrie, 'Commerces et expéditions militaires de la France et de Venise au moyen âge', *Mélanges historiques*, iii, 99; Bongars, *Gesta Dei*, ii, 1–2, 8. In general, Tyerman, 'Holy Land and the Crusades', pp. 105–12. By 1400 there was almost complete unanimity in condemnation of internecine feuding in Christendom, including papal wars, by those eager to promote resistance to Muslim advances. It is no coincidence that apologists of papal policy have tended to concentrate on earlier periods.

245. Sanudo, *Secreta*, in Bongars, *Gesta Dei*, pp. 5, 37, 273–81.

246. Bibliothèque Nationale MS Latin 3293, fol. 243r col. ii.

247. For Peter of Blois, M. Markowski, 'Peter of Blois and the Conception of the Crusade', *Horns of Hattin*, pp. 261–9.

248. Roger of Howden, *Gesta Henrici*, ii, 15–19 for *Audita Tremendi*.

249. Above, pp. 69, 72.

250. Caesarius of Heisterbach, *Dialogus Miraculorum*, ed. J. Strange (Cologne, Bonn and Brussels 1851), i, 12–13: *Distinctio Prima: De Conversione*, ch. vi.

251. Jacques de Vitry, *Historia Occidentalis*, pp. 20–1; Bongars, *Gesta Dei*, i, 1048.

252. William the Breton, *Gesta Philippi Augusti, Oeuvres de Rigord et de Guillaume le Breton*, ed. H.-F. Delaborde (Paris 1882–83), i, 303–4.

253. J. L. Cate, 'The English Mission of Eustace of Flay', *Etudes d'histoire dédiées à la memoire de Henri Pirenne* (Brussels 1937), pp. 67–87, esp. 71.

254. Brundage, *Canon Law and the Crusader*, pp. 179–83; Baldwin, *Masters, Princes and Merchants*, i, 22, 37, 220, 272.

255. Jordan, *Louis IX, passim.*

256. Tyerman, *England and the Crusades*, pp. 146–51; for Simon's spiritual life, see J. R. Maddicott, *Simon de Montfort* (Cambridge 1994), pp. 77–105.

257. F. M. Powicke, *The Thirteenth Century, 1216–1307* (Oxford 1962), p. 80.

258. For contrasting accounts of Henry III and the crusade, Tyerman, *England and the Crusades*, pp. 111–32; Lloyd, *English Society and the Crusade*, esp. 198–232.

259. Housley, *Italian Crusades*, p. 109 and, generally, pp. 1–14, 252–7; for convenient citations of debate on this, Mayer, *Crusades*, pp. 312–13.

260. An extreme example is the use, without comment, of Martino da Canale's description of 'all the great men of Venice . . . and the whole of the Venetian *popolo*' taking the cross in 1256 by the otherwise severe critic of antipapal chroniclers, Housley, *Italian Crusades*, p. 126.

261. Housley, *Italian Crusades*, p. 109. The *e silentio* argument (Housley, *Later Crusades*, p. 266) that if there had been serious criticism more of it would have survived, appears a trifle desperate. Cf., generally, S. Reynolds, 'Social mentalities and the case of scepticism', *TRHS*, 6th Ser., i (1991), pp. 21–41.

262. Housley, *Later Crusades*; Tyerman, *England and the Crusades*, pp. 302–70; Riley-Smith, *The Crusades*, pp. 240–57.

263. F. Cardini, 'Crusade and "Presence of Jerusalem" in Medieval Florence', *Outremer*, ed. B. Kedar, H. Mayer and R. Smail (Jerusalem 1982), p. 341 and n. 44.

264. See above, 'Papal leadership', pp. 41–9. See now J. Richard, *Histoire des croisades* (Paris 1996) for an argument that accepts the pluralist definition but insists on the spiritual and ideological primacy of the Holy Land.

265. Mayer's essential point ('what is at issue is not Church doctrine but the extent to which society found that doctrine acceptable'), *Crusades*, p. 313.

266. K. Setton, *The Papacy and the Levant*, i (Philadelphia 1976), esp. chs. 9–15; Housley, *The Avignon Papacy and the Crusades*; Tyerman, *England and the Crusades*, pp. 229–301.

267. S. Schein, *Fideles Crucis: The Papacy, the West and the Recovery of the Holy Land 1274–1314* (Oxford 1991); C. J. Tyerman, 'Sed nihil fecit? The last Capetians and the recovery of the Holy Land', *War and Government in the Middle Ages*, ed. J. Gillingham and J. C. Holt (Woodbridge 1984), pp. 170–81; C. J. Tyerman, 'Philip V of France, the Assemblies of 1319–20 and the Crusade', *Bulletin of the Institute of Historical Research*, lvii (1984), pp. 15–34; C. J. Tyerman, 'Philip VI and the recovery of the Holy Land'.

268. For some French examples, Bibliothèque Nationale MSS Collection Bourgogne 72, fol. 72r (the duke of Burgundy's conditional vow and refusal to contribute to a compulsory crusade tax in 1314); Bibliothèque Nationale MSS Collection Doat, vol. 12, fol. 4v (for Louis X's assurance of his intention to go on crusade made to persuade the clergy to pay the crusade tithe granted at Vienne in 1312); *Chronographia regum Francorum*, i, 211 (for 1313 reluctance to grant money before action was apparent);

Tyerman, 'Philip V and the Assemblies of 1319–20'; cf. English attitudes, Tyerman, *England and the Crusades*, pp. 229–58.

269. As Philip V of France warned Louis, count of Clermont in 1319, Archives Nationales JJ 60, no. 100.

270. Schein, *Fideles Crucis*, pp. 74–5, 109–11, 137–8, 154, 197–202, 208, 210–11, 217, 240–3. For the discussion of merger at the Council of Lyons (1274), J. Delaville le Roulx (ed.), *Cartulaire général de l'ordre des Hospitaliers* (Paris 1899), iii, 597, no. 4156.

271. Mézières, *Epistre lamentable*, esp. pp. 467–505.

272. Christiansen, *Northern Crusades*, pp. 223–33.

273. For English examples, see Tyerman, *England and the Crusades*, pp. 202, 311–15, 318, 319, 353–8; on the Hospitallers, see, in general, the work of Dr Anthony Luttrell, e.g. his article on the Order at Rhodes in Setton (ed.), *History of the Crusades*, vol. iii. Regional differences are noted by Housley, *Later Crusades*, p. 376.

274. Above, n. 63; Housley, *Later Crusades*, pp. 249, 251, 264, 266.

275. Tyerman, *England and the Crusades*, p. 256 and n. 120.

276. Siberry, *Criticism of Crusading*, pp. 190–201.

277. Barber, 'Crusade of Shepherds', pp. 2–4, 7, 16; Ralph Niger, *De re militari*, ed. L. Schmügge (Berlin 1977); G. B. Flahiff's studies, 'Ralph Niger: an introduction to his life and works' and 'Deus non vult: a critic of the Third Crusade', *Medieval Studies*, ii (1940), 104–26, 162–88; Siberry, *Criticism of Crusading*, pp. 11–13 and refs; W. F. Wakefield, *Heresy, Crusade, Inquisition* (London 1974), p. 210.

278. Throop, *Criticism of the Crusade, passim*; Schein, *Fideles Crucis*, pp. 15–50.

279. Siberry, 'Criticism of crusading in fourteenth-century England', pp. 127–32; Luttrell, 'Chaucer's Knight and the Mediterranean', esp. pp. 152–60.

280. Brundage, *Canon Law and the Crusader*, pp. 68–114, 131–8; Purcell, *Papal Crusading Policy*, pp. 99–132; Maier, *Preaching the Crusades*, pp. 135–60.

281. Lunt, *Financial Relations of the Papacy with England*, i, 430–4; Lloyd, *English Society and the Crusade*, pp. 22, 149, 151, 178; Tyerman, *England and the Crusade*, pp. 105–6; cf. Matthew Paris's outrage, *Chronica majora*, iv, 133–4.

282. See the collected references in Siberry, *Criticism of Crusading*, pp. 193–96.

283. A point made by Maier, *Preaching the Crusades*, p. 155.

284. M. J. Epstein, 'Ludovicus deus regnantium: perspectives on the rhymed office, *Speculum*, liii (1978), 322.

285. Mézières, *Epistre Lamentable*, pp. 458–9, 470–2.

286. Sanudo, *Secreta*, Bk iii, pt iv, Bongars, *Gesta Dei*, ii, 130–48 (where he follows William of Tyre closely, probably through the mediation of Jacques de Vitry's *Historia Orientalis*); Piloti, *De Modo*, pp. 313, 320–1. For 'cult' of Godfrey de Bouillon, cf. the romances and tapestries describing his exploits owned by the earl and countess of Gloucester in the 1390s, A. Goodman, *The Loyal Conspiracy* (London 1971), pp. 81–2.

287. Bongars, *Gesta Dei*, ii, 98–281; C. J. Tyerman, 'Marino Sanudo Torsello and the lost crusade: lobbying in the fourteenth century', *TRHS*, 5th ser., xxxii (1982), 57–73. For a French collection of tracts, Bibliothèque Nationale MS Latin 7470 (presented to Charles IV); for an English compilation of slightly later vintage, British Library MS Cotton Otho D. V.

288. Iorga, *Philippe de Mézières*, pp. 71 (and n. 1), 73–4.

289. *Le Songe du Vieil Pèlerin*, ed. G. W. Coopland (Cambridge 1969), i, 196, 398–9; 487, 515–16, 632; ii, 222–3 for the advice to read about Godfrey's exploits.

290. Torzelo's *Avis*, and Bertrandon de la Broquière's critique, *Le Voyage d'Out remer de Bertrandon de la Broquière*, ed. C. Schéfer, *Recueil de voyages et de documents pour servir à l'histoire de la geographie depuis le xiiie jusqu' à la fin du xvie siècle*, pp. 263–6, 267–74; Germain, *Discours d'Oultremer*, pp. 338–9.

291. Piloti, *De Modo*, pp. 314, 320, 362–3; Broquière, *Voyage d'Outremer*, pp. 2, 230; most of the work, however, concerns the Ottomans, the author actually meeting Murad II, pp. 176–99, although he too refers to topographical and historical details gleaned from the 'livre de Goddefroy de Buyillon', p. 138 (cf. p. 152).

292. Charrière, *Négociations de la France dans le Levant*, pp. cxxviii-cxxxi; cf. Housley, *Later Crusades*, pp. 47–8, 125, 390, 397.

293. R. de Maulde la Clavière, ed., *Chronique de Louis XII par Jean d'Auton* (Paris 1889–95), i (Pièces Annexes), 396–7.

294. *Chronique de Louis XII*, ii, 166–7.

295. Tanner, *Decrees of Ecumenical Councils*, pp. 595, 607, 609–14, 651, 653–4, 796–7.

296. Philippe de Vitry, *Le Chapel des Fleurs de Lis*, ed. A. Piaget, *Bibliothèque de l'Ecole des Chartes*, xxvii (1898), 55–92.

297. Mézières, *Songe*, i, 5; A. S. Atiya, *The Crusade in the Later Middle Ages* (London 1938), p. 183; Luttrell, 'Chaucer's Knight and the Mediterranean', pp. 131–2, 139, 149–50.

298. Luttrell, 'Chaucer's Knight and the Mediterranean', pp. 144–7, 154–9; Tyerman, *England and the Crusades*, pp. 262–5 (noting Luttrell's corrections).

299. M. Keen, *Chivalry* (Yale 1984), pp. 194–5 and refs.

300. Abbé Lebeuf, *Histoire de la ville et de tout le diocèse de Paris: Rectifications et Additions*, ed. F. Bournon (Paris 1890), i, 63–5; *Chronique parisienne anonyme*, pp. 29–30; X. de Boisrouvray, 'L'église collégiale et la confrérie du St. Sépulchre à Paris 1325–1791', *Positions des Thèses de l'École nationale des Chartes* (Paris 1953), pp. 33–5.

301. T. Smith, *English Gilds*, Early English Text Society xl (London 1840), pp. 11, 22, 114.

302. A. Sabarthes, 'Les seigneurs de Palaja', *Bulletin philologique et historique* (1920), p. 198; in general, Tyerman, 'The French and the Crusade', pp. 340–51 for details.

303. *Cartulary of the Priory of St. Denys near Southampton*, ed. E. O. Blake (Southampton 1981), i, 88; ii, 181–2; *Archives historiques de la Gironde* (Bordeaux 1859–), xlix, 324–34.

304. Archives Nationales J 404, no. 34.

305. *The Chapter Act Book of the Collegiate Church of St. John of Beverley*, ed. A. F. Leach, Surtees Society ii (Durham 1903), 136; U. Robert, *Testaments de l'Officialité de Besançon*, i (Paris 1902), 233–5.

306. Archives Nationales J 404, no. 22; *Archives historiques de la Gironde*, xvii, 138–40; xlix, 324–34.

3 Proteus Unbound: Crusading Historiography

1. *RHC Occ.*, iii, 723.
2. For a useful discussion of these themes, Riley-Smith, *First Crusade*, esp. ch. 6.
3. Cf. the comments of B. Smalley, *Historians of the Middle Ages* (London 1974), ch. 9, esp. pp. 122–3.
4. The tradition, a long one, includes Fulcher of Chartres; the author of the *De Expugnatione Lyxbonensis* ; William of Tyre; Jacques de Vitry; Villehardouin; Joinville; Marino Sanudo Torsello; Philippe de Mézières, etc.
5. David Hume, *History of Great Britain* (London 1761), i, 209, cf. p. 211.
6. E.g. in 1463, D. Wilkins, *Concilia Magnae Britannicae et Hibernicae* (London 1733–37), iii, 588.
7. *Registrum Abbatiae Johannis Whethamstede*, ed. H. T. Riley, RS (London 1872–73), i, 333–4.
8. Housley, *Later Crusades*, pp. 421–2.
9. In general, R. Schwoebel, *The Shadow of the Crescent: The Renaissance Image of the Turk* (Nieuwkoop 1967); J. W. Bohnstedt, *The Infidel Scourge of God: The Turkish Menace as seen by German pamphleteers of the Reformation Era*, Transactions of the American Philosophical Society (Philadelphia 1968); K. Setton, *Papacy and Levant* (Philadelphia 1976–84), vols. ii–iv; Housley, *Later Crusades*, esp. pp. 99–100, 380, 383–8, 390–1, 393, 398, 409; cf. R. Black, *Benedetto Accolti and the Florentine Renaissance* (Cambridge 1985), esp. pp. 226–40; R. Black, 'La Storica della Prima Crociata di Benedetto Accolti', *Archivio Storico Italiano*, cxxxi (1973), 2–25. A. S. Atiya, *The Crusade in the Later Middle Ages* (London 1938), chs ix, xi, xix.
10. Schwoebel, *Shadow of the Crescent*, p. 223.
11. Schwoebel, *Shadow of the Crescent*, p. 217; Setton, *Papacy and Levant*, iii, 179 n. 28, 189–90 and n. 72; S. A. Fischer-Galati, *Ottoman imperialism and German Protestantism* (Harvard 1959), esp. pp. 9–10; Heath, *Crusading Commonplaces*.
12. Fischer-Galati, *Ottoman Imperialism*, esp. p. 117.
13. Bohnstedt, *Infidel Scourge*, pp. 14, 34–5, and 41–6 for text of Kretz's sermon.
14. M. J. Heath, 'Erasmus and War against the Turks', *Acta Conventus neo-Latini Turonensis*, ed. J.-C. Margolin (Paris 1980), pp. 991–9; Heath, *Crusading Commonplaces*, p. 88; R. H. Bainton, *Erasmus of Christendom* (London 1970), pp. 190 and nn. 19, 245; *Opus Epistolarum Des. Erasmi Roterodami*, ed. P. S. Allen *et al.*, viii (Oxford 1934), no. 2285, pp. 382–5.
15. Fischer-Galati, *Ottoman Imperialism*, pp. 17–18; Housley, *Later Crusades*, p. 380; Bohnstedt, *Infidel Scourge*, pp. 12, 14, 20, 32, 46–51; Heath, *Crusading Commonplaces*, p. 15; cf. Luther's original stance attacked in the papal bull *Exurge Domine* (1520) with his later thoughts, *Vom Kriege widder die Türken* (1529) and his *Exhortation* of 1541; on the impact of these changes, Heath, 'Erasmus and War', pp. 991–3; J. Pannier, 'Calvin et les Turcs', *Revue historique* clxxx (1937), 268–72.
16. Setton, 'Leo X and the Turkish peril', *Proceedings of the American Philosophical Society*, cxiii (1969), 367–424; J. Riley-Smith, *The Crusades* (London 1990), pp. 248–9; Tyerman, *England and the Crusades*, pp. 360, 362.

17. *Dictionnaire de droit canonique*, ed. R. Naz, iv (Paris 1949), col. 781; Setton, *Papacy and Levant*, iii, iv, chs 12, 13, 18 *passim*; Housley, *Later Crusades*, pp. 312–15, 410–20.

18. Quoted by J. Lock, 'How many Tercios Has the Pope?', *History*, lxxxi (1996), 202.

19. E.g. Kretz's sermon talked of martyrdom but not indulgences, Bohnstedt, *Infidel Scourge*, pp. 43–4; Heath, *Crusading Commonplaces*, pp. 10, 24, 88.

20. Setton, *Papacy and Levant*, iii, iv form the basis for Housley, *Later Crusades*, esp. pp. 118–50, 260 and Riley-Smith, *Crusades*, pp. 241–50; cf. Tyerman, *England and the Crusades*, pp. 346–54, 359–62.

21. Cf. Heath, *Crusading Commonplaces*, pp. 21–2.

22. F. L. Baumer, 'England, the Turk and the common corps of Christendom', *American Historical Review*, (1944–45), 26–48, esp. 31, 36–8, 43–7; Tyerman, *England and the Crusades*, pp. 348–50; for James VI's youthful Virgilian epic of 1585, *The Poems of James VI of Scotland*, ed. J. Craigie (Edinburgh 1955–58), xlviii, 197–257.

23. *A Lytell Cronycle: Richard Pynson's Translation (1520) of Hethoum's 'La Fleur des histoires de la terre d'Orient*, ed. G. Burger (Toronto 1988), esp. pp. xxxv–xxxvi.

24. Bohnstedt, *Infidel Scourge, passim*; Fischer-Galati, *Ottoman Imperialism*, pp. 17–18.

25. H. Wolter, 'Elements of Crusade spirituality in St Ignatius', *Ignatius of Loyola; His Personality and Spiritual Heritage*, ed. F. Wulf (St Louis 1977), pp. 97–134; N. P. Tanner, 'Medieval Crusade decrees and Ignatius's Meditation on the Kingdom', *Heythrop Journal*, xxxi (1990), 505–15. I am grateful to Dr Tanner for bringing these references to my attention.

26. Jacques de Vitry, *Historia Orientalis*, ed. F. Moschus (Douai 1597), Preface to Reader.

27. J. Foxe, *Acts and Monuments*, ed. S. R. Cattley (London 1837–41), iv, 18–21, 27–8, 33–4, 38, 52–4, 69, 113, 120–1.

28. Reinerius Reineccius Steinhemius, *Chronicon Hierosolymitanum* (Helmstadt 1584); Dresser's commentary appears in Part II.

29. Herold was from Basel; for a summary, see Housley, *Later Crusades*, p. 420.

30. Published at Hanau (in Cassel).

31. For Bongars's researches at Corpus Christi College, Cambridge, see MS letter attached to the Bodleian copy of the *Gesta Dei*, E. 2. 8. Art-Seld.

32. Pannier, 'Calvin et les Turcs', 278–86.

33. 'Periculosissimis ita gloriosissimis expeditionibus', from the Dedicatory Preface.

34. Pierre de Bourdeille, seigneur de Brantôme, *Oeuvres complètes*, ed. L. Lalanne, ix (Paris 1876), 433–4; cf. the pointed comparison of sixteenth-century freedom with how restrictive crusading was for the women left behind, p. 450.

35. *The Works of Francis Bacon*, ed. J. Spedding *et al.*, vii (London 1859), pp. 1–36.

36. *Advertisement, Works of Francis Bacon*, vii, p. 24.

37. Heath, *Crusading Commonplaces*, pp. 53, 103–4.

38. See, especially, Bk V, chs ix–xvii. Fuller's work went into four editions between 1639 and 1651.

39. Maimbourg's *History* went into a third edition in 1680 and was translated into English by Nalson in 1685. For references, see, in Nalson's translation, 'Letter to the Reader'; Maimbourg's 'Letter to the King of France'; the Second Advertisement to the French edition (where the sources are listed); and pp. 2–3, 200–1, 407–10.

40. G. C. Müller, *De Expeditione Cruciatis Vulgo Von Kreutz Fahrten* (Nuremburg 1709), pp. 3–6, 11, 20, 25–7, 33.

41. J. D. Schoeplin, *De Sacris Galliae Regum in Orientem Expeditionibus* (Strasbourg 1726).

42. Hume, *History*, i, 209.

43. D. Diderot, *Dictionnaire Encyclopédique, Oeuvres complètes* (Paris 1821), xiv, 496–511.

44. Voltaire, *History of the Crusades*, English trans. (London 1753), pp. 49, 52, 54, 57, 59, 66, 68, 74, 76, 84–5, 88, 91–2, 95, 108–10, 114, 119, 127.

45. E. Gibbon, *Decline and Fall of the Roman Empire*, chs lviii–lxi; ed. Milman, Guizot and Smith, vol. vii (London 1862), pp. 178–349; cf. F. Schiller, *Über Volkwänderung, Kreuzzüge und Mittelalter, Werke*, ed. R. Roxberger (Berlin and Stuttgart 1886).

46. Gibbon, *Decline and Fall*, ch. lxi; Milman *et al.* eds, vii, pp. 346–9.

47. Quoted by E. Siberry, 'Images of the Crusades in the Nineteenth and Twentieth Centuries', *Illustrated History of the Crusades*, pp. 365–85.

48. For the British dimension, M. Girouard, *The Return to Camelot* (London 1981); cf. J. Prawer, *Histoire de royaume Latin de Jérusalem* (Paris 1969–70), i, 3–5.

49. For Sybel, see below, pp. 119–20.

50. C. Mills, *History of the Crusades* (London 1820), i, vi, 33; ii, 341, 371.

51. Mills, *History*, ii, 218, 348–51, 373–5.

52. See the entry on Mills in the *Dictionary of National Biography*.

53. H. Stebbings, *The History of Chivalry and the Crusades* (Edinburgh 1830).

54. J. F. Michaud, *Histoire des croisades* (6th edn, Paris 1841), ii, 206.

55. Michaud, *Histoire*, iv, 411; vi, 370–1.

56. Michaud, *Histoire*, vi, 371.

57. See nn. 47 and 48 above; cf. the comments of T. S. R. Boase, 'Recent developments in crusading historiography', *History*, xxii (1937), 110–25.

58. Siberry, 'Images of the Crusades', pp. 371, 376.

59. In 1786, Thomas Jefferson called for 'a crusade against ignorance', quoted in the *Oxford English Dictionary* (Oxford 1971 edn), p. 1221; for a recent account of evangelical 'crusades', J. Wolffe, *The Protestant Crusade in Great Britain* (Oxford 1991).

60. Siberry, 'Images of the Crusades', pp. 377–8.

61. On the Courtois forgeries, see R.-H. Bautier, 'La collection de chartes de croisade dite "Collection Courtois"', *Comptes rendus des scéances de l'Académie des Inscriptions et Belles Lettres* (1956), pp. 382–6; cf. the article on Courtois and Bautier's exposure of him and his accomplices in *Bibliothèque de l'École des chartes*, cxxxii (1974); D. Abulafia, 'Invented Italians in the Courtois Charters', Edbury, *Crusade and Settlement*, pp. 135–43.

62. J. Gillingham, *Richard the Lionheart* (London 1978), p. 300.

63. L. Von Ranke, *Übungen (Historical Exercises)* of 1837; von Sybel, *Geschichte des ersten Kreuzzuges* (1st edn, Leipzig 1841). For an interesting early discus-

sion of the effect of Sybel's work, E. Barker, 'The Crusades', *Encylopaedia Britannica*, 11th edn (1910–11), pp. 550–1.

64. *Peter der Eremite* (Leipzig 1879); Hagenmayer also edited Ekkehard of Aura (Tübingen 1877); the *Gesta Francorum* (Heidelberg 1890); Fulcher of Chartres, *Historia Hierosolymitana* (Heidelberg 1913) and letters written during the First Crusade, *Epistolae et chartae ad historiam primi belli sacri spectantes* (Innsbruck, 1901); Blake and Morris, 'A hermit goes to war' of 1984.

65. For a recent discussion, J. Riley-Smith, 'The Crusading Movement and Historians', *Illustrated History of the Crusades*, pp. 1–12.

66. T. A. Archer and C. L. Kingsford, *The Crusades* (London 1894).

67. Boase, 'Developments in crusading historiography'.

68. Cf. Siberry, 'Images of the Crusades', pp. 384–5; it could be argued that the emphasis on Christian nationhood had academic origins in the late nineteenth century, P. E. Russell, 'The Nessus-Shirt of Spanish history', *Bulletin of Hispanic Studies*, xxxvi (1959), 219–25, or even earlier, P. Linehan, *History and the Historians of Medieval Spain* (Oxford 1993), pp. 1–21, but esp. pp. 15–20 for Francoism; cf. R. Fletcher, 'Reconquest and Crusade in Spain', *TRHS*, 5th ser., xxxvii (1987), 31–3.

69. L. Madelin, 'La Syrie franque', *Revue des deux mondes* (1917); L. Madelin, *L'expansion française: De la Syrie au Rhin* (Paris 1918); Boase, 'Developments in crusading historiography'.

70. R. Grousset, *Histoire des croisades* (Paris 1934–36), iii, 763; cf. comments by J. L. La Monte, 'Some problems in Crusading historiography', *Speculum*, xv (1940), 56–75; Boase, 'Developments in crusading historiography'.

71. J. Richard, *The Latin Kingdom of Jerusalem* (English trans. Amsterdam 1979; orig. French edn 1953), i, pp. v, ix; ii, p. 463.

72. J. Prawer, *The Latin Kingdom of Jerusalem: European Colonisation in the Middle Ages* (London 1972), pp. ix, 524 and, specifically as well as generally, pp. 469–533; Prawer, *Histoire du royaume Latin*, i, 6–8, esp. p. 8 for clear parallels with modern Israel; cf. 'The Crusading Kingdom of Jerusalem – The First European Colonial Society? A Symposium', *Horns of Hattin*, pp. 341–66 for a discussion of Prawer's thesis by some crusader heavyweights.

73. Barker, 'The Crusades', p. 550.

74. *Gesta Francorum*, ed. R. Hill (London 1962), p. xv.

75. D. Lloyd George, *The Great Crusade: Collected War Speeches 1915–18* (London 1919); D. Eisenhower, *Crusade in Europe* (London 1948); Siberry, 'Images of the Crusades', p. 381–5.

76. La Monte, 'Some problems', p. 60; Pirie-Gordon wrote anonymously so that the association would be more easily made.

77. Newbolt's infamous poem 'Vitaï Lampada' of 1897, verse 2:

> The sand of the desert is sodden red –
> Red with the wreck of the square that broke;
> The gatling's jammed and the colonel dead,
> And the regiment blind with dust and smoke.
> The river of death has brimmed its banks,
> And England's far and Honour a name,

> But the voice of a schoolboy rallies the ranks:
> Play up! Play up! And play the game!

78. *Time Magazine*, 4 January 1982, p. 31.
79. Riley-Smith, *Crusades*, p. 256; J. Riley-Smith, 'Revival and Survival', *Illustrated History of the Crusades*, pp. 386–91.
80. S. Runciman, *History of the Crusades* (Cambridge 1951–54), iii, 480.
81. Riley-Smith, *Crusades*, pp. 256–7; Mayer, *Crusades* (1st edn trans. 1972), p. 281.
82. Runciman, *Crusades*, iii, 130.
83. S. Lloyd, 'Crusading movement', *Illustrated History of the Crusades*, pp. 36, 64; Archer and Kingsford, *The Crusades*, pp. 450–1, and generally, 446–51. (In respect of research and scholarship, however, there is no comparison between Lloyd, who is very good, and Archer and Kingsford, who were, in this instance, not.)
84. *DNB* entry for Mills; Riley-Smith, 'Revival and Survival', illustration p. 390.
85. La Monte, 'Some problems', p. 58.
86. William of Tyre, *Historia*, Bk xxiii, Preface; adaptation based on translation by E. Babcock and A. Krey (New York 1941), ii, 506; cf. William's exemplary, if formal, protestations in his Prologue to the whole work, trans. Babcock and Krey, i, 53–9.

SELECT BIBLIOGRAPHY

Primary Sources

Most surveys of crusading contain adequate or extensive lists of primary sources, including those in translation. The great nineteenth- and twentieth-century collections, the *Recueil des Historiens des Croisades (RHC)* series or the *Monumenta Germaniae Historica (MGH)*, contain most of the major crusade texts, even if not always in the best editions. What follows is a selection of texts that illustrate one of the central themes of this book, the process whereby the image and ideal of the crusade were invented by observers and later historians. Some of these will, therefore, be strictly primary; others not.

Benedetto Accolti, *La Storica della Prima Crociata, RHC Occ.*, v
J. Bédier and P. Aubry, *Chansons de croisade* (Paris 1909)
H. Bonet, *Tree of Battles*, ed. G. W. Coopland (Liverpool 1949)
J. Bongars, *Gesta Dei Per Francos* (1611)
Jehan Cabaret d'Orville, *La chronique de bon duc Loys de Bourbon*, ed. A.-M. Chazaud (Paris 1876)
De expugnatione Lyxbonensis, ed. and trans. C. W. David (New York 1936)
J. Foxe, *History of the Turks* in *Acts and Monuments* (1563–83)
Fulcher of Chartres, *Historia Hierosolimitana*, ed. H. Hagenmeyer (Heidelberg 1913); trans. F. R. Ryan, ed. H. S. Fink (Knoxville 1969)
T. Fuller, *History of the Holy War* (1st edn 1639)
Gerald of Wales, *Journey Through Wales*, trans. L. Thorpe (London 1978)
Jean Germain, *La discours du voyage d'Oultremer*, ed. C. Schéfer, *Revue de l'Orient Latin*, iii (1895)
Gesta Francorum, ed. R. Hill (London 1962)
E. Gibbon, *The Decline and Fall of the Roman Empire* (1st edn 1776–88)
Guibert of Nogent, *Gesta Dei Per Francos, RHC Occ.*, iv.
Günther of Pairis, *Historia Constantinopolitana*, ed. Comte Riant, *Exuviae sacrae Constantinopolitanae*, i (Geneva 1877)
Henry of Livonia, *Chronicon Livoniae*, ed. L. Arbusow and A. Bauer (Hanover 1955); trans. J. Brundage (1961)
D. Hume, *History of England* (1762)
Jacques de Vitry, *Historia Occidentalis*, ed. J. F. Hinnebusch (Fribourg 1972)
Jacques de Vitry, *Historia Orientalis*, ed. J. Bongars, *Gesta Dei Per Francos*, i (1611)

Jacques de Vitry, *Lettres*, ed. R. B. C. Huygens (Leiden 1960)
Jean de Joinville, *Histoire de St Louis*, ed. N. de Wailly (Paris 1868); trans. M. R. B. Shaw (London 1963)
L. Maimbourg, *Histoire des croisades* (1675)
Matthew Paris, *Chronica majora*, ed. H. R. Luard (London 1872–84)
F. Michaud, *Histoire des croisades* (1817–41)
C. Mills, *History of the Crusades* (1820)
Oliver of Paderborn, *Historia Damiatina, Die Schriften*, ed. H. Hooeweg (Tübingen 1894); trans. J. J. Gavigan (1948)
Philippe de Mézières, *Epistre lamentable et consolatoire*, ed. K. de Lettenhove, *Oeuvres de Froissart*, xvi (Paris 1872)
Philippe de Mézières, *La Songe du Vieil Pèlerin*, ed. G. W. Coopland (Cambridge 1969)
E. Piloti, *De modo, progressu etc. . . . pro conquesta Terrae Sanctae*, ed. Baron de Reiffenberg (Brussels 1846)
J. P. Pitra, ed., *Analecta Novissima* (Paris 1885–88), for sermon extracts
R. Reineck, *Chronicon Hierosolymitanum* (Helmstadt 1584; intro. to Part Two by M. Dresser)
Robert of Rheims, *Historia Iherosolimitana, RHC Occ.*, iii
H. von Sybel, *Geschichte des ersten Kreuzzuges* (1841)
Marino Sanudo Torsello, *Secreta Fidelium Crucis*, ed. J. Bongars, *Gesta Dei Per Francos*, ii (1611)
Geoffroi de Villehardouin, *La conquête de Constantinople*, trans. M. R. B. Shaw (London 1963)
Voltaire, *Histoire des croisades* (final version 1756)
William, Archbishop of Tyre, *Chronicon*, ed. R. B. C. Huygens *et al.* (Turnhout 1986) (before Huygens's edition this was usually known as the *Historia*; this was trans. E. Babcock and A. Krey, New York 1943)

Secondary Sources

(As each chapter is fully noted, only a few obvious works are listed here)

A. S. Atiya, *The Crusade in the Later Middle Ages* (London 1938)
J. W. Baldwin, *Masters, Princes and Merchants: The Social Views of Peter the Chanter and his Circle* (Princeton 1970)
E. O. Blake and C. Morris, 'A hermit goes to war: Peter and the origins of the First Crusade', *Studies in Church History*, xxi (1984)
J. A. Brundage, 'Crucesignari: the rite of taking the cross in England', *Traditio*, xx (1960)
J. A. Brundage, *Canon Law and the Crusader* (Madison 1969)
M. Bull, *Knightly Piety and the Lay Response to the First Crusade* (Oxford 1993)
E. Christiansen, *Northern Crusades* (London 1980)

P. Cole, *The Preaching of the Crusades to the Holy Land 1095–1270* (Cambridge, Mass. 1991)

G. Constable, 'The Second Crusade as seen by contemporaries', *Traditio*, ix (1953)

H. E. J. Cowdrey, 'Pope Urban II's preaching of the First Crusade', *History*, iv (1970)

H. E. J. Cowdrey, 'Canon Law and the First Crusade', *Horns of Hattin*, ed. B. Kedar (Jerusalem 1992)

D. D' Avray, *The Preaching of the Friars* (Oxford 1985)

C. Erdmann, *The Origin of the Idea of the Crusade* (Princeton 1977, trans. of 1935 classic)

M. Gervers, *The Second Crusade and the Cistercians* (New York 1992)

J. Gilchrist, 'The Erdmann thesis and the Canon Law', *Crusade and Settlement*, ed. P. Edbury (Cardiff 1985)

J. Gilchrist, 'The papacy and war against the Saracens 795–1216', *International History Review*, x (1988)

M. J. Heath, *Crusading Commonplaces* (Geneva 1986)

E.-D. Hehl, *Kirche und Krieg im 12 Jahrhundert* (Stuttgart 1980)

N. Housley, *The Italian Crusades* (Oxford 1982)

N. Housley, 'Crusades against Christians', *Crusade and Settlement*, ed. P. Edbury (Cardiff 1985)

N. Housley, *The Avignon Papacy and the Crusades* (Oxford 1986)

N. Housley, *The Later Crusades* (Oxford 1992)

N. Iorga, *Philippe de Mézières et la croisade au xive siècle* (Paris 1896)

W. C. Jordan, *Louis IX and the Challenge of the Crusade* (Princeton 1979)

M. Keen, *Chivalry* (Yale 1984)

H. C. Lea, *History of the Inquisition* (New York 1900–01)

S. Lloyd, *English Society and the Crusade 1216–1307* (Oxford 1988)

W. E. Lunt, *Papal Revenues in the Middle Ages* (New York 1965)

A. Luttrell, 'Chaucer's Knight and the Mediterranean', *Library of Mediterranean History*, i (1994)

C. T. Maier, *Preaching the Crusades* (Cambridge 1994)

H. E. Mayer, *The Crusades* (trans. Oxford, 1972, 1988)

M. Markowski, 'Crucesignatus: its origins and early usage', *Journal of Medieval History*, x (1984)

M. Markowski, 'Peter of Blois and the Conception of the Crusade', *Horns of Hattin*, ed. B. Z. Kedar

C. Morris, 'Propaganda for War: The Dissemination of the Crusading Ideal', *Studies in Church History*, ed. W. Shiels (Oxford 1983)

J. Muldoon, *Popes, Lawyers and Infidels* (Liverpool 1979)

K. Pennington, 'The rite for taking the cross in the twelfth century', *Traditio*, xxx (1974)

M. Purcell, *Papal Crusading Policy* (Leyden 1975)

J. Richard, *Saint Louis: Crusader King of France* (Cambridge 1992)

J. S. C. Riley-Smith, *What Were the Crusades?* (2nd edn, London 1992)

J. Riley-Smith, *The First Crusade and the Idea of Crusading* (London 1986)

J. Riley-Smith, ed., *Oxford Illustrated History of the Crusades* (Oxford 1995)

H. Roscher, *Papst Innocenz III und die Kreuzugge* (Göttingen 1969)

S. Runciman, *A History of the Crusades* (Cambridge 1951–54)

F. H. Russell, *The Just War in the Middle Ages* (Cambridge 1975)

R. Schwoebel, *The Shadow of the Crescent: The Renaissance Image of the Turk* (Nieukoop 1967)

K. Setton, gen. ed., *History of the Crusades* (Madison 1969–)

K. Setton, *The Papacy and the Levant* (Philadephia 1976–84)

E. Siberry, *Criticism of Crusading* (Oxford 1985)

P. Throop, *Criticism of the Crusade* (Amsterdam 1940)

C. J. Tyerman, 'The Holy Land and the Crusades of the Thirteenth and Fourteenth Centuries', *Crusade and Settlement*, ed. P. Edbury (Cardiff 1985)

C. J. Tyerman, 'Some Evidence of English Attitudes to the Crusade in the Thirteenth Century', *Thirteenth Century Studies*, i, ed. S. Lloyd (Woodbridge 1987)

C. J. Tyerman, *England and the Crusades 1095–1588* (Chicago 1988, 1996)

M. Villey, 'L' Idée de la croisade chez les juristes du moyen âge', *Relazioni del X Congresso internationale di scienzo storiche*, iii (1955)

INDEX

Absolom, archbishop of Lund, 31
Acre: siege of (1190), 75; loss of
    (1291), 3
Adam von Beham, papal legate, 32
Adhemar, bishop of Le Puy, 69
Aildred, abbot of Rievaulx: *De
    Amicitia,* 25
Aimery of Lusignan, 26
Alan of Lille, 63
Albert of Aachen, chronicler, 11, 20,
    64, 107, 119, 120
Alexander III, pope, 14, 21, 24, 65
Alexander IV, pope, 41
Alexius I Comnenus, Byzantine
    emperor, 47, 112
Alfonso Enriquez, king of Portugal,
    16, 17
Allenby, Edmund, British general,
    124
Almer, Robert, of Kent, 79
Ambrose, St, 17
America, conquest of, 38, 41, 103
Anacletus, anti-pope, 15
Angles of Mons, 123
Anna Comnena, Byzantine
    chronicler, 112
Apostolic Poverty, 26, 64, 67, 85–6
Archer, T. A., 120, 125
Armada, Spanish (1588), 103
Ascalon, siege of (1153), 28
Astley's Amphitheatre, 118
Augustine of Hippo: theories of
    just war, 17

Bacon, Francis, 55, 109
Baldric of Dol, chronicler, 11, 107

Baldwin, archbishop of
    Canterbury, 66, 69
Baldwin III, king of Jerusalem, 28
Baring-Gould, S., 117
Barker, E., 123
Basel, 71–2
Beatrice, countess of Flanders, 75
Beaumanoir, Philippe de Rémi de,
    52: *Coutumes de Beauvaisis,* 52,
    58–9, 61
Bede: *Ecclesiastical History,* 12
Beirut, bishop of, 66
Belgrade, defence of (1458), 79
Benedict XII, pope, 46–7
Bernard, abbot of Clairvaux, 8, 9,
    12, 13, 15, 18, 20, 22, 25, 62, 65,
    70, 86, 102
Bernard Gui, inquisitor, 50, 77
Bertrandon de la Broquière, 95
Bohemund of Taranto, prince of
    Antioch, 13: crusade of
    (1108), 13, 23
Bologna, university of, 57
Bonaparte, Napoleon, emperor of
    the French, 114
Bonet, Honoré: *Tree of Battles,* 39
Bongars, Jacques, editor and
    diplomat, 107–8, 109
Boniface of Savoy, archbishop of
    Canterbury, 12
Boucicaut, Jean le Maingre, Marshal
    of France, 84, 96
Bracton, Henry of: law book
    attributed to, 58, 60
Brantôme, Pierre de Bourdeille,
    seigneur de, 108–9

Brian FitzCount, 8–9, 18
Brundage, J. A., 22
Bruno of Segni, papal legate, 13
Burchard of Worms, canonist, 12

Caesarius of Heisterbach,
    Cistercian, 86
Caffa, 37
Calixtus II, pope, 16, 40
Calvin, John, 104, 107–8
Canute VI, king of Denmark, 31
Carolingians, Frankish rulers, 12
Caxton, William, printer, 104
Cerne, monks of, 65
chansons of the crusades,
    16, 18, 25, 27, 84
Charles I, king of Sicily and
    count of Anjou, 42
Charles IV, king of France, 46
Charles V, Holy Roman
    emperor, 103
Charles VI, king of France, 95
Charles VIII, king of France, 95
Chastellain, Georges, chronicler, 55
chastity belts, 76
Chaucer, Geoffrey, 48
Chavigny, Jean-Aimes de, 109
chivalry and the crusade, 18, 25, 26,
    84, 94–5, 96, 98, 114–16, 123
Chrétien de Troyes, poet, 25
Clanchy, M., 22
Clement III, pope, 36, 71
Clement IV, pope, 44
Clement V, pope, 74, 90, 97
Clement VI, pope, formerly Pierre
    Roger, 37, 70, 72, 73, 82, 85
Clement VII, anti-pope, 47
Clermont, council of (1095), 15, 62,
    63, 65, 69, 78, 118
colonialism, 117, 120, 122–3
confession, 30, 64, 67, 81
Conrad III, king of Germany, 19
Conrad IV, king of Germany, 44
Constable, G., 21
Constance, council of (1414–18), 91
Constantinople, 18, 49: fall of
    (1453), 100, 105
Courtois, E.-H., forger, 118

Cross, the: as crusading symbol,
    21–3, 26–8, 38, 40, 50, 52, 53, 62,
    71–2, 73, 74, 76–83, 85, 86, 87;
    adoption of, 19, 20, 21–3, 30, 32,
    36, 39–40, 48, 52, 56, 59, 61–2,
    64, 66, 67, 68, 69–70, 71–2, 74, 75,
    78–83
crucesignati, 5, 20, 27–8, 32, 38, 41,
    45, 50, 56, 57–8, 61–2, 68, 69,
    76–83, 86, 90, 105, 111: as thieves,
    murderers, rapists, etc., 59, 82
Crusade the: First, 4, 8–13, 16–21,
    24, 28, 63, 64, 99, 106, 107, 119;
    Second, 8–11, 13, 15, 18, 25, 108;
    of 1128–9, 13; Third, 11, 18, 24,
    26, 27, 28, 31–2, 56, 57, 62, 63,
    65, 66, 78, 92, 106, 112, 114, 118;
    Fourth, 18, 27, 46, 48, 62; Fifth,
    47, 53, 62, 64, 67–8, 93, 107; of
    Frederick II (1228–9), 48; of
    Richard of Cornwall (1240–1), 34,
    93; of the Shepherds (1251), 45,
    51, 92; and Canon Law, 10; and
    history, 94–6, 100, 104; lack of
    definition of, 2, 4–5, 9–10, 12–15,
    17, 19, 20–9, 30, 32, 33, 38–9, 40,
    45, 46, 49–55, 58, 60–1, 73, 77,
    78, 90; language of, 27–8, 49–55,
    56, 60–2, 76–83, 106; and
    liturgical rituals, 32, 36, 38, 68–9,
    70–2, 74, 81, 88, 105 (*see also*
    Cross, adoption of); organisation
    of, 26, 31, 32–3, 35–7, 39, 43, 44–
    5, 64, 67, 93 (sclerosis of, 47); as
    pilgrimage, 10, 15, 21–3, 34–5, 40,
    49, 50, 51, 52, 53, 56, 60–1, 79,
    86; propaganda for, 33, 48, 71–3,
    94–6; vows, 39–41 (redemption
    of, 36, 44–5, 59, 67, 81–2, 83, 93);
    women and, 75–6
crusades, in Africa, 32, 44, 45, 46,
    48: Albigensian, 27, 32, 33, 35,
    38, 42, 46, 50, 52, 66, 77, 79, 82,
    87, 105, 111; against Aragon, 32,
    46; in the Baltic, 3, 15, 16, 18, 32,
    34–5, 37, 41, 44, 46, 48, 50, 77, 79,
    87, 91, 92; against Bosnians, 32,
    42, 44, 87; against Christians, 35,

crusades – *continued*
42, 67, 77; against Greeks, 32, 34,
37, 41–2, 44, 45, 50; against
heretics, 32, 35, 42, 44, 48, 67,
105, 112; against the
Hohenstaufen, 32, 34, 37, 42, 44,
45, 46, 67, 68, 77, 78, 89, 111;
against the Hussites, 42, 48, 54,
55, 78; in Italy, 34, 37, 42, 43–4,
46, 48, 50, 54, 67, 77, 78, 79, 82,
87, 89, 90, 92, 96; against the
pope, 32, 45; in Spain, 15, 16, 17–
18, 32, 41, 48, 77
crusaders, charters of, 10, 11, 20–1,
118: God's disapproval of, 93;
indulgences of, 9, 14–5, 16, 17–18,
30–1, 35, 37–8, 39, 40–1, 67, 68,
73, 74, 76, 82, 84, 85, 89, 93, 97,
102, 103, 111; as martyrs, 10–11;
motives of, 10, 25; privileges of, 4,
5, 14–15, 16, 17–18, 19, 20, 23–4,
27–8, 30–1, 32, 35, 37, 40–1,
55–62, 68, 71, 73, 74, 78, 81, 83,
97; wives of, 40, 75
crusading: criticism of, 13–14, 25, 44,
45–6, 52–3, 68, 87–94, 102,
105–15, 124, 125; decline of, 56,
62, 88–98; lack of papal control
over, 23, 44–6, 47–9, 66, 80, 84,
90; lack of spontaneity of, 69–70;
malleability of, 33, 40, 44–7; as a
minority interest, 2; as a movement, 4; papal authorization of, 9;
as a vocation, 10
Cuthbert, St, cross of, 77
Cyprus, 18

Damietta, 53
Danes, 31–2
De expugnatione Lyxbonensis, 16–18
De Gaulle, Charles, 122
De legibus et consuetudinibus, law book
attributed to Ranulf Glanvill, 24, 56
*De profectione Danorum in
Hierosolymam,* 31–2
Despenser, Henry, bishop of
Norwich, 12: crusade of (1383),
47, 51, 53–4, 55, 78, 82

Diderot, Denis, 111–12
Digby, Kenelm, 115
Directorium ad passagium faciendum,
51
Dolcino, heretic, 50
Dominic, St, 77
Dorylaeum, battle of (1097), 75
Dresser, Matthew, scholar, 105–6
Dubois, Pierre, pamphleteer, 84, 107

Edward I, king of England, 60
Edwin, king of Northumbria, 12
Eisenhower, Dwight D., US
general, 123
Eleanor of Aquitaine, queen of
France and of England, 75, 108
Eleanor of Castile, queen of
England, 75
Eleanor of Montfort, countess of
Leicester, 75
Elizabeth I, queen of England, 103
England, 45–6, 48, 58, 60, 92
Erard de Valéry, 50
Erasmus of Rotterdam, 101, 102,
103, 105
Erdmann, C., 8
Esbern, Danish noble, 31–2
Etienne de Bourbon, preacher, 82
Etienne de Niblens, 25
Eudes de Châteauroux,
papal legate, 67, 83
Eugenius III, pope, 9, 13, 14, 18, 20,
21, 24, 40, 65
Eustace, abbot of Flay, 66, 85, 86
Evesham, battle of (1265), 78
exempla from sermons, 27, 28, 67, 73,
75–6, 82, 94
Ezzelino of Romano, 44

Faisal, emir, 114
fascists and the crusade, 121–2
First World War, 123
Flanders, 47
Florence, 89
Foxe, John, Anglican propagandist,
105, 106
Francis I, king of France, 54–5, 95
Franco, F., 121–2

Fréauville, Nicholas, cardinal, 70
Frederick I, king of Germany and
    emperor, 106, 112, 121,
Frederick II, king of Germany and
    emperor, 32, 33, 34, 42, 44, 45,
    47, 48, 52, 74, 89, 111, 112
Frederick III, king of Germany and
    emperor, 82
friars, the, 43, 44, 45, 63, 93
Fulcher of Chartres, chronicler,
    9, 107
Fulk, bishop of Toulouse, 77
Fulk V, count of Anjou and king of
    Jerusalem: crusade of, 13, 22
Fulk of Neuilly, preacher, 62, 63, 64,
    85, 86
Fuller, Thomas, Anglican divine, 110

Garcia, Peter, heretic, 92
Gelasius II, pope, 16
Genoa, 15, 75, 79
Gentili, Alberic, war theorist, 104
Geoffrey de Lucy, 60
Geoffrey FitzPeter, English
    justiciar, 59
Geoffrey of Monmouth: *History of the
    Kings of Britain*, 16
Geoffrey of Villehardouin,
    chronicler, 27
George Podiebrad, king of Bohemia,
    101
Gerald of Wales, chronicler, 28, 69,
    70, 72, 86
Géraud, H., 118
Gesta Francorum, 21, 107, 119, 123
Gibbon, Edward, 3, 55, 109, 111–13,
    114, 125
Gilbert, V., 124
Gilbert of Tournai, preacher, 67
Gilchrist, J., 10, 19
gilds and confraternities, 96–7
Godehilde of Tosni, 75
Godfrey de Bouillon, 85, 94, 95
Godric of Finchale, hermit, 21–2,
    23, 79
Gotthardt, St, battle of (1669), 3
Gower, John, 48
Grabois, A., 20

Graham, Billy, 69
Granada, 41, 122
Gratian, canonist, 11: *Decretum*, 11, 19
Great Schism, the, 47, 48, 53–4, 87,
    88, 92
Greenland, 32
Gregory VII, pope, 12, 19
Gregory VIII, pope, 14, 21, 31, 36,
    57, 71, 85
Gregory IX, pope, 38, 67–8:
    Decretals, 38
Gregory X, pope, 43, 59, 90, 92
Gregory XIII, pope, 102
Grotius, Hugo, war theorist, 104
Grousset, R., 122
Guibert of Nogent, chronicler, 8,
    26, 99, 107, 110
Guignes, Joseph de, 113
Guillaume Durand the Elder, 80
Guillaume le Veneur, 22
Günther of Pairis, chronicler,
    63, 71–2, 86

Haakon IV, king of Norway, 34
Habsburgs, the, 101
Hadrian IV, pope, 14–15
Hagenmeyer, H., 119, 120
Hattin, battle of (1187), 26, 27, 28, 76
Henry, archbishop of
    Strasburg, 62, 66
Henry I, king of England, 11, 21
Henry II, king of England, 14, 66,
    69, 85
Henry III, king of England, 32, 42,
    45, 46, 66, 78, 87
Henry IV, king of France, 107
Henry VI, king of England, 101
Henry VIII, king of England, 54,
    103, 104
Henry Knighton, chronicler, 51
Henry of Huntingdon, chronicler, 15
Henry of Livonia, chronicler, 33–5
Henry the Lion, duke of Saxony, 20
Heraclius, patriarch of Jerusalem,
    65–6, 69
Herold, Joannes, 106
Hervey de Glanvill, 18, 19
Hillary, Sir William, 117

Holy Land, the, as pre-eminent goal
    of crusading, 34, 37, 38, 43, 45–6,
    47, 48, 60–1, 67, 80–1, 82, 84–5,
    89–90, 92, 96, 97
Horn, Andrew: *Mirror of Justice*, 62
Hospitallers, of the Order of St John,
    92, 96, 105, 110, 111
Hostiensis, canonist, 3, 38, 40, 50,
    68, 79, 83
Housley, N., 3, 4
Hubert, Master, preacher, 68
Hubert Walter, bishop of Salisbury
    and archishop of Canterbury, 12
Hugh, count of Bar, 49
Hugh V, duke of Burgundy, 80
Hugh de Fonte, *crucesignatus*, 79–80
Hugh de Payens, founder of the
    Templars, 13, 65
Hugh II du Puiset, 24
humanists and the crusade, 95–6,
    100–1, 102, 106
Humbert of Romans, preacher, 46,
    67, 68, 70, 72, 73
Hume, David, 55, 100, 111–12
Hundred Years War, 47, 88

Ida, margravine of Austria, 75
Inab, battle of (1149), 13
Incas, the, 109
Innocent III, pope, 10, 15, 28, 31,
    35–6, 37, 38, 39, 40, 41, 42, 45,
    49, 53, 63, 66, 67, 71, 75, 76, 86,
    93, 103
Innocent IV, pope, 38, 42, 44, 45,
    58, 59, 76, 83
Innocent VIII, pope, 80
Inquisition, the, 30, 39, 112
interpreters, 70
Isidore of Seville, 17
Ivo, bishop of Chartres, 11, 24

Jacques de Vitry, bishop of Acre,
    cardinal, preacher and chronicler,
    51, 53, 62, 63, 64, 67, 68, 69, 72,
    75, 76, 83, 86, 94, 105, 107, 119:
    Historia Orientalis, 64
James VI of Scotland and I of
    England, 104

Jarento, abbot of St Bénigne,
    Dijon, 65
Jaruzelski, Wojcieck, Polish leader,
    124
Jean de Joinville, chronicler, 46, 52,
    61, 70, 84, 110, 112
Jean Germain, bishop of Châlon, 51,
    95: *Discours du voyage d'Oultremer*,
    51
Jerome, St, 17
Jerusalem: fall of (1099), 125; (1187),
    31; as goal of crusade, 2–3, 5, 6,
    14, 15, 16, 17, 19, 26, 34, 49, 52,
    56, 60–1, 71, 80–1, 95, 96, 106,
    112, 124, 126; as goal of
    pilgrimage, 15, 20, 24, 56, 60, 96–7
Jewell, John, bishop of Salisbury, 104
Jews, 26, 36, 57, 115
John, king of England, 48, 74, 78
John VIII, pope, 15
John X, pope, 12
John XII, pope, 12
John XXII, pope, 46, 47, 72, 73, 74,
    78, 82, 90
John XXIII, anti-pope, 54, 92
John Chrysostom, St, 17
John Hunyadi, of Transylvania, 47
Josias, archbishop of Tyre, 62, 66
Josserand, lord of Brançion, 84
Juan de Segovia, conciliarist, 101
Julius II, pope, 103
just war, 17, 38–9

Kingsford, C. L., 120, 125
Kretz, Matthias, preacher, 102

Ladislaus, king of Naples, 42, 92
Ladislaus V, king of Hungary, 48
La Monte, J. L., 125
Langland, William, 48
Langres, Godfrey de la Roche,
    bishop of, 65
Las Novas de Tolosa, battle
    of (1212), 41
Lateran, councils of: First (1123), 16,
    21; Fourth (1215), 35, 37; Fifth
    (1512–17), 96
Lautrec, 62

Lewes, battle of (1264), 78
Leo IV, pope, 15
Leo IX, pope, 54, 102, 103
Lepanto, battle of (1571), 3, 104
Lesbos, 96
liberation theology, 124
Lille, 46, 78
Limoges, 62
Lincoln, battle of (1217), 77
Lisbon, capture of (1147), 16–18, 62, 65
Lloyd, S., 125
Lloyd George, David, 123
Lollards, 96
Louis I, duke of Bourbon and count of Clermont, 74, 81
Louis II, duke of Bourbon, 78
Louis VII, king of France, 10, 14, 18, 19, 20, 48, 70, 79, 86, 116
Louis VIII, king of France, 52
Louis IX, king of France, 33, 45, 48, 50, 59, 61, 70, 75, 79, 83, 87, 94, 96, 112, 113, 115, 116
Louis X, king of France, 97
Louis XII, king of France, 95–6
Louis XIII, king of France, 108
Louis XIV, king of France, 110
Louis Philippe, king of the French, 117
Loyola, Ignatius, 104
Lucinge, Réné de, 103
Lucius II, pope, 12
Lucius III, pope, 14
Ludwig IV, king of Germany, 47
Luther, Martin, 101, 102, 103, 105
Lyons, councils of: First (1245), 37; Second (1274), 37, 92

Maccabees, the, 18
Madelin, L., 122, 123
Mahdia, attack on (1087), 16
Maimbourg, Louis, 110–11
Malatesta da Verruchio of Rimini, 43
Malta: knights of, 115, 117, 125; siege of (1565), 104
Mansourah, battle of (1250), 34, 75
Manuel I Comnenus, Byzantine emperor, 14

Margaret of Provence, queen of France, 75
Markowski, M., 21
Martin, abbot of Pairis, 63, 66, 71–2
Martin V, pope, 54, 91, 92
Mathieu d'Escouchy, provost of Peronne and chronicler, 51
Matthew Paris of St Alban's, chronicler, 33–4, 35, 48, 68, 110
Maximilian I, Holy Roman emperor, 54
Mayer, H. E., 1–3, 125
medievalism, 114–18
Mercadier, mercenary, 118
Messina, 18
Michaud, J. F., 116–17, 118, 119, 125
Military Orders, 13, 19–20, 78, 91–2, 94–5, 96
Mills, C., 115, 125
Mise of Amiens, the (1264), 46
Mohacs, battle of (1526), 101
Mohammed, prophet, 105
Mongols, the, 44, 67
Morris, C., 13, 14
Moschus, François, 105
Müller, George Christoph, 111
Murray, R. H., 117

Nalson, John, 111
Napoleon III, 122
nationalism and crusading, 106–8, 110–11, 116–18, 121–2
Nazis and crusading, 121
Newbolt, H., 124
Nicetas Choniates, Byzantine chronicler, 110
Nicholas IV, pope, 90
Nicopolis, crusade and battle of (1396), 51–2, 78, 84, 95, 105
Niger, Ralph, crusade critic, 92
Norman Conquest, invention of, 119
Norwich, 77
Noue, François de la, 54, 101

Odo of Deuil, chronicler, 10, 18
Oliver of Paderborn, scholasticus of Cologne, preacher and chronicler, 62, 64, 67, 107

Oporto, Pedro Pitoes, bishop of, 17, 62, 65
Orderic Vitalis, chronicler, 12, 19, 21
orientalism, 113
Orkneys, bishop of, 15
Oswald, king of Northumbria, 12
Oswy, king of Northumbria, 12

papal bulls and decrees, 102: *Eis qui Hierosolymam* (1123), 40; *Quantum praedecessores* (1145), 9, 14, 20, 24, 40, (1165) 14; *Immensum pietatis opus* (1150), 13; *Inter Omnia* (1169), 14; *Cor nostrum* (1181), 14, (1184/5), 14; *Audita tremendi* (1187), 14, 24, 31, 57, 58, 65, 85; *Quia Maior* (1213), 35, 36, 37, 39, 41, 48, 54, 58, 63, 64; *Ad Liberandam* (1215), 35, 36–7, 38, 40, 58, 59, 74, 96; *Excommunicamus* (1215), 37; *Redemptor Noster* (1316), 37; of John XXII (1316), 74
Paris, university of, 57, 63, 64, 86
Paschal II, pope, 11, 13, 23
Paul III, pope, 102
Paul IV, pope, 103
Pelagius, cardinal and papal legate, 47
Peronne, 59
Peter of Blois, polemicist, 26–9, 85: *Passio Reginaldi*, 26–9
Peter the Chanter, don, 63
Peter the Hermit, 62, 64, 65, 94, 119, 120
Peter the Venerable, abbot of Cluny, 12
Pheasant, Vows of the (Lille 1454), 52, 78
Philip I, the Fat, king of France, 24
Philip II, king of France, 58, 59, 66, 79, 94
Philip II, king of Spain, 103
Philip III, king of France, 42
Philip IV, king of France, 74, 89
Philip V, king of France, 46
Philip VI, king of France, 46, 62, 95, 97

Philip d'Aubigny, 34
Philippe de Mézières, propagandist, 73, 82, 84, 91, 94–5, 96
Philippe de Vitry, poet and musician, 96
Pierre de Fontaines, lawyer, 60
Pierre de la Palud, patriarch of Jerusalem, 70
pilgrimage, 13: armed, 5, 6, 9, 20
Piloti, Emmanuele, Cretan merchant, 84, 94, 95
Pirie-Gordon, H., 124
Pisa, 16: council of (1135), 15
Pius II, pope, 100
Pius V, pope, 102, 103
Poitiers, council of (1106), 13
Powicke, F. M., 87
Prawer J., 122–3
preaching and preachers, 44–5, 46, 53, 62–74
Protestants and crusading, 101, 102, 103–8, 109, 110
Prutz, H. G., 121
pullani, suspicion of, 14
Pynson, Richard, printer, 104

Radulphus Glaber, chronicler, 11
Raimbold Croton, crusader, 11, 12
Rainald von Dassel, archbishop of Cologne, 12
Ralph, abbot of Coggeshall, chronicler, 49
Ralph, bishop of Bethlehem, 12
Ralph of Caen, chronicler, 11
Ranke, L. von, 116, 119, 120
Raymond of Aguilers, chronicler, 107
Raynald of Châtillon, 26–9
Reineck, Reinier, editor, 106–7
Renard Crest, *crucesignatus*, 75: and his wife, 75
Rhodes, siege of (1522), 101
Richard, earl of Cornwall, 45
Richard, J., 122
Richard I, king of England, 23, 32, 87, 94, 118
Riley-Smith, J. S. C., 2–3, 124–5

Robert II, count of Flanders, 12
Robert II, duke of Normandy, 11, 21
Robert Curzon, papal legate and
   preacher, 53, 67, 86
Robert d'Arbrissel, preacher, 65
Robert of Clari, chronicler, 27
Robert of Rheims, chronicler, 63,
   64, 99, 107, 110
Roger of Howden, chronicler, 49
Röhricht, R., 120, 121
Rossi, Ugolino, bishop of Parma, 81
routiers, 15
Rudolph, renegade preacher, 65
Runciman, S., 13, 116, 124–5
Rutebeuf, poet, 53

Saladin, sultan of Egypt, 26–8, 32,
   112, 113, 121
Saladin Tithe (1188), 27, 39, 57, 66
Santarem, siege of (1147), 16
Sanudo, Marino Torsello of Venice,
   propagandist and chronicler, 33,
   51, 52, 79, 84, 85, 94, 95, 107
Saragossa, siege of (1118), 16
Schiller, Friedrich, 113
Schoeplin, J. D., 111
Scott, Walter, 114–15
Second World War, 123
Segovia, synod of (1166), 15
Selim I, Ottoman sultan, 101
Shakespeare, William, 108
Siberry, E., 117
Sibylline prophecies, 18
Simon de Montfort, earl of Leicester,
   33, 45, 77, 78, 87
Smalley, Beryl, 89
Standard, battle of the (1138), 15
Stebbings, H., 115
Stedinger peasants, crusade against, 67
Suger, abbot of St Denis, 12, 110
Suleiman the Magnificent,
   Ottoman sultan, 101
Sullivan, Sir Arthur, 117
Sybel, H. von, 114, 119–20, 121
Syria, French mandate in, 114, 122

Tasso, Torquato, 108
Templars, the (Order of the Knights

of the Temple of Solomon), 8,
   19–20, 31, 74, 91, 114
Teutonic Knights, Order of, 41, 78,
   91, 121
Thomas Aquinas, 40
Thomas Basin, chronicler, 51
Thomas Becket, archbishop of
   Canterbury, 13
Thomas of Marle, 15
Torzelo, John, 95
Tournai, 59, 74
Trent, council of, 102
Truce of God, 24
Tunis, siege of: (1270), 46, 48, 52;
   (1390), 51, 78
Turks, the, 37, 41, 48, 54, 78, 81, 82,
   84, 88, 90, 95, 96, 97–8, 100–5,
   107–8, 109, 110–11, 113, 125
Tyre, 20

Ulric Bucel, 25
Ulrich von Hutten, 101
uniforms, crosses as, 78
Urban II, pope, 2, 9, 13, 15, 16, 24,
   26, 47, 62, 63, 64–5, 73, 78, 85,
   93, 109, 118

Varangeville (Normandy), priest of,
   61, 79
Varna, battle of (1444), 105
Venice, 20
Versailles, peace conference of
   (1919), 114
Vézelay, 20, 22, 62, 70
Vienna, siege of (1529), 101, 106
Vienne, council of (1312), 37, 90
Villani, Giovanni, chronicler, 46
Villey, M., 79
Vladimiri, Paul, Polish spokesman, 91
Voltaire, 111–12

Wales, 66
Walter Cantelupe, bishop of
   Worcester, 44, 45
Walter Map, courtier, 25
White Company of Toulouse,
   the, 77, 86
Wibald of Corvey, 19

Wilhelm II, kaiser of Germany, 121
Wilken, Frederick, 114
William, archbishop of Tyre,
    chronicler, 9, 20, 21, 51, 64, 94,
    107, 110, 119, 124, 126
William Clito, 21

William Longsword, 34
William of Tudela, poet, 27
wills and legacies, 76, 97
Wisden, J., 118
Wyclif, John, 48, 54: *De Cruciata*, 54
Wynkyn de Worde, printer, 104